WOMEN HOLD UP
HALF THE SKY

WOMEN HOLD UP HALF THE SKY

Selected Speeches of Nicola Sturgeon

Foreword by
Val McDermid

Edited
by
ROBERT DAVIDSON

SANDSTONE PRESS

First published in Great Britain in 2021 by
PO Box 41
Muir of Ord
IV6 7YX
Scotland

www.sandstonepress.com

ISBN: 978-1-913207-60-1
ISBNe: 978-1-913207-61-8

Sandstone Press is committed to a sustainable future.
This book is made from Forest Stewardship Council ® certified paper.

Cover design by Ryder Design
Typeset by Iolaire, Newtonmore
Printed and bound by CPI Group (UK) Ltd, Croydon, CR0 4YY

For Ian and Kim Davidson

CONTENTS

Foreword by Val McDermid   xi

Introduction   1

1: **MY PLEDGE TODAY IS SIMPLE BUT HEARTFELT**   9
Holyrood, Edinburgh, 19th November 2014

2: **BRIDGE TO A BETTER FUTURE**   14
The Royal Society of Edinburgh, 25th February 2015

3: **CONNECTIVITY AND INTEGRATION**   26
Kirkwall, Orkney, 1st June 2015

4: **THE IMPORTANCE OF EQUALITY**   31
Washington DC, 10th June 2015

5: **WE NEED MEN TO SHOW LEADERSHIP**   36
Napier University, Edinburgh 25th June 2015

6: **WOMEN HOLD UP HALF THE SKY**   41
Beijing, 27th July 2015

7: **60,000 EXCITED LITTLE MINDS**   48
Wester Hailes Education Centre, 18th September 2015

8: **OUR RESPONSE WILL BE JUDGED BY HISTORY**   59
St Andrews House, Edinburgh, 4th September 2015

9: **HUMAN RIGHTS ARE NOT ALWAYS CONVENIENT
BUT . . .**   64
Pearce Institute, Govan, 23rd September 2015

10: **SCOTLAND AND ALCOHOL**   74
*Edinburgh International Conference Centre
7th October 2015*

11: **A VISION FOR THE HIGHLANDS AND ISLANDS**   79
Isle of Skye, 21st October 2015

12: **FOOD BANKS AND THE HEALTH OF THE NATION**   88
Edinburgh 30th October 2015

13: **RESPONDING TO THE PARIS ATTACKS**   93
Holyrood, Edinburgh, 17th November 2015i

14: **THE IMPORTANCE OF NATURAL CAPITAL**   97
Edinburgh International Conference Centre,
23rd November 2015

15: **WORKERS' RIGHTS ARE HUMAN RIGHTS**   103
Glasgow University, 24th November 2015

16: **THE IMPORTANCE OF THE EUROPEAN UNION**   114
St John's Smith Square, Westminster 29th February 2016

17: **STEP IT UP FOR GENDER EQUALITY**   123
Holyrood, Edinburgh, 5th March 2016

18: **REFLECTIONS ON THE EU REFERENDUM**   130
Edinburgh, 25th July 2016

19: **THE DEFINING CHALLENGE OF OUR TIME**   142
Reykjavik, Iceland 7th October 2016

20: **A SPECIAL AND UNBREAKABLE BOND**   149
Leinster House, Dublin, 29th November 2016

21: **THE UNDERPINNING PRINCIPLE OF THE STATE**   157
Stanford University, California, 4th April 2017

22: **WOMEN IN CONFLICT RESOLUTION**   169
United Nations Building, New York, 5th April 2017

23: **THE IMPORTANCE OF TRUTH**   174
University of Strathclyde, Glasgow 12th April 2017

24: **DIVERSITY IN THE MEDIA**   181
Edinburgh International Conference Centre 17th August 2017

25: **THE ROLE OF INCOME TAX**   190
Edinburgh, 2nd November 2017

26: **HISTORICAL SEXUAL OFFENCES, AN APOLOGY**   195
Holyrood, Edinburgh 7th November 2017

27: **THE BEST POSSIBLE PLACE TO BE**   199
Verity House, Edinburgh, 16th January 2018

28: **A HUNDRED YEARS OF WOMEN'S SUFFRAGE**   205
Holyrood, Edinburgh, 6th February 2018

29: **ON CHILD POVERTY AND CHILDREN'S RIGHTS**   210
Beijing, 10th April 2018

30: **THE IMPORTANCE OF INTERNATIONAL
        COLLABORATION**   217
Shanghai, 11th April 2018

31: **CATHOLIC EDUCATION IN SCOTLAND**   225
Glasgow University, 4th June 2018

32: **OUTWARD-LOOKING AND OPEN FOR BUSINESS**   235
Mansion House, London, 29th January 2019

33: **HONOURING THE EDINBURGH SEVEN**   240
Surgeons' Hall, Edinburgh, 30th January 2019

34: **THE MARINE ECOLOGY**   246
University of Strathclyde, Glasgow, 20th February 2019

35: **A CALL TO SERVICE**   252
Assembly Hall on the Mound, Edinburgh, 22nd May 2019

36: **TWENTY YEARS OF DEVOLUTION**   259
Edinburgh, 18th June 2019

37: **THE COUNTRIES MOST AFFECTED**   267
Glasgow Caledonian University, 28th June 2019

38: **GROWTH IS NOT AN END IN ITSELF**   272
Edinburgh, 29th July 2019

39: **THE IMPORTANCE OF LITERATURE**   276
Edinburgh International Conference Centre, 25th August 2019

40: **A CUP OF KINDNESS**   281
Brussels, 10 February 2020

A note on the transcriptions   291
Acknowledgements   295
Index   297

FOREWORD

What are political speeches *for*? Propaganda or information? Personal advantage or public interest? Winning over voters or damning opponents? Charming us or conning us, or both?

All of the above, obviously. But from time to time, a politician comes along who's less interested in the fact of power than in what you can do with it. Even more rarely, we're confronted with a politician who believes above everything else that they should use their power for the benefit of their citizens. And beyond that group, when the opportunity arises.

In the mouth of such a politician, the political speech becomes something different. It becomes something worth listening to, because it escapes the bounds of self-interest or narrow party concerns. It informs us and it challenges us to take a hard look at our own preconceptions.

This is a collection of speeches that does just that.

In these pages, we see Nicola Sturgeon's passions laid bare. There's no empty sloganeering here. Instead, we see a programme for government that's underpinned by her aspiration for a fairer, healthier, happier nation. Of course, at the heart of it is her absolute conviction that the best route to achieving that is via independence.

But whether you agree with that keystone of her ambition, it's hard to deny the humanity, decency and necessity of the things she advocates in these speeches. Whether she's talking to heads of governments about Scotland's place in Europe or to the Scottish Grocers' Federation about food banks, the positions she outlines are always informed by compassion and sometimes by an anger that's visible between the lines. These are not empty emotional manipulations either; they're always accompanied by ambitions and suggestions for making things better. As she herself says, 'We are more likely to make progress in the right direction by aiming high than we ever will by being over-cautious.'

So what are those passions we see laid bare here? Independence for Scotland, obviously. Social justice; equal educational opportunities; the importance of literacy and literature; equal access to health and social care; tolerance; feminism; workers' rights; holding out a hand to refugees; and building a strong and green economy to sustain all of these.

It may seem an idealistic and unrealistic set of goals. But in the years since Nicola Sturgeon has been First Minister, her government has made many steps in the right direction. They've also made mistakes, just like every other government in human history. Any political system relies on human beings to deliver. And human beings are . . . well, only human.

But another benefit of a collection of speeches like this is that it looms in the landscape as an irrefutable monument to what Nicola Sturgeon has promised to do her best to deliver. Speeches like this are hostages to fortune; they allow both her rivals and her friends to hold her feet to the fire when her government falls short.

I've been fortunate to spend enough time in the company of Nicola Sturgeon to know that what we see is what we get. I've never seen the slightest sign of some 'secret Sturgeon' sneering behind her hand at the people she governs or engaging in Machiavellian intrigues for her own benefit. The woman who emerges in private is the woman we see through the lens of these speeches. Except that in private, she's funnier than the political speech allows.

If you want to get to know the woman who leads the Scottish Government, this is a good place to start.

Val McDermid
Edinburgh
March 2021

INTRODUCTION

A beloved cousin who died too soon told me that freedom is a myth for as long as other people are in your life. Call that statement cynical or call it a platitude, it encapsulates much that is relevant to any independence debate.

Take freedom, which can only be a temporary condition because, when the newly liberated party meets with others, or accepts obligations as they must surely do, their choices are constrained. Independence, on the other hand, thrives on interactions and choice, and is in constant development with new challenges, new relationships and changing values. Freedom is static where independence must constantly adapt. Freedom is hampered by obligations where independence is fulfilled by them. Winnie Ewing, one of my great heroes, famously and frequently declared, 'Stop the world, Scotland wants to get on'.

The independence debate in Scotland has too easily and too often been characterised as passionate, hand-on-heart nationalism, which perhaps has its place in an energising myth, but the real business is about decision-making and direction. Nationalism is a noun badly in need of an adjective because, as I think is obvious, there is serious qualitative difference between the cultural and ethnic varieties.

It was Scotland's fourth First Minister, Alex Salmond, who introduced the term civic nationalism to the debate, which followed the acceptance by Jack McConnell, his predecessor, of a national need for immigration, for 'others', to counter a shrinking population level. These contributions, in my view, along with shared sovereignty within the European Union, shifted the argument from heritage and tradition onto the Enlightenment values

I

of tolerance and equality, along with the economy. In this way the implicit question in my cousin's statement, not so much who are the 'others' as who are 'we', was answered positively: whoever is in our territory.

So much for freedom, the 'others' and myth. The final element in my cousin's statement is time, the idea that change will happen in time. A Scottish Parliament seemed a forlorn hope through the 1980s. Margaret Thatcher's first Scottish Secretary, George Younger, declared that 'devolution is dead' often enough and with such authority that most ideas would have stuck. This one did not.

Politicians will try to 'draw a line under it' when a sliver of the vote goes their way, as happened after the 1979 referendum on John Smith's Scotland Act, but are vulnerable to the slow regeneration of hope against a background of perceived injustice. Devolution became a central tenet of the Labour Party in Scotland under the leadership of Donald Dewar whose jousts with Mrs Thatcher's second Scottish Secretary, Malcolm Rifkind, became an unmissable feature of Scottish political life.

Two more Scottish Secretaries would hold office, Michael Forsyth and Ian Lang, before Labour regained power in 1997 under Tony Blair and Gordon Brown. The second devolution referendum followed on the 11th September that year, one of the great days of my life, and nothing could be the same after a vote of 74% in favour of the proposal.

Donald Dewar became the first First Minister but, after only seventeen months in office, tragically died following a brain haemorrhage. Henry McLeish followed but stood down after only a year. Jack McConnell steadied the ship, remaining in office until 2007, when the Scottish National Party was returned as a minority government. Alex Salmond achieved majority status in the election of 2011 and remained in office until after the Independence Referendum of 2014.

If ever a format was tired it was the Westminster model, weighed down as it was, and remains, by weary traditions and ritual. Five of the fifteen post-war prime ministers to 2020 attended Eton. Three more went to costly fee-paying schools. Its second house has historically been filled, as Lloyd George put it, by men (now also women) 'chosen accidentally from the ranks of the unemployed', by political appointments, and by some who simply bought their peerages from the ruling party.

In comparison, the Scottish Parliament is proportional and ferociously modern, banning smoking in public places, legalising equal marriage, ending period poverty for all women – first in the world to do so – and introducing Britain's first gender-balanced cabinet. It is directly answerable to the Scottish people, accessible to all, and housed in a remarkable new building that acknowledges the past but is fit for the 21st century.

Utterly dominant in debate, Alex Salmond swept all before him until, throughout Scotland and the United Kingdom, extending to the United States and beyond, he came to be respected as the genuine voice of the nation and, with that, both his authority and that of the office grew. Where the parliament might formerly have carried with it a suggestion of municipality, it now had the textures of real authority. Where the First Minister's role once had a sort of Lord Provost colouring, it took on presidential overtones. Administration and leadership had conjoined.

Scotland's head of state remains the monarch, for long a politically silent figure. The Prime Ministerial incumbent is the most obvious surrogate, but the Thatcher years alienated the office from many Scottish people. There was a void and Alex Salmond filled it. His deputy throughout these years in office would be his successor, the author of these speeches, Nicola Sturgeon.

Born in 1970, she describes herself in the first as a 'working-class girl from Ayrshire'. After joining the Scottish National Party as a teenager, she took her law degree from the University of Glasgow. Later she worked for the Drumchapel Law Centre in the same city, reinforcing the working-class outlook that would be so beautifully expressed in her Jimmy Reid Lecture (Speech 15). However, she would move beyond the ideas of her parents' generation, as will be seen.

When the Scottish Parliament reconvened in 1999 she was among the first intake of MSPs. An intake, incidentally, that included more women than had ever been elected to Scottish seats at Westminster. John Swinney took over as leader of the party in 2000 when Alex Salmond relinquished the position but stood down after four unsuccessful years. Mr Salmond resumed the leadership from his Westminster base with Nicola Sturgeon not only deputy but also leader in the Scottish Parliament. Together they won the Scottish election of 2007 and he returned in triumph with her at his side. From then until late 2014 they formed an invincible and inseparable pairing.

Between 2007 and 2012 she served as Cabinet Secretary for Health and Wellbeing, after which she covered Infrastructure, Investment and Cities, but other things were going on in her life. In 2010 she married party official Peter Murrell to form what was often described (not always approvingly) as a 'power couple'. Of more relevance to these speeches is that she continued her lifetime's habit of reading widely and voraciously and so, it seems to me, exposed her mind to more progressive thinking than do most political leaders. Any list of dedicated readers among such would include John Fitzgerald Kennedy, Barack Obama, and Donald Dewar himself, a distinguished minority of a liberal, progressive persuasion. They could write well, too.

Familiar with the Scottish canon, she also read contemporary literature from such as Chimamanda Ngozi Adichie, Arundhati Roy, and Ali Smith, authors she would interview at the Edinburgh International Book Festival. When, as First Minister, she began to tweet her current reading, always appreciatively, her account became a point of interest to readers and publishers across Britain. Between this, and her direct relationships with both left and right in the political spectrum, her socialism transmuted into a more socially progressive brand of politics with feminism at its core, a feminism that was in her leadership from the start but that became increasingly apparent as her authority grew. That said, the speeches that follow are equally imbued with practical solutions.

Beginning in late 2014 with her acceptance of the post of First Minister, the speeches presented here end early in 2020 with her address to the European Policy Centre. By that time, Scotland had been removed from the European Union as part of the Brexit process, but was still within the period of transition. To my mind, this closing speech is among the most heartening of the forty in this book.

Others of special note include Speech 4 on equality, and Speech 6, which takes its title, as does the book, from an aphorism usually ascribed to Chairman Mao[1], but that may in its turn have been lifted from common currency. It is used here, regardless of its provenance, because it is appropriate, beautiful, and true. Speeches 8 and 9 accurately reflect not only the feelings of Scottish people on the plight of refugees, but also those of humanitarian thinkers across Europe and America. Speeches 10 and 12 speak to the health of the nation, which was and remains a preoccupation of the Scottish Government.

Speeches 16 and 18 were delivered on either side of the EU referendum and are of historic importance.

I am especially fond of Speech 23 as it predates other fine writing on a subject – the importance of truth – that would in previous times have seemed so transparently obvious it would not have required elucidation. More detailed writing would follow from others, but here is an early warning from Scotland's First Minister.

Speeches 28 and 33 could stand as representative of feminist writing in Scotland and are a joy to read. So too are Speeches 19 and 34 on the environment, and 38 which is related. Speeches 29 and 30 were given in China on a visit which was criticised on the grounds of that country's human rights violations, but that address

1.   Mao Zedong, Chairman of the Communist Party of China 1949–1976.

those very rights while seeking to establish common ground and build bridges.

The period contains many events of local (meaning British) and international significance. In 2014, David Cameron was still Prime Minister, relieved that No had prevailed in Scotland's first independence referendum. In 2015 he won a British General Election for the Conservative Party, ending their coalition with the Liberal Democrats. In the same election, the Scottish National Party won a historic victory, taking 56 of the 59 available seats on fifty per cent of the vote, an astonishing performance.

2016 was bung full politically. The Scottish National Party won handsomely again in the Scottish election but lost its overall majority. When the EU (Brexit) referendum was run Leave won by a tiny majority, although much controversy would ensue over the illegal gathering and use of data and, indeed, the misuse of truth. Noting that Scotland emphatically voted Remain, the author J. K. Rowling, a defender of the Union in 2014, tweeted 'Goodbye UK'. Many others wrote at greater length but with no additional eloquence.

David Cameron resigned and was replaced by Theresa May who promptly activated Article 50 of the Lisbon Treaty[2], committing to what had been an advisory vote without consideration of the nations who had voted to remain, Scotland and Northern Ireland, or their parliaments. The Labour Party supported the move. Negotiations were entered with the European Union and, frankly, chaos reigned.

In 2019 Theresa May stepped down to be replaced by Boris Johnson who called a general election late in the year, on 12th December, when a divided Labour Party presented the main opposition ... except in Scotland ... and won by a landslide. At 11.00 pm on the 31st January 2020 Britain formally left the EU

2. Article 50 has five parts, the first of which states that 'any member state may decide to withdraw from the (European) Union in accordance with its own constitutional requirements.'

and began its long flounder through the transitional period.

All that said, it would be wrong to view these speeches as a commentary on events. Rather they represent a national leader meeting obligations and responding to changing times. Closing, as they do, when the far right was in the ascendant across much of the world, not least in America, and a global pandemic was about to strike, they address the international condition almost as much as that of a small nation off the coast of Europe. There is resistance, but the values of the past are slowly, globally, falling away and there can be no return to whiteness, island mentality, or patriarchy. The future formation will be diverse, European, and feminist, and is heralded in the following pages.

To my mind, the story of the Enlightenment continues in these speeches. We might say the New Enlightenment. Reading and rereading them, I was increasingly impressed not only by Nicola Sturgeon's command of detail but also by the guiding spirit that shines through, and came to see that the Scotland I want dwells here among the thickets of details and ideas. Open-minded and warm-hearted, industrious, fair; a forward-looking and progressive nation. Above all, she speaks from the same common humanity that inhabits the social tradition she imbibed with her mother's milk. Essentially, a humane outlook that has survived all manner of change and, I dare say, will continue to do so.

1

MY PLEDGE TODAY IS SIMPLE BUT HEARTFELT

Given to the Scottish Parliament
Holyrood, Edinburgh, 19th November 2014

> In this, her first speech as First Minister, Nicola Sturgeon (NS)
> spoke to a noticeably cheerful debating chamber, which held an
> overall majority for her party. After referring to the origins of
> the parliament, she paid tribute to her four predecessors in office,
> including a fulsome appreciation of her career-long friend and
> mentor Alex Salmond. She also struck the principal keynote not
> only of her political life to date, but also her prospective tenure:
> gender equality.

Presiding Officer, I thank you for your kind words, and my fellow
members of Parliament for giving me the honour and privilege of
being your nominee as the next First Minister of Scotland. My
pledge today, to every citizen of our country, is simple but heartfelt. I will be First Minister for all. Regardless of your politics or
point of view my job is to serve you, and I promise to do so to the
best of my ability.

This is a special and proud moment for me, a working-class
girl from Ayrshire given the job of leading the Government of
Scotland. It is also a big moment for my family, and I am delighted
that they join me here today... particularly delighted, relieved
even, to note that (so far) my niece and nephews appear to be on
their best behaviour!

I am so grateful to my family, but especially to my Mum,

Dad, sister, and husband, for the unwavering support they have given me in everything I have chosen to do. Now that I am First Minister, I suspect that I am going to need that support more than ever, but I am lucky in knowing that it will always be there. I also want to thank my constituency office staff for the invaluable work they do for me and for my constituents in Glasgow Southside.

Presiding Officer, like you, I have been a member of this Parliament since its re-establishment in 1999, which means that I have had the opportunity, at close quarters, to watch and learn from all of my predecessors as First Minister. Each of them in their own unique ways have been passionate and diligent advocates for Scotland. I have the greatest respect for all of them, the late Donald Dewar, Henry McLeish, Jack McConnell, and Alex Salmond, and am genuinely humbled that my name will be added to that distinguished list.

That our Parliament and Government, in just fifteen short years, have come to be so firmly established and, dare I say, respected in our national life, is testament to the quality of their stewardship and leadership. However, I am sure members will understand why I want to pay a particular tribute to Alex Salmond today.

Without the guidance and support that Alex has given me over more than twenty years, it is unlikely that I would be standing here. I owe him a personal debt of gratitude and it is important to me to put my thanks on the public record today. His place in history as one of Scotland's greatest leaders is secure, and rightly so. However, I have no doubt that he has a big contribution yet to make to politics in Scotland. I will continue to seek his wise counsel and, who knows, from time to time he might seek mine too.

To become First Minister is special and a big responsibility. To make history as the first woman First Minister is even more so, and I am reminded of a quote from Florence Horsburgh, a Conservative MP for Dundee. In 1936 she became the first woman to reply to what was then the King's Speech in the House of Commons. She said:

'If in these new and novel surroundings, I acquit myself but poorly, when I sit down I shall at least have two thoughts for my consolation – it has never been done better by a woman before, and whatever else may be said about me, in the future from henceforward, I am historic.'

I can sympathise with the sentiment but hope not to need any such consolation! Indeed, I much prefer this quote from the same speech: 'I think of this occasion as the opening of a gate into a new field of opportunity.'

I hope that my election as First Minister does indeed help to open the gate to greater opportunity and that it sends a strong, positive message to girls and young women. Indeed, to all women across our land. There should be no limit to your ambition or what you can achieve. If you are good enough and work hard enough, no glass ceiling should stop you achieving your dreams.

What I do as First Minister will matter more than the example set by simply holding the office. Leading on equal representation, and encouraging others to follow, addressing low pay, improving childcare, are the obligations I now carry, and I am determined to discharge them on behalf of women across our country.

My niece, who is in the public gallery today with her brother and cousins, is eight years old. She does not yet know about the gender pay gap, or underrepresentation, or barriers such as high childcare costs that make it so hard for women to work and pursue careers. My fervent hope is that she never will and that, by the time she is a young woman, she will have no need to know about any of these issues because they will have been consigned to history. If, during my tenure as First Minister, I can play a part in making that so, for my niece and for every other little girl in this country, I will be happy indeed.

I am taking on the responsibilities of First Minister at an exciting time in our nation's history. All of us, regardless of party, have been inspired and challenged by the flourishing of democracy that we have witnessed during and since the referendum[3]. Democratic politics in Scotland has never been more alive, and the expectations that people have of their politicians and their parliament have never been higher. There is a burning desire across our country to build a more prosperous, fairer, and better Scotland and not only among those who voted Yes. Those who voted No want a better country too, and I intend to lead a government that delivers on those aspirations.

My role as First Minister will be to help build a Scotland that all who live and work here can be proud of. A nation both social democratic and socially just; a Scotland confident in itself, proud of its successes and honest about its weaknesses; a Scotland of good government and civic empowerment; a Scotland vigorous and determined in its resolve to address poverty, support business, promote growth and tackle inequality. These are the points against which my government will set its compass, and I earnestly believe that, in doing so, we will reflect the wishes, hopes and desires, even the dreams, of the Scottish people.

Of course, we will have our differences in this chamber as to the best way forward. We must never shy away from robust debate but should strive always to be constructive and respectful. I want all members to know that when we are on common ground (and I want to find as much of that as possible), you will find in me a willing and listening ally.

It will surprise no-one to hear that I will always argue the case for more powers, indeed the full powers of independence, for this Parliament. I believe that the more we are able to do the better we can serve the people, but will do my utmost to govern well with the powers we have.

My daily tasks will be to protect and improve our NHS, support our businesses at home and abroad, ensure that all children get the chance to fulfil their potential, and keep our communities safe from crime.

3.   In the independence referendum of 18th September 2014.

I intend to lead a government with purpose, that is bold, imaginative, and adventurous, although tough decisions must be made and I may not always get them right. It is not necessarily the case that all manner of things shall be well. There will be challenges, but I will strive to meet them positively and with fortitude, inspired and sustained each day by the potential of this country and the people who live here.

I want to end with another quote, this time from the Earl of Seafield, the Chancellor who signed away Scotland's sovereign independence in 1707. As he did so, he lamented, "There's ane end of ane auld sang". That song lay lost for 292 years, until we reconvened this parliament in 1999, but this First Minister intends to ensure that we adorn it with new verses that tell of a modern and confident Scotland, fit for purpose and fit for all her people.

Together, let us now get on with writing that story.

2

BRIDGE TO A BETTER FUTURE

Given to the David Hume Institute
The Royal Society of Edinburgh, 25th February 2015

> Speaking to the subject 'the sort of country we want Scotland
> to be' NS picked up on her constant themes of education and
> equality, seeming to balance the infrastructure project she
> inherited, the Queensferry Crossing, with her own intended
> signature project of increased care and learning provisions. Both
> the longest and most data-heavy speech included, this speech
> is impressive not only for its detail and scope, but also in its
> idealistic faith in the power of education to level upwards. Also
> interesting is the first use in this selection of the word 'wellbeing'
> that would later become almost an organising principle of her
> government.

When we were choosing whether to vote Yes or No[4] last year, we
engaged in one of the most passionate, wide-ranging and fundamental debates that any nation can have. We had to ask ourselves
what kind of country we wanted to live in. We thought of our
concerns about the present, and hopes and dreams for the future,
and came to our conclusions. Anyone travelling the country then,
as I did, heard time and time again, from No voters as well as Yes,
an overwhelming desire to build a better and fairer society as well
as a wealthier one.

The referendum did not turn out as I hoped, but that assessment

---

4.   The referendum on Scottish independence held in September 2014.

and reassessment has strengthened and energised our country. The challenge now is to harness its energy to build a better Scotland, to turn those aspirations into reality.

When I became First Minister, nearly one hundred days ago, I set out a programme for government based on the three priorities of prosperity, participation, and fairness. We aim to build prosperity because a strong economy underpins the wellbeing of every community in Scotland, and encourage participation because we want to empower and enable people to improve their own lives and those of others. We will promote fairness because we know there are too many barriers standing in the way of too many people, whether from background, income, geography, gender, or disability. We also know that inequality is bad, not only for individuals and society, but also for our economy.

The OECD [Organisation for Economic Co-operation and Development] estimates that inequality reduced the UK's economic growth by nine percentage points between 1990 and 2010. To put it simply, if we succeed in making Scotland more equal, we will not only raise the life chances of this and the next generation, but also enhance our economic prosperity.

That is why I strongly believe that a strong economy and a fairer society should no longer be viewed as competing, but instead as mutually reinforcing objectives.

As leader of the Scottish Government, I am determined that we will use all the powers at our disposal, now and in the future, to progress these twin goals but, of course, we cannot ignore the wider context. The hard fact of the matter is that the current UK Government's spending cuts, largely endorsed by the main opposition party, make tackling inequality more difficult.

The cuts we have seen so far have had a disproportionate impact on women, disabled people, and families on low incomes. The UK parties' plans for even more austerity would hurt those groups again, and it seems to me that no politician can be taken seriously on poverty and inequality if they are not also prepared to challenge the current Westminster model. It is also important to make that challenge because austerity has been bad for the economy. Low growth is the major reason that the government has missed its deficit reduction targets by a total of £150 billion ... which is why the Scottish Government has set out an alternative approach based on limiting real terms spending growth to 0.5% a year.

A policy of very modest spending increases would see the debt and deficit reduce as a proportion of national income every year from 2016–17, and free an additional £180 billion across the UK (over the next parliament), which could be used to invest in infrastructure and innovation, protect the public services we all depend on and ease the pressure on the most vulnerable.

By offering an alternative to the austerity agenda, we can ensure that fiscal consolidation is consistent with the wider vision of a society striving to become more equal as part of becoming more prosperous and fiscally sustainable. Education is a vital part of that vision.

Education is, and will continue to be, a defining priority for the government I lead. It is also a personal passion. The education I received at Dreghorn Primary, Greenwood Academy, and Glasgow University, is the major reason I am able to stand here as First Minister of Scotland. So, it is important to me personally that every young girl and boy growing up today, regardless of their background, gets the same chances that I did.

This evening, I will talk about how we achieve that, focussing in turn on the early years ... on school education ... and then opportunities for young adults. In doing that, I will point towards areas where we need to do better, but my starting point is an optimistic one.

This country is incredibly fortunate. A commitment to education is ingrained in our history, part of our DNA and our very sense of ourselves. We pioneered the idea of universal access to school education and sparked the Enlightenment, the spirit of which still inspires the David Hume Institute. Hume himself argued that 'The sweetest . . . path of life leads through the avenues of science and learning'. We discovered, relatively early, that education does not just sweeten life or bring enlightenment. Widening access to education also brings economic benefits. During the 18th and 19th centuries, because Scotland educated more people to a higher level than most other countries, we pioneered the industrial revolution and provided a disproportionate number of the world's great thinkers, scientists, and inventors.

In many ways, our education system still lives up to its reputation. Actually, it is better than ever. More children are better educated than at any time in our history. Higher exam passes are at record levels. Curriculum for Excellence[5] is being successfully implemented. School leaver destinations are the best on record. Of the students who left school in 2014, more than nine out of ten are in employment, training, or education. We have more world-class universities per head than any other country except Switzerland.

A survey last summer from the Office of National Statistics showed that, in terms of college and university qualifications, Scotland has the best-educated workforce anywhere in Europe and that is a remarkable asset. It is an incredible advantage for Scottish businesses looking to recruit and overseas companies looking to invest. It also provides a firm foundation for future economic growth.

We all understand that, although these achievements are hugely significant, they are not the whole story. So today, I want to highlight some of the areas where we can and must do better. In particular, I want to focus on how inequality in attainment, starting in the very early years, and persisting into adulthood, weakens our society, holds back our economy, and constrains the life chances of too many fellow citizens.

The basic problem can be illustrated with just one statistic. In terms of qualifications, school leavers from the most deprived

5. Scotland's national education curriculum from nursery through to the end of secondary.

twenty per cent of Scotland only do half as well as those from the least deprived areas. None of us should accept a situation where so many people are unable to realise their full potential. It lets too many young people down and diminishes us all. Those figures relate to school education, but the challenges start before that. The Growing Up in Scotland Study calculated the difference in vocabulary between children from low-income and high-income households. By the age of five, the gap was already thirteen months.

The first step in tackling the attainment gap, is to make sure every child gets the best possible start in life.

I will talk about formal care and learning in a moment, but the issue is much broader than that. We need to think about the wellbeing of babies and parents from pregnancy onwards, which is why our Early Years Collaborative is so important. Since it was established in 2012, it has brought together health workers, carers, parenting organisations and others from every part of the country. It ensures that evidence and research is shared, so that approaches which work in one area can be adopted elsewhere.

The Collaborative has already identified several priorities, and community planning partnerships are now working on these. For example, we are looking at better early assistance for pregnant mothers; encouraging better attachment between mothers and young children; and helping parents to support learning. All of this will have a big impact not only on attainment, but also on children's happiness and emotional wellbeing.

The Collaborative is attracting international attention. It is helping to ensure that good practice becomes common practice. It is already helping to create a better future for young children in Scotland.

The establishment of the Collaborative has accompanied a significant investment in early years learning and care. In August, we will further extend funded childcare places to disadvantaged two year olds, having already expanded the care available to three and four year olds from 412 hours a year in 2007 to 600 now.

By the end of the next parliament, it will be more than 1100 hours, meaning that funded childcare will match primary school provision.

There are two significant things about this increase. The first is its economic impact. I was struck by a comment President Obama made in his State of the Union Address last month. He argued that: 'It's time we stop treating childcare as a side issue, or as a women's issue, and treat it like the national economic priority it is', making the fundamental point that childcare is an economic necessity. I would describe it as essential economic infrastructure, as fundamental in its own way to enabling parents to work as the transport infrastructure that gets them there every morning. Better childcare empowers parents, especially mothers, to return to work, and that is why, last November, the CBI [Confederation of British Industry] cited more childcare as the top priority in their 'Plan for a Better Off Britain'.

The second point is perhaps even more important. Childcare is not just about enabling parents to return to work. It is about providing the caring and learning environment that every child needs to flourish. We already know that, by age five, children attending early learning and childcare settings with high inspection ratings have better vocabulary skills than their peers, regardless of their family's income level. Vocabulary skills are a key indicator of later attainment. So, by improving the quality of learning and care by supporting workforce guidance and development we will improve attainment and reduce social inequalities. Curriculum for Excellence does not start in Primary 1. It starts at age three in our nurseries.

The key point is this. Early Learning and childcare promote opportunity twice over, enabling parents to enter the workforce and provide a better standard of living while helping all children to make the most of their potential later in life. It is one of the best investments any government can possibly make. In my view, it is central to any enlightened view of what modern Scotland should look like and that is why it is such a driving priority of my government.

Today I confirm my intention that spending on early learning and care will double over the course of the next parliament, in addition to the extra capital spending we will provide.

The great capital investment project of this parliament is the Queensferry Crossing. If I am re-elected next year, I intend that the great infrastructure project of the next parliament will be even more transformational. It will be the investment in care and learning facilities needed to ensure early years provision matches primary school provision. These facilities will create a bridge to a better future for children and families across the country.

High-quality learning and care in the early years will help reduce the attainment gap in schools, but we need to do more within schools as well. Understanding how much we owe to the passion, commitment, and expertise of our teachers, we are determined to invest to protect teacher numbers.

Teachers are the major reason for the significant successes I mentioned, the implementation of curriculum for excellence, the record exam results, and the high number of school leavers in education, employment, or training, but we need to do more to support them and their schools. Especially schools with significant intakes from more deprived communities.

In January we introduced free school meals for all primary school children, because making nutritious lunches available to everyone, without the stigma of means testing, will benefit every child's health, education, and wellbeing. Two days ago, I visited Blue Gate Fields Junior School in Tower Hamlets, which participated in the London Challenge attainment initiative. 70% of its pupils are eligible for free school meals, almost three times the average for England. Notwithstanding that, it is in the top 20% of schools in England for reading, and in the top 40% for writing and maths. Ofsted has reported that it is 'an outstanding school in almost every respect'.

Some of the coverage around my visit expressed surprise that I was learning from London, but I have never pretended that Scotland has a monopoly on wisdom in education or any other area. Just as other countries study Scotland's Curriculum for Excellence, and the Early Years Collaborative, so we should be prepared to adopt good ideas from elsewhere. We are not just looking to London. In Canada, Ontario has achieved dramatic improvements in literacy and numeracy.

Not all the lessons of the London Challenge can or should be used in Scotland, but some are applicable. Leadership has been a factor in the success of many, and I also see great examples of good leadership in schools across Scotland. Because we are looking to build on that, I announced on Monday that the new Qualification for Headship, which will come on stream later this year, will be mandatory for all headteachers by 2018/19.

One lesson that London and Ontario demonstrate, is that when efforts and resources are targeted it is possible to achieve dramatic improvements. Therefore, I launched the £100 million Scottish Attainment Challenge two weeks ago. The fund will be focussed initially on primary schools in the local authorities with the highest concentration of pupils living in deprived areas, aiming to improve literacy, numeracy, health, and wellbeing.

If we can close the attainment gap when children are young, the benefits will continue into secondary school and beyond. The real prize though, is not simply the additional £100 million we are investing. It lies in the potential to apply what we learn from the programme across the £4 billion school education budget. The Challenge will add to the other steps taken, such as our national numeracy and literacy drive 'Read, Write, Count', and our funding of attainment advisers in every local authority.

What the Scottish Attainment Challenge does, together with those other steps, is provide new impetus and focus on closing the attainment gap. We are making support available to all schools, while also placing additional assistance and resources where they are needed most. We are raising standards everywhere but want to see the biggest improvements in the places with the greatest need. That, in my view, is a moral imperative. It is not acceptable that any child is held back because of their background or the circumstances of their birth.

Free higher education tuition has become a touchstone of this government's commitment to equality of opportunity. As someone who benefited from it, I am determined to preserve the principle that access to university is decided by ability to learn, not ability to pay.

Protecting the principle of free education, vital though it is, is still not enough. We also need to remove the other barriers that prevent too many young people from our most deprived communities pursuing a university education... and we have work to do! Children from the most deprived fifth of communities make up only a seventh of undergraduate intakes.

When I became First Minister, I unambiguously set the ambition that a child born in one of our most deprived communities should, by the time he or she leaves school, have the same chance of going to university as one born in our least deprived communities. Let me stress that. The *same* chance. Not just a better chance than they have today, but the same chance as anyone else. In other words, where you are born and brought up and your parents' circumstances must not be the driver of how likely you are to go to university.

The work outlined for early years and in our schools will be fundamental to achieving that ambition, as will work by the government and our universities. This year the government funded 730 additional places to widen access for students from more disadvantaged backgrounds, but to ensure we are doing everything we can, as early as possible, we are establishing a Commission on Widening Access.

The Commission will propose milestones, measure progress, identify improvements, and be central to ensuring that our ambition of equal access becomes a reality. That is part of a far broader approach to post-school learning. After all, the key test we need to apply is not whether learning takes place in college, at work, or in university. It is whether the learning is relevant, engaging, and widens people's opportunities.

Since 2007 we have focussed colleges on promoting skills which help people to work and support economic growth. The number of students gaining recognised qualifications has increased by a third in the last five years. We retained educational maintenance allowances when the UK Government scrapped them in England, invested in modern apprenticeships directly tied to job opportunities, and launched a national campaign to promote youth employment.

All of this has achieved results. We currently outperform the rest of the UK on all three youth employment indicators: higher youth employment, lower unemployment, and lower economic inactivity rates ... but, still, we need to do more.

Last year, the Commission for Developing Scotland's Young Workforce published its final report and we are investing £28m between this year and next to implement its recommendations. We have already established an 'Invest in Young People' group, bringing together industry, local government, further education, and trade unions. It is worth setting out what all this will mean.

A closer relationship between industry and education, enabling courses to reflect what companies need. Apprenticeships up from 25,000 a year at present to 30,000 a year by 2020. Better careers advice at an earlier age. Support for employers (for example, to gain the investors in people accolade). Concerted action to improve participation of underrepresented groups so the gender segregation in too many modern apprenticeships (where only 5% of engineering apprentices are female, and just 3% of childcare apprentices are male) eventually diminishes and disappears. Men and women will choose work to match their talents and interests, rather than outdated expectations.

From supporting mothers in the early stages of pregnancy, to helping people gain their first experience of work, the overriding message I want to leave you with tonight is that my government is committed to doing everything it can to promote opportunities and reduce inequalities.

Of course, this commitment is not something that government, schools, colleges, and universities can achieve on their own, although our role is hugely important. It must be part of a shared endeavour. Earlier today, I announced a further £6m of funding for the Scottish Council of Voluntary Organisations, to deliver its Community Jobs Scotland programme. Using that money, it will deliver at least 1,000 job training opportunities across all thirty-two local authority areas. At least three hundred will be for vulnerable young people, such as care leavers and ex-offenders. A further hundred will be for disabled people. It is a good example of how the third sector is working with us to help young people into work.

Businesses also have an important part to play. When we launched the 'Make Young People Your Business' campaign we got, from many companies, a magnificent response that has made a difference to many young people's lives. What those companies found was that employing young people brought significant benefits. Doing the right thing was in their own best interests. Business will not have a role in every part of education, but we will seek to work together on issues where they do have an interest, whether entrepreneurship in schools or the delivery of modern apprenticeships.

The approach to education I have outlined tonight is part of a wider approach to sustainable growth, which will also be clear in the Government Economic Strategy being published next week. Fundamentally though, it is about achieving the basic ideal that I think of when I am asked the question: what kind of country do you want Scotland to be?

To put it simply, I want Scotland to be a land of opportunity. A country where every individual, regardless of background or race or gender, gets the chance to fulfil his or her potential.

Can that be achieved? Yes, and education is the key. I quoted David Hume earlier. In the same passage he goes on to say that 'whoever can either remove any obstruction (to education), or open up any new prospect, ought... to be esteemed a benefactor to mankind'.

The removal of obstructions to education, and the opening of new opportunities, has been the focus of many of the major initiatives of my first hundred days as First Minister, and will receive sustained attention for as long as my government holds office. Education is not only part of our sense of ourselves, it is the key to a better future for young people growing up today, and it must be at the heart of the fairer and more prosperous country we all seek to build.

3

CONNECTIVITY AND INTEGRATION

Given to the Convention of the Highlands and Islands[6]
Kirkwall, Orkney, 1st June 2015

Since at least the 1960s, intermittent attention had been given by successive governments to infrastructure development in the Highlands and Islands. A plan for growth was published within that decade, the Cromarty Firth was bridged in the 1970s, the Kessock Bridge built in the 1980s, the Dornoch Bridge opened in 1991. However, even by the 21st century, roads between communities and to the south were inadequate and ferries too expensive. Land ownership and use had been a barrier to progress for generations, as well as a political fault line. Later, digital communication brought new challenges and opportunities to rural communities. Having been, no doubt, sensitised by her years as Cabinet Secretary for Infrastructure, Investment and Cities, implicit in these comments by NS is the idea that the Highlands and Islands have traditionally been seen as somehow a land apart and that a greater integration with the rest of Scotland was overdue.

---

6. Founded in 2007, The Convention of the Highlands and Islands (CoHI) seeks to strengthen alignment between the Scottish Government and member organisations to support sustainable economic growth. Members include local authorities, Highlands and Islands Enterprise, the University of the Highlands and Islands and others.

The Scottish Government's Programme for Government, and the economic strategy we published in March, emphasise the importance of creating a fairer nation as well as a more prosperous one. It therefore stands to reason that we want every part of Scotland to prosper and are determined to ensure that jobs and opportunities are available in rural and island communities. While welcoming this discussion on the specific challenges we face, I do wish to mention two issues which are important across the whole country.

The first is connectivity: improving the transport and digital links which connect island and rural communities with the wider world. The second is empowerment: how we give local authorities and local communities more power to take decisions for themselves.

To start with connectivity. Perhaps the biggest and quickest change will come from the investment in next-generation broadband. Here in Kirkwall, the first broadband exchanges came into use in February and 2,400 properties are now connected to a local fibre network. More work will start soon in Westray, Sandwick, Orphir and Birsay[7]. By the end of next year, seventy-five per cent of properties on Orkney will have access to next-generation broadband, as will eighty-four per cent of properties in the Highlands and Islands. We see the broadband project as being truly transformational.

Without public money, no commercial broadband would have been planned in Orkney or in many other places. What is now being achieved is hugely significant, but we are clear that connecting eighty-four per cent of the Highlands should be seen as a staging post rather than a final destination, and that is why Community Broadband Scotland is working with development trusts to explore how to deliver broadband services to the remoter islands. It is also why we welcome this opportunity to discuss with you how to extend broadband provision further.

7. Westray is an island to the north of Orkney Mainland, the largest Orkney island. Sandwick, Orphir and Birsay are locations on Orkney Mainland.

We are determined that your digital infrastructure will enhance the sustainability and prosperity of your communities, and that the Highlands and Islands will not be left behind.

We are also investing heavily in road, rail, air, and sea links. Dualling the A9 between Perth and Inverness, upgrading eighty miles of single carriageway, is the biggest transport project, by cost, in Scotland's history, and its three billion pounds of investment is a true reflection of the importance we attach to it. We are also starting work on dualling the A96 and making improvements to the A82.

For rail links, as part of the new Scotrail franchise, hourly services between Inverness and the Central Belt will start in 2018. Journey times will also be shortened. The sleeper franchise will have new rolling stock from 2018 and changes to the timetable mean that the Fort William service now connects with trains from Oban. An order for two more ferries is likely to be confirmed shortly, and we have renewed the Air Discount Scheme for a further four years to the end of March 2019. All this represents an unprecedented investment in the transport and digital infrastructure of the Highlands and Islands. It will not resolve every difficulty or eliminate every inconvenience, but it should bring benefits for tourists, businesses, and individuals across the area.

Our investment in connectivity is a crucial part of how we create a fairer and wealthier nation.

The second point is that we want to involve and empower communities as much as possible. In the run up to the [independence] referendum, we saw an engagement in politics on a scale unprecedented in the recent history of these islands. That did not happen because the referendum created something new, but because it spoke to something enduring: the desire to build a better country. Now, we need to find new ways of harnessing that democratic energy, not just in the great constitutional questions of our time, but also in the day-to-day decisions made by and for communities.

Community empowerment is one of the key themes of the Programme for Government. It can bring benefits right across Scotland but is arguably even more important in those areas furthest from the Central Belt. It is appropriate that several of the actions we are taking will have particular benefits in the Highlands and Islands. Land reform is a good example.

The Scottish Government is trebling the size of the Scottish Land Fund, which supports community buy-outs. We have set a target that 1,000,000 acres of land should be in community ownership by 2020 and are introducing a Land Reform Bill later this month.

Responses to our consultation paper showed strong public support for such legislation. The Land Reform Bill will modernise the legal framework of rights and responsibilities in such issues such as land use, access, ownership, and development. It will help to ensure that the ownership and use of land is in the public interest. That it contributes to the collective benefit of the people.

Land reform is just one element in a much wider programme of encouragement. Our Community Empowerment Bill gives community organisations the right to ask if they can purchase, lease, manage or use land and buildings which belong to public bodies. It also enables us to require public bodies to promote participation by members of the public in the decisions that affect them. It refocuses the purpose of community planning to how public sector bodies work with themselves, and with others, to improve outcomes and tackle inequalities.

Of course, we are making specific steps to ensure that the needs of island communities are recognised and addressed. The 'Empowering Scotland's Island Communities' prospectus, which the previous First Minister, Alex Salmond, launched here in Kirkwall last June, was the most comprehensive empowerment package for our Islands put forward by any government. Since then we have appointed a Minister for the Islands and established an Islands Area Ministerial Working Group, which will meet here tomorrow to discuss transport. Later this summer we will launch a consultation on greater powers for Scotland's islands, which will offer the perfect opportunity to share ideas about the future powers of the islands. We want to understand the best way to work with you to promote your economy, harness your resources, and enhance the wellbeing of your communities.

Finally, the work we have been doing is linked to our policy on the Crown Estate. The Scottish Government's current focus is on ensuring that the devolution of the Crown Estate to the Scottish Parliament takes place in a workable way. We do not believe the current Scotland Bill truly reflects the spirit of the Smith Commission proposals but, once we have achieved that devolution, we will consult on how the new body will operate.

I am committed to working closely with local authorities to involve communities in the day-to-day running of the Crown Estate's assets, and planning for coastal and island councils to benefit from a hundred per cent of the net revenue generated within twelve miles of the shore. People will have a greater say in managing their local coastline, and communities will get greater benefit from the natural resources on their doorstep.

The principle in all of this is clear. People who live in local communities are in the best position to take decisions about those communities and giving more powers to them is an essential part of creating a fairer and more prosperous Scotland.

It should be clear from this short summary that there is a huge amount happening, and that consultation on the islands, new powers at local level, and unprecedented investment in infrastructure will create new opportunities. This convention has never been more important or more relevant. This government will work with you to understand priorities, address challenges, and seize opportunities for the Highlands and Islands.

4

THE IMPORTANCE OF EQUALITY

Given to the World Bank
Washington DC, 10th June 2015

In her first visit to the United States as First Minister, NS appeared on *The Daily Show*, hosted by Jon Stewart, following three American presidents[8], two vice-presidents[9], prime ministers Tony Blair and Gordon Brown, and Hillary Clinton. To the surprise of many, her party had almost swept the board in the general election held a month previously, taking 56 of the available 59 Scottish seats. After the defeat of the Independence proposition in 2014, her party now found itself on the crest of a wave with its leader a figure of world standing, often mentioned in the same breath as the German Chancellor, Angela Merkel. In New York, she hosted a fundraising event dedicated to the restoration of Glasgow School of Art, and in Washington addressed an influential audience at the World Bank.

It is a pleasure to speak to you today about the economy and equality, a subject that is of interest around the world and where the research and insights of the World Bank and IMF [International Monetary Fund] are directly relevant to Scotland's experience.

Scotland, like many countries, faces a paradox. Deep inequalities exist in our society and are reflected in reduced educational

---

8. Four after the 2020 presidential election: Carter, Clinton, Obama, and now Biden.
9. Al Gore and Joe Biden.

outcomes, poorer health, and lower life expectancy, while at the same time we are a wealthy nation with vast economic potential. We have an international reputation in economic sectors such as life sciences, creative industries, energy, food and drink, and tourism, and the value of our international exports has increased by twenty per cent in the last three years with the US and the European Union their main destinations.

Recent research by the (independent) UK Office of National Statistics showed that we have the most highly educated workforce in Europe, which is one of the reasons why, within the UK, we are second only to London in attracting international investment.

Like many other countries, we face significant challenges. We are still dealing with the legacy of the recession. Output and employment are above their pre-recession peak, but full-time employment and real wages are not.

Like most advanced economies we face longer-term, structural challenges. We need to ensure skilled and well-paid job opportunities, adapt to an ageing population, and make progress to the low-carbon age. Productivity has been a consistent preoccupation of the Scottish Government in recent years, but is an area in which we have had success. In 2007 the productivity gap between Scotland and the rest of the UK was six per cent. It has now largely closed, but we still lag countries such as Sweden, Germany, and the USA. We need to do better, to ensure that economic opportunities are more widely available and economic growth benefits more people.

Compared with the other OECD [Organisation for Economic Co-operation and Development] countries, Scotland would rank fifteenth in terms of GDP per head, and twentieth for income equality in terms of our Gini coefficient[10]. On both ratings we are ahead of the UK, but there is room to do better. We want to increase our competitiveness but also to create a fairer society with a better distribution of income.

What we increasingly recognise is that competitiveness and

10.　A measure of statistical dispersion representing income or wealth inequality.

equality are not separate issues. They are connected, and we would have a more competitive economy if we had a fairer society.

That conclusion draws on recent evidence from the IMF and the OECD. The OECD estimated that rising income inequality in the UK reduced economic growth in output per head by nine percentage points between 1990 and 2010. That is approximately £1,600 for every person. IMF research, examining 173 countries over fifty years, has shown that more unequal countries tend to have lower and less durable growth.

Christine Lagarde argued last year that 'by making capitalism more inclusive, we make capitalism more effective', and that idea is also influencing US economic policy. President Obama said in his State of the Union address, 'we don't just want everyone to share in America's success, we want everyone to contribute to our success'.

What these sources recognise is that inequalities of income and opportunity undermine growth prospects in the longer term. Countries become more competitive if they make use of the talents of all their people, which is why the Scottish Government's revised economic strategy focuses on increasing competitiveness and tackling inequality. Objectives that are equally important because they are interdependent.

The theoretical basis of the strategy is well-founded and widely accepted. Professor Joseph Stiglitz, former chief economist at the World Bank, serves on my Council of Economic Advisers and has said that 'tackling inequality is the foremost challenge that many governments face. Scotland's Economic Strategy leads the way in identifying the challenges and provides a strong vision for change'.

What that means in practice, is that we focus on what we call the four 'I's: innovation, internationalisation, investment and inclusive growth.

Looking at innovation, Scotland has more world-class universities per head of population than any country in the world except Switzerland. What we are now trying to do is improve the links between our universities and our businesses. We are establishing innovation institutes to develop new technologies in growth areas where we have identifiable opportunities (such as stratified medicine, industrial biotechnology, and big data), while also trying to reduce the barriers to access. So that more people have a fair chance to go to university or become entrepreneurs.

We promote international trade, not only because exports create jobs in Scotland, but also because companies looking to international markets are more likely to innovate. We also prioritise investment in skills and infrastructure, which has not been easy. Facing an incredibly tough public spending environment we have protected spending on the skills, broadband and transport infrastructure that will be essential to future economic growth and, in all of this, have tried to ensure that growth is inclusive. That it reaches all regions of the country, across all sectors and that it benefits all in our society.

Recent research from the OECD supports this approach. It recommends tackling inequalities at source while promoting competitiveness, so our efforts apply across a range of policies from early years, childcare and education, to entrepreneurship and innovation.

We have a dedicated Minister for Fair Work focussing on how businesses, trade unions and the private sector can collaborate to improve productivity and promote well-paid employment, and are seeking to improve inter-generational equality by increasing attainment, early years interventions, and improving childcare.

Our investment in childcare has a significant additional benefit. It helps remove barriers to women participating in the workforce. Three years ago, we launched a major initiative on women's employment, an area which is receiving increasing attention across the globe. The World Bank's 'Gender at Work' report emphasised that closing the gender gap in employment does not benefit only women. It benefits their families, businesses, and the wider community.

The G20 has a target to reduce the gender gap in employment

by a quarter by 2020. Scotland has more than halved the gap in the last three years: from 9.1% to 4.2%. We currently have the second-highest female employment rate in the European Union but recognise that we need to do more. Women are still more likely to be low-paid, and gender segregation is apparent in some occupations. We want companies to commit to having gender-balanced boards by 2020. That said, we are making progress and, by doing so, giving more people a fair chance of good employment. We are making better use of people's talents and skills and, at the same time, permanently boosting the productive capacity of our country.

The final point I want to emphasise is that our economic strategy is not only about policies. It is about our approach. Because we work in partnership with business the government does all it can to support and promote business. Businesses and government together help to establish a fairer society.

Seventy years ago, in the wake of World War II, West Germany developed what became known as Rhine capitalism. It encouraged competitive markets but combined them with strong social protections. It instilled a sense of partnership between workers, trade unions, businesses, and the public sector. As a result, the German economy has been characterised by innovation, high productivity, and strong exports.

What we are aiming to create in Scotland is in some ways similar. While investing in the innovation and infrastructure essential to productivity growth we are also creating an inclusive society. One which harnesses the talents of all our people, and which shares the benefits of growth more equally. We are confident that we are on the right path, but we know we have a huge amount to learn.

5

WE NEED MEN TO SHOW LEADERSHIP

Given at Launch of 50:50 by 2020
Napier University, Edinburgh 25th June 2015

> The 50:50 by 2020 voluntary scheme, promoting gender equality in boardrooms across all sectors, was initiated by the Scottish Government and launched by NS before an audience that included private, third and public sector directors as well as students with a direct interest in the working environment into which they would soon enter. Implicit in her speech is a phrase most often associated with Hillary Clinton, that 'women's rights are human rights', and therefore men have their part to play. In addition to the scheme's intended social and economic benefits it would become a sort of political flagship, frequently cited as an indicator of the Scottish Government's progressive inclinations.

It is especially good to see so many young people here today, since this event is about the jobs market you will enter, the career paths you will choose, and the ambitions you will be able to fulfil. On becoming First Minister I made it clear that I want to make major and lasting progress towards true gender equality, and towards shattering the glass ceiling for good and all. However, that is only part of a wider aspiration.

I also want to ensure that every person in this room, and across Scotland, can fulfil their potential. That nobody is held back by their background, race, religion, sexual orientation, disability, or any other factor. Gender equality is a vital part of that wider work, and fair representation in the boardroom (which is the focus of today's event) is another, of achieving gender equality more generally.

There have been some encouraging figures in recent months which show that, on some measures, Scotland is already performing relatively well. If you look at female participation in the workforce, which has been a major focus for the government in the last three years, we have higher levels of female employment than any country in the European Union except Sweden. The gap between male and female employment rates has more than halved in the last three years: from 9.1 percentage points to 4.2. In the rest of the UK, the gap is ten.

Challenges remain. Underemployment is more common among women. When we look at the gender gap for full-time employment, we find that it is not four percentage points, or anything like it. It is fifteen. Some forty-five years after the passing of the Equal Pay Act, the gap between men and women remains far too high at nine per cent. Women are less likely than men to enter senior management positions and they are less likely to sit on boards and hold executive positions.

There is still much work to be done and, since there is no single solution, we are adopting a range of measures. We are encouraging more women to take up science and maths subjects at school. We are addressing career segregation in terms of the modern apprenticeship subjects that people choose. We are investing in childcare by helping parents to contribute in the workplace. We are encouraging, and looking at how we better support, talented and able women to become executives and senior managers.

As part of all of this, we want to see as many women as men in board positions. Not just because it is right, although it is, but because it will help drive the wider and deeper change that we need to see at all levels of society and the economy. This is an area where the Scottish Government is leading by example.

The Cabinet is, in many respects, the Scottish Government's

board, and when I became First Minister, I appointed a gender-balanced cabinet. In fact, my Cabinet is one of only three in the developed world with as many women as men and they, just like the men, are there on merit. There were two reasons to do this.

The first reason is that it sends an important message. It demonstrates to any young woman thinking about entering politics or public life, that there are no limits to what they can achieve if they are good enough and work hard enough. The second point is this. All the evidence suggests that gender-balanced boards, because they better reflect the talents at our disposal, make better decisions.

In my view, that principle applies to other organisations, as well as the government, which is why we have initiated this 50:50 by 2020 commitment. We are encouraging companies, third sector organisations and public sector bodies across the country to make a commitment that, by 2020, fifty per cent of their board members will be women. We are promoting this message through three basic arguments.

First argument: gender equality is the right thing to do. Basic fairness demands that women should have the same opportunities as men. That on its own would make this pledge worth signing.

Second: gender equality is good for the economy. For Scotland, as for any nation, our greatest resource is our people, and we cannot afford to underuse the skill and talent of more than half of our population. That point is increasingly recognised around the world. When I was in the USA earlier in the month, I discussed this with both the World Bank and the International Monetary Fund. In fact, Christine Lagarde, the Director of the IMF, made the point very clearly in Brussels last week. She said that 'if you care about greater shared prosperity, you need to unleash the economic power of women'.

Third and final (and obviously a crucial point): gender equality is good for individual organisations. Companies are more likely to be successful when they draw from as wide a range of talent as possible. It is the best way of getting the best people.

Seventy-seven public sector organisations have already signed this pledge, and I am delighted about that because I want the public sector to lead by example. I am also delighted that, so far, forty-four third sector organisations and sixteen private companies have signed up too. They have a hugely important role to play.

This should be viewed as a partnership between the private sector, third sector, and public sector. Organisations learn from each other. I understand that many businesses and organisations, while being committed to the principle of gender balance, will have concerns about their ability to overcome the challenges to achieve 50:50 by 2020. It will be important to learn from those who have or are in the process of overcoming these challenges themselves.

To those who might worry about signing lest they fall slightly short, I would say this. As in any area of life, we are more likely to make progress in the right direction by aiming high than we ever will by being overcautious. So, in the interest of sharing experience and ambition, I am delighted that four businesses will join us for the panel discussion: Alliance Trust Savings, The Gate Interactive, Virgin Money and Quorum Network Resources.

In welcoming men as well as women to the panel, let me make this point. Women cannot, and should not be expected to, win the battle for gender equality on their own. We need men who are already in senior positions to show leadership, too.

· The final point I want to make is that the discussion we will have this afternoon is just one example of the much wider partnership that the Scottish Government tries to build with business, the third sector and the wider public sector.

Scottish Government and our enterprise agencies are working with businesses to build a stronger economy, to help companies to innovate, export and expand and, as part of that, are encouraging and helping companies to adopt progressive employment practices. Measures which are good for society, but which also benefit a business's reputation and its bottom line. These includes gender equality as well as measures like the living wage and encouraging employees to have a say in how the company is run.

This partnership approach is already seeing success. Around this time last year, thirty organisations had achieved accreditation as living wage employers. There are now more than two hundred. Hard evidence that businesses want to do the right thing for their employees and for themselves.

Today is a real milestone for the cause of gender balance, with 137 organisations signed up to this groundbreaking 50:50 pledge. I am sure they will be joined by many more in the months and years ahead.

At the start of my speech I mentioned how many young people there are in today's audience. My ambition for all of you is that you will have a fair chance to succeed. That you will know that, if you work hard and have the ability, there is nothing to stop you realising your dreams. The 50:50 pledge will contribute, and I believe that its adoption will make businesses and other organisations more successful. It will make Scotland's economy more prosperous and our society fairer.

6

WOMEN HOLD UP HALF THE SKY

*Given to the Chinese People's Association for Friendship with
Foreign Countries*
Beijing, 27th July 2015

On a trade mission to China and Hong Kong, NS gave this
keynote speech to an audience of more than a hundred women
from Chinese academia, business, and government. Touching
on familiar themes, she spoke in impressive detail not only of
measurable progress in gender equality but also of the many
continuing challenges. Citing the inspirational example of
Malala Yousafzai, similarly inspirational words of Mary
Robinson, and the guidance and support offered by the United
Nations, she closed by pointing in the direction of opportunity.
Before that, though, she demonstrated how a country like
Scotland, small and without complete sovereignty, can and does
contribute to the global struggle against ignorance and poverty,
and on that basis speaks to larger nations as a moral equal.

I am delighted to speak to the Chinese Friendship Association
today, and grateful for the good work you do in strengthening the
ties between our Scottish Affairs Office in Beijing and the Chinese
Government's State Council, knowing that ours is just one example
of your good work in forging friendships around the world. I am
especially pleased to be speaking about gender equality, as this is a
highly appropriate time and location.

It is twenty years since Beijing hosted the fourth World

Conference on Women, a conference that famously included the affirmation that human rights are women's rights, and that women's rights are human rights. The Beijing Platform for Action rallied governments and international organisations around the world to do more and, in Scotland, led us to establish our first ever framework against domestic violence.

I wish to talk today about how we make a reality of the beautiful Chinese saying that 'women hold up half the sky', and discuss some of the steps we are taking in Scotland before addressing wider international issues. First though, I want to look back across those twenty years since the Beijing conference. Not so much in terms of the progress made on women's rights, but in terms of China's own achievements.

In 1995, China's GDP per head was a seventh of what it is now, and its economy has gone from being less than a third of the USA's, to being of comparable size, progress that has transformed global trade. Perhaps most importantly of all, hundreds of millions of people have been lifted out of poverty. China accounts for around three quarters of the world's total decline in extreme poverty over the past thirty years.

China has always had extraordinary human resources, but in 1995 was still only beginning to realise its full economic potential. Twenty years later, as its economy continues to expand, the consequences are proving to be momentous and beneficial not just to China, but to the wider world.

Although the following comparison is not exact, it is worth thinking about. The world has been changed dramatically, and for the better, because China is making greater use of the productive potential of more than 900 million working age people.

There are currently over two billion working age women across the world, but there is virtually no country, on any continent, where women have equal economic opportunities to men. When Christine Lagarde, Director of the International Monetary Fund, spoke in Shanghai earlier this year she stressed the importance of gender equality in contributing to higher, more sustainable growth. The IMF has calculated that, if women participated in the labour market to the same extent as men, income per person would increase by a quarter in south Asia, and by a seventh in Europe, Central Asia, and East Asia.

For virtually every nation, fully empowering women is probably the single simplest way to sustainably increase productive potential. Gender equality can help to transform the global economy.

Just as women's rights are human rights, so women's innovations are human innovations. Women's wealth-creation is human wealth-creation. Women's prosperity is human prosperity. Societies impoverish themselves when they stifle the talent of half of their population.

Just as everyone benefits from gender equality, so everyone should help to promote it. This is not just a job for government, and it is certainly not just a job for women. Everyone can play a part in making it clear that violence against women is unacceptable. Everyone can refuse to perpetuate prejudice and discrimination. Everyone can help to combat gender stereotyping whether at work, school, or in the home.

Some important aspects of gender equality are about simple things: how we play with children; how we talk with them as they are growing up; what they are encouraged to do by families, friends, and the media.

Some of you may have young daughters or nieces. If you do, I suspect you will have the same hopes for them that I do for my own niece. That she does not have to face everyday sexism, gender pay gaps, and underrepresentation in positions of influence. My hope is that the men and women of my generation will have addressed those problems before she even becomes aware of them. At heart, that is not just an economic issue, although the economic argument is important, it is a question of fundamental, universal human rights. About giving everyone an equal chance to live in dignity, fulfil their potential and realise their dreams.

Those combined moral and economic imperatives explain why gender equality has become such an important feature in the Scottish Government's approach to economic growth. To give some idea of how much we have already achieved, it is worth noting that the nations of the G20, including both China and the United Kingdom, have a collective commitment. They have pledged to reduce the gender gap in employment by a quarter in ten years' time.

In Scotland, we have more than halved the gender gap in just three years, from ten percentage points to four percentage points, and our female employment rate is the second best in the European Union. Despite that progress, women in Scotland are still less likely to be on company boards or senior management posts, and more likely to be in low-paid professions.

Although women make up more than half of all higher education students in Scotland, they make up just a seventh of engineering and technology students, and less than a fifth of computer science students. We are still underusing the talents of half our population.

So, we are acting on all stages of people's careers. Encouraging women to take up more science and engineering courses at school and university and doubling our investment in childcare to help parents into work. We have launched a major initiative at boardroom level, called 50:50 by 2020, and ask organisations to make the commitment that in five years' time, half of their board will be women. As a government, we are leading by example with a cabinet of five men and five women. According to the United Nations, it is one of only three gender-balanced cabinets in the developed world.

Finally, we are doing all we can to support women overseas through our international development work in places such as Pakistan and Malawi. In Pakistan we have established a scholarship programme for up to 250 women from poor backgrounds, inspired by Malala Yousafzai's stand on girls' education. Delivered with the British Council, it enables women to study Masters-related courses in Education and Energy, and is one of the ways in which we are hoping to encourage a new generation of female leaders in education, industry and wider society.

Much of the work we do in Scotland will strike a chord here in China, where gender equality is incorporated in the constitution. Women account for forty-five per cent of your workforce, and you recognise the importance of women being fully involved in decision-making. Chu Guang, speaking at the United Nations, argued recently that it is 'an important guarantee for women's empowerment'.

As with all societies, certainly including Scotland's, there is more that China can do. To give one example, women are still significantly underrepresented among key decision-makers in business and government. The truth is that virtually all countries are on a journey towards true gender equality, but none have completely arrived. We need to learn from each other how best to make progress.

Twenty years ago, the fourth women's summit in Beijing was an important part of that dialogue, that learning process. So, it is appropriate that, in September, China is marking its twentieth anniversary by co-hosting, with the United Nations, the Global Leaders' Meeting on Gender Equality and Women's Empowerment.

China's willingness to show leadership is especially important at this present time. In September, world leaders will agree the new Sustainable Development Goals in New York. In December, they are due to decide future action on climate change in Paris. Gender equality is important to both and must be at the heart of sustainable development.

The previous Millennium Development Goals[11] contributed

---

11. The new millennium goals laid down by the United Nations are: eradication of extreme poverty, universal primary education, gender equality, reduce child mortality, improve maternal health, eradication of HIV/AIDS and other diseases, environmental sustainability, and a global development partnership.

to the advancement of women by improving girls' access to education. However, improving the status of women and girls remains critical, and includes tackling violence against women and properly valuing their work. Therefore, I am delighted that the draft sustainable development goals address the empowerment of women more effectively than their predecessors.

As UN Secretary General Ban Ki-Moon has said, 'removing the barriers that keep women and girls on the margins of economic, social, cultural, and political life must be a top priority for us all: businesses, governments, the United Nations and civil society'.

As we look towards the Paris summit in December, we must remember that there is a significant gender dimension to climate change. The worst impacts are disproportionately felt by women, who are more likely to be subsistence farmers and affected when crops fail, who carry water and walk further in times of drought. It is girls who are more likely to stop going to school when tough times force the family to work even harder.

As we tackle and mitigate climate change, we need to ensure that women are equally represented when it comes to taking decisions. To quote Mary Robinson, the President of the Mary Robinson Climate Justice Foundation: 'Women are at the heart of effective solutions to addressing the impacts of climate change. They are the most convincing advocates for the policy solutions that they require and have a right to participate in decision-making processes.'

That basic principle applies beyond the context of climate change. Women's rights are not something that can primarily be considered and taken account of by men. Women and men should have equal opportunities to lead and take decisions, and this should be seen as a basic right to be recognised by communities, companies, and governments around the world. The point is that whether in a small village in a developing country, or in the technology and engineering firms of the advanced economies, we all benefit when women are able to contribute their ideas, expertise, leadership and talent as freely as men.

I began this speech by referring to the Chinese saying, 'women hold up half the sky'. However, women should not just be supporting the sky. We should be reaching for it. We need to ensure that young girls and women today feel confident that if they have the ability, and work hard enough, there are no limits to what they can achieve.

In the twenty years since the last Beijing summit, the world has seen extraordinary change. When we think about the progress made by China or consider the communications revolution that has transformed so much of what we do, we are reminded that there are virtually no limits to human ingenuity. It seems paradoxical therefore, that we do not always show the same ingenuity and resolve when it comes to our greatest resource: the full potential of our people.

For all the progress we have seen in the last two decades, virtually no country enables women to participate equally in the workplace, which is why gender equality, as well as being a fundamental issue of human rights, is also one of the great economic opportunities of the 21st century.

7

60,000 EXCITED LITTLE MINDS

Launching the Scottish Government's Attainment Challenge
Wester Hailes Education Centre, 18th September 2015

The Scottish Government Attainment Challenge aims to raise
the attainment levels of children in deprived areas and in this
way close the attainment gap. In this speech, NS recognised
the difference in life chances of children raised in wealthier
areas against those raised in poorer circumstances. Taking this
opportunity to praise all involved for the real progress that had
been made, she also spoke frankly of how much had still to be
achieved and its importance. She also referenced the late Jimmy
Reid in whose memory she would, later in the year, give a lecture.
Literacy and literature were always (and still are) close to her
heart and the following year she would begin the First Minister's
Reading Challenge for children.

This week is the first week of term for many young people,
including almost 60,000 children who are entering Primary One.
60,000 excited little minds, eager to learn and curious about the
world around them. Our duty to them is sacred.

Earlier today, I visited Clovenstone Primary and found myself,
inevitably, thinking back to my own school days. I was fortunate
that my education at Dreghorn Primary and Greenwood Academy
in Ayrshire was first class. My teachers were superb and the quality
of education, together with wonderful parents who encouraged
me to see horizons beyond their own, are the reasons that this

working-class girl from Ayrshire stands here today as First Minister of Scotland.

It matters to me, deeply and personally, that every young girl and boy growing up, regardless of where they were born or family circumstances, gets the same chances that I did. It also matters to us as a nation.

Scotland pioneered the idea of universal access to education in the 17th and 18th centuries and that commitment has been part of our sense of ourselves ever since, but there is more to it than pride in our past. Excellence in education is essential to our prosperity, competitiveness, and future success. Since this is the first school year to begin since I became First Minister I want to make clear that the government intends to ensure that our proud educational traditions are renewed and refreshed for the modern age. They should stand not as a symbol of the past but a hallmark of our future.

I want to be able to say, with confidence and evidence, that there is no better place in the world to be educated, and this claim holds true for all young people regardless of background or circumstance. In outlining how the government will help children to have the best possible start in life, I will set out two overarching priorities.

The first is straightforward. We want to raise standards everywhere, for every pupil in every school in the country. The second follows from the first. We want to raise standards most quickly where improvement is most needed, and to close the gap in educational outcomes between pupils from the most and least deprived parts of Scotland. Before talking about how to do that, I want to emphasise an important truth that is too often overlooked.

Despite the challenges we face, Scotland's schools are a success story. The last eight years have been tough. The recession followed by deep public spending cuts have created pressures for the Scottish Government, for local government, and for many families... and yet education in Scotland has made progress.

The introduction of Curriculum for Excellence has been a

major step forward and is now attracting international attention. It gives teachers more flexibility, provides a broader education for young people, and sets higher standards for achievement than ever before.

More than five hundred schools have been rebuilt or refurbished since 2007, a fifth of all school premises in the country and two hundred more than in the previous eight years. Funding has been provided to maintain teacher numbers. In 2006, more than fifteen thousand Primary One children were in classes of more than twenty-five. Now, the figure is below five hundred.

In 2007, just forty-five per cent of students stayed on at school until 6th year. Now, the proportion is sixty-two per cent, an increase made possible by retaining the educational maintenance allowance that was abolished in England. This step benefits 35,000 school pupils and college students yearly, and we are seeing better outcomes than ever before.

School leaver destinations are the best on record. Of the students who left school last year, more than nine out of ten were in employment, education, or training, nine months later. Two weeks ago, young people in Scotland gained a record number of passes at Higher and Advanced Higher, but the successes have not just been about Highers. More people received Awards, National Certificates and National Progression Awards, and qualifications relating to wider skills for life and work. From childcare to construction, in leadership and personal finance, we are providing a more flexible school environment with more qualifications providing routes into work.

Preparing young people for work is going to be an even bigger focus in the future, and we are working increasingly closely with employers. By implementing a national plan for developing the young workforce and widening access to our universities, we are expanding what young people can learn and where they can learn it. In our last national performance report, ninety per cent of schools were graded satisfactory or better. To suggest, as some have done, that ninety per cent of schools are merely satisfactory is to ignore the 'or better' part of the categorisation. In fact, the percentage of schools with a grading of just satisfactory was twenty-one per cent. Sixty-nine per cent of schools were graded as good, very good, or excellent.

Let me be clear that I am not satisfied with that. None of us should be. Given the work we are doing, I want to see the percentage of schools in the good or better category rise on a yearly basis. Education Scotland is reviewing its approaches to inspection and will advise me specifically on any changes they consider would support that wider improvement work.

However, the basic picture is clear. In every part of the country Scotland has good schools, good teachers, and our young people are good learners. Standards have risen, continue to rise, and are testament to the work not only of our local authorities but also the contributions of many other individuals and organisations. The third sector, youth workers and community learning and development staff all work increasingly closely with schools. Most of all, it is a tribute to the dedication of teachers, parents, and students across the country.

Wester Hailes Education Centre is a great example of this progress. In 2009 only six per cent of school leavers here gained at least one Higher. Last year, forty-three did. It is a place where better schooling and better results are leading to better life chances. Two points follow.

The first is that it is impossible to think about that success without appreciation of the expertise, commitment, and passion of the teachers here . . . led by Sheila Paton until recently, and now by Stuart Heggie. I also met great teachers at Clovenstone Primary this morning, led by Carolyn Didcock.

In schools across the country, how much we owe our teachers and headteachers is apparent, which is why we are investing in their professional development through Teaching Scotland's future, and why we have established the Scottish College for

Educational Leadership. Supporting teachers and headteachers to be local leaders, drivers of change and improvement, is an essential part of supporting our young people. So, next month will see the start of our new Masters-level qualification for headship which, by the summer of 2019, will be mandatory.

The second point is that the success we have seen here at Wester Hailes, and across Scotland, must encourage us to aim for even greater improvements. Although standards have risen across the board, we need to do more. The recent SSLN [Scottish Survey of Literacy and Numeracy] report, suggesting that standards of literacy have fallen, was of significant concern to me, as it should be to all who care about the future of our young people.

Much of the attainment work we are undertaking is focussed on literacy and numeracy. We know though, that there is a significant attainment gap between different parts of Scotland. There is evidence that progress is being made, but not far or quickly enough.

In 2008, just over two in ten students from our most deprived areas obtained at least one higher or equivalent. Last year, the figure was almost four in ten. However, for students from the most affluent areas, the figure was not four out of ten. It was eight out of ten. In other words, when it comes to Highers, school leavers from the most deprived twenty per cent of Scotland currently do half as well as school leavers from the most affluent areas.

That is quite simply unacceptable, and we must strive to improve. My aim, to put it bluntly, is to close that attainment gap completely. It will not be done overnight, but it must be done. Its existence is more than economic and social. It is a moral challenge that goes to the very heart of who we are and how we see ourselves as a country.

Five years ago, I went to the funeral service of Jimmy Reid, the great trade union activist, in Govan Old Parish Church. Billy Connolly was one of the speakers, and he told a story about going for walks with Jimmy in Govan when they were young. This was probably in the 1950s, in the constituency I now represent. Jimmy would point to a tower block and say: 'Behind that window is a guy who could win Formula One. And behind that one there's a winner of the round-the-world yacht race. And behind the next one... and none of them will ever get the chance to sit at the wheel of a racing car or in the cockpit of a yacht.'

It is a beautiful way of expressing how poverty can stifle aspiration but, despite our many achievements, still too relevant today, and not only relevant to the exceptional occupations Jimmy mentioned.

To look at a profession like medicine... The most deprived twenty per cent of Scotland provides one in five of Scotland's school leavers, but just one in twenty successful entrants for medicine and dentistry courses. That underrepresentation is not a reflection of young people's talent. It reflects the fact that, for all the great work done in our schools, too many children's life chances are more influenced by where they live than by how talented they are, or how hard they work. If we are missing many of the talented medics of the future, it does not take much imagination to guess what else we are missing: engineers, computer coders, life scientists, artists, teachers. Even MSPs and MPs.

The attainment gap does not simply hold back young people who deserve a fair chance to fulfil their potential. It impoverishes us. Closing that gap is a defining challenge for the government I lead, and for our society.

Everyone in this room will be aware that a huge amount of what we need to do goes beyond the education system. By the time children enter school, at the age of five, the gap in vocabulary between the poorest and wealthiest families can already be eighteen months. Therefore, when UK Government cuts to tax credits and welfare hurt many households, the work we do to support children and families matters hugely. It is vital to tackle poverty and use the Scottish Parliament's new welfare powers to support parents through investment in health visitors for young children, and early reading projects such as Bookbug.

Our major expansion of early learning and childcare is one of the best investments we can make as a country.

School education and how it relates to people's home and family circumstances is hugely important and is the focus of my remarks today. While we must recognise and address the factors beyond the school gates, we must never be content to shrug our shoulders and accept that these factors make under-attainment in our schools inevitable. We must see school education as one of the most powerful tools at our disposal to overcome the disadvantages associated with poverty. We must make a reality of the adage that education is the great leveller in life.

I want to outline today some of the work we are doing to increase standards in all schools and, crucially, raising them most quickly in the areas where they are most needed. We are focussing some of our key initiatives on primary schools because we believe that, by closing the attainment gap when children are young, the benefits will continue into secondary school and beyond.

We will focus on young people's literacy, numeracy, health and wellbeing, and will ensure that the education system adapts to the career paths and work patterns of the future. That will be a major theme in developing the young workforce, but we must ensure that all children have a good grounding in the most essential skills. Children's ability to read, write and count, to be confident, healthy, and happy learners, underpins their success in all other subjects. So, I will talk about our plans for improving literacy and numeracy and begin with a fundamental point.

When it comes to the education of our young people, to improving attainment and closing the gap, what matters is what works. All our attainment initiatives within Scotland encourage schools to learn from each other, and the Scottish Government is happy to learn lessons from around the world. In the last six months I have visited successful and improving schools in Tower Hamlets in London and Brooklyn in New York.

However, if you believe that what matters is what works, you must accept something else. We need information about children's attainment to measure progress consistently, acutely in primary and early secondary school. Virtually all local authorities recognise the importance of standardised assessment for those age groups, and thirty out of thirty-two currently use it. Standardised assessment helps teachers by providing factual information to support their judgement. However, local authorities may use different systems, which makes it more difficult to get a clear and consistent picture.

We are now developing a National Improvement Framework. I will say more about how it will address this issue of clear and consistent information when I set out my Programme for Government to the Scottish Parliament, but its basic purpose will be to provide clarity by measuring where we are succeeding and where we need to do more. In doing that it will enable us to raise standards more quickly and, as a result, help to change the future for young people across our country. The improvement framework will underpin all the other steps we are taking.

Last year, we launched Raising Attainment for All, a voluntary programme now covering more than 250 schools in twenty-four local authority areas. Not only about significant extra funding, which is not always possible in the current spending climate, it is more about helping schools to try new things and learn from each other.

The schools themselves identify what they will do to improve standards, and then assess whether those actions are working. One school is focusing on setting aside time so that children can read for pleasure; another is prioritising written work among a certain age group; another might work on improving numeracy; others are trying different approaches according to their particular needs. These ideas and examples are shared so that whatever works best can be used more widely.

Raising Attainment for All has been working well over the last year, but we know we need to do more and are supporting the recruitment of an attainment adviser in every local authority area, while launching two further initiatives for primary schools. The Read Write Count literacy and numeracy campaign began yesterday and, in the coming months, all children in Primary One will be sent a pack of books and learning materials. Primaries Two and Three will receive a pack in 2016.

The campaign encourages young children and recognises the crucial importance of parents. Providing hints for possible activities, whether reading to the children at bedtime or playing counting games in the supermarket, it also includes special sessions, targeted in areas of greater deprivation, which will bring parents and carers together with teachers.

Most importantly of all in this context, the Scottish Government announced earlier in the year that we would allocate an additional £100m over the next four years to a Scottish Attainment Challenge. The Challenge will focus specifically on, and provide additional funding for, literacy, numeracy, health and wellbeing in primary schools in our most deprived areas.

A large proportion of the Attainment Fund has been allocated to the seven local authorities which have the highest concentration of pupils living in poverty. Each of those authorities is developing its own plans according to its own priorities. Most of the extra funding is being used to recruit more staff: teachers, classroom assistants, learning support specialists and family link workers. As a result, schools will be able to provide even better support for children and parents in the areas where it is most needed.

West Dunbartonshire will provide targeted support as children move from nursery to primary, and from primary to secondary schools. It will also recruit more maths specialists to improve teaching in primary school. Dundee's plans include a strong focus on music, drama, and dance. Glasgow is recruiting ninety additional teachers and looking at staff development, among other issues. The point is that each local authority has flexibility, and the Scottish Government, together with each authority, will closely monitor the results. The evidence of what works will be shared.

Of course, the fund is not solely for those seven local authorities. Today I can confirm that it will support fifty-seven more schools in another fourteen local authority areas, taking the total number of primary schools benefiting to more than three hundred.

One of the reasons I visited Clovenstone Primary today, is that it is one of the Edinburgh schools which will benefit. A school which already has a strong focus on literacy and numeracy, it is working increasingly closely with parents and the wider community. This funding will enable it to do even more for its students, including the boys and girls I met who were starting Primary One today.

The final area we are focusing on is aspiration, and I want to be clear about exactly what is meant here. It is all too easy to think it is the job of adults to give children aspirations, as though they would not have them otherwise. Most young people are full of ambition and dreams. Often lacking as they get older though, are the information, support, and role models to make them see that those aspirations are achievable.

We are putting together an aspirations package for schools, and will work with organisations such as the Children's University, as well as local employers and entrepreneurs, to ensure that young people have access to the experience, knowledge and networks that can help them realise what they might achieve. A practical approach to help them understand the work they need to do to realise their ambitions, this is also consistent with the aims of the Commission for Developing Scotland's Young Workforce. It is another way of giving our young people a fair chance to succeed, to find work which makes good use of their talents, and enable them to lead productive, fulfilling, and happy lives. More than anything else, that is what this government wants to achieve.

I spoke earlier about Jimmy Reid's reflections on the wasted potential he saw when he was growing up in Govan. His famous Glasgow University Rectorial address, in 1972, captured the same point differently, but just as well: 'The untapped resources of the

North Sea are as nothing compared to the untapped resources of our people.'

Every young person should have the same advantages that I did while growing up in Ayrshire. They should know that if they have the talent, and work hard enough, they will be able to fulfil their potential. That is a challenge for schools, local government, indeed for society as a whole, and it is one on which my government is determined to show leadership.

8

OUR RESPONSE WILL BE JUDGED BY HISTORY

Given to a humanitarian summit including the refugee community, third sector, local authorities, religious and political leaders, and others
St Andrews House, Edinburgh, 4th September 2015

The news of the tragic death by drowning of three-year-old Alan Shenu[12], and the accompanying photograph, precipitated much thinking and feeling on the refugee crisis that now reached from Syria into Europe. No immediate or even long-term solution was apparent, but the crisis had to be met somehow. Millions of refugees were widely described as migrants, even illegal migrants, a term that shifted the responsibility of sanctuary, and blame for their fate, away from political authority onto the victims themselves. By using the simple phrase 'language and terminology matter' NS not only illuminated this point but also accepted appropriate responsibility for the country she led. Her speech is an exercise in humanitarian thinking, equalled by few other national leaders other than Angela Merkel.

I am delighted to be joined here in St Andrews House by so many from our aid agencies, humanitarian organisations and churches, people and organisations who do outstanding work in helping those in need overseas and welcoming those in need of asylum. I am also delighted that we are joined by some who have found a

---

12.   Alan was originally identified as Aylan Kurdi, with Kurdi being an indicator of ethnic background.

safe and welcoming home here in Scotland. Lastly, let me welcome the leaders of the opposition parties, and representatives of local government, whose presence signals our shared determination to contribute a practical, cross-party response to a humanitarian crisis that is shocking the world.

Let us be in no doubt, what we are witnessing today is on a scale not seen in Europe since the Second World War. The United Nations estimates that up to a third of a million people have tried to cross the Mediterranean in the last few months alone. Nearly three thousand have died in the process. Desperate people are travelling through Turkey, Greece, and the Balkans into Hungary as they try to get to Austria and Germany.

The images of people suffocating in the backs of trucks, of children drowning, of people losing their lives as they try to cross from Calais to Britain, haunt us daily, and will haunt our consciences and reputations for generations if we do not act to help those in desperate need.

I am not suggesting that solutions are easy, nor am I suggesting that we can help everyone. We know that we cannot, but that is no excuse for not doing everything we can. Yes, the long-term solution must be peace and stability in the countries from which people are fleeing. Yes, we must tackle the criminal gangs and traffickers who profit out of human misery. We must do all of that, but we cannot leave our fellow human beings to perish in the meantime.

In Scotland, we have a long and proud tradition as a welcoming and tolerant nation. A country where, down the generations, thousands of people fleeing persecution, war, and desperate circumstances, have found refuge, a place of safety and a home to call their own.

Scotland is richer for the contribution they have made, but that welcoming and tolerant tradition is not unique to our country. It is something that we have long shared with our neighbours across these islands. Britain down the generations has distinguished itself in the welcome it has given to refugees. Just this year, we marked the passing of Sir Nicholas Winton, who organised the *kinder-transport*, bringing 10,000 children to the UK from Nazi occupied territory. That proud history of compassion and leadership, as well as our human despair at the images we see daily on our TV screens, makes it desperately dispiriting to see the UK Government struggle to show leadership in this refugee crisis.

Let me be clear, that is exactly what this is: a refugee crisis. Language and terminology matter. It is important that we do not describe this as a migration crisis. Immigration and asylum are not the same things.

In my view, treating the refugees and asylum seekers as migrants is making it difficult for David Cameron [UK prime minister at the time] to show leadership. Instead of being a humanitarian response to a refugee crisis, it has become part of a pejorative debate on immigration. One policy step the Prime Minister might take is to remove refugees from his target on net migration.

The people we see crowding railway stations and wading ashore on Europe's southern and eastern frontiers are not willing migrants. They are desperate, frightened, and vulnerable human beings forced to flee their homelands, and the fact that so many are prepared to risk their lives and the lives of their children should be proof enough of that.

The image this week of three-year old Aylan Kurdi washed ashore on a Turkish beach is heart-breaking beyond words. It moved me and countless others around the world to tears and is now seared into the collective consciousness of the world. It is a demonstration, in the starkest and cruellest terms possible, of the reality of this crisis. A chain of human misery stretching from the south-eastern boundaries of the EU all the way to North Africa, Syria, Afghanistan, and other countries.

As I said earlier, there are no easy answers to this crisis. Its causes are complex and varied and will not be solved overnight. However, I do believe we need a better response. These people are 'real' asylum seekers. They are 'genuine' refugees, and we have a moral responsibility to them. We cannot, and must not, walk on the other side of the street while a human catastrophe of enormous proportions unfolds on our doorstep.

As an EU member state, we have a duty as well as a moral obligation to meet our responsibilities by accepting a fair and proportionate share of refugees. We cannot leave others to shoulder the responsibility alone. Indeed, the contrast between the UK's stance and that of other EU nations, Germany in particular, could not be more stark.

Despite those concerns, I am encouraged that there does appear to be a change of approach after a distinct and understandable change in public opinion in recent days, with a general acceptance that we simply must do more to help.

If that change is matched by the Prime Minister and his government, as has been suggested, it will be a welcome development. I note David Cameron's comments from Lisbon earlier this morning but, welcome as they are, we need to hear more detail of what he is proposing. This problem is unprecedented in its nature, but it is not beyond resolution if we act firmly with a response that matches the scale of the crisis.

As I said in a letter to the Prime Minister last night, the scale of such a humanitarian emergency is immense but not insurmountable. We recognise the need for long-term, coordinated action to tackle the causes, but that cannot preclude an immediate humanitarian response.

With our neighbours and friends across the EU, we have a moral obligation to offer a place of safety to desperate people fleeing conflict and persecution. I welcomed the expansion of the Syrian Vulnerable Person Relocation Scheme, but it is not sufficient to address a crisis that transcends politics. We need practical, collective, and co-ordinated action to deliver help to those who need it.

Today's summit will be a chance to examine how we in Scotland can play our part, informed by what we will hear at first-hand from those with most experience.

It has been suggested that we should ready ourselves to accept a thousand refugees, and I believe we should do so, not as a cap or limit but as a starting point for meaningful discussion on how much we can contribute. The practicalities of accepting refugees, including questions about how they can be accommodated, are important issues and I look forward to hearing the views of those gathered here today. I also look forward to finding practical ways to galvanise the public desire to help and will make clear that the Scottish Government, working with our partners in local government, will provide practical help and assistance.

Our response to this crisis today, in Scotland, the UK and across the EU, will be judged by history.

I hope that we can make future generations as proud of us as we are of Sir Nicholas Winton and his generation, and that our proud traditions have not perished in a narrow debate about immigration. Instead, when the world is looking for leadership, courage, and a simple display of common humanity, we will be found standing eagerly at the front of the queue, not cowering timidly at the back. As First Minister of Scotland, my message is a simple one. We stand ready, in the best traditions of this nation, to offer sanctuary to those who so desperately need it.

9

HUMAN RIGHTS ARE NOT ALWAYS CONVENIENT BUT...

Given to an audience of civic leaders and human-rights activists including Baroness Shami Chakrabarti, director of Liberty
Pearce Institute, Govan, 23rd September 2015

In June of 2015, prime minister David Cameron threatened to withdraw the United Kingdom from the European Convention on Human Rights, in full knowledge that acts of the Scottish Parliament were obliged to comply with it and that human rights were a devolved responsibility. Later in the year NS gave this speech in the Convention's defence. Remarkable in its scope and historical reference, it was reported across the United Kingdom, and indeed the world. Shami Chakrabarti would say 'The First Minister of Scotland shows international leadership today. She vows to defend the Human Rights Act, the European Convention on Human Rights and the vulnerable against the powerful everywhere'. She had 'waited a long time for a senior politician in power to make a speech like that.' So had many others.

Thank you very much indeed, Shami, and thank you all for joining us on this important occasion. I am delighted that we are here in the Pearce Institute, which I know well. Before the boundary commission got their hands on my constituency it was situated within it. For decades, the Pearce Institute has been at the heart of the community in Govan.

It is also a pleasure, for both Shami and me, to speak here in the Mary Barbour room, because a hundred years ago this year Mary Barbour's army, as they were known, led the Glasgow rent strikes. Strikes that asserted the right of tenants to be protected from exploitative rent rises, in which groups of women drove away sheriff officers as they tried to evict tenants. The strikers forced the UK Government to impose rent caps and, in doing so, won a significant victory for the fundamental right to decent housing and decent lives. I can think of no more appropriate place to be launching a defence of human rights.

Mary Barbour exemplifies the sense of solidarity and social justice that has characterised the best elements of Scotland's political tradition and is so relevant to what we are here to talk about this morning. The cause of human rights is also the cause of social justice and is founded on the recognition that all human beings have equal worth and are entitled to the same fundamental protections and freedoms. Today I want to talk about the importance of the protections granted by the European Convention on Human Rights and by the Human Rights Act and am going to make three fundamental points.

The first is that repealing or weakening the provisions of the Human Rights Act, as the current UK Government intends to do, would be a monumental mistake. It would remove important protections from people within the UK and deeply damage the UK's reputation overseas. Secondly, I will explain how the Scottish Government will respond to any UK Government proposals by seeking to ensure that human rights protections are retained in Scotland, and how we will do all we can to ensure they are retained across the UK. Finally, I will point out that far from being a burden on government, the European Convention on Human Rights sets minimum standards that we should be looking to build on. The Scottish Government is doing that by placing social and economic rights at the heart of our policy making, but I want to start with a basic point.

The European Convention on Human Rights is a considerable achievement of post-war Europe, perhaps its finest. It was a direct response to the atrocities seen before and during World War II and has been remarkably effective in defining common principles and standards that are now agreed by almost all countries across the continent. Far from looking to row back from it, we should be proud that politicians across the UK played such a leading role in its formation. Winston Churchill championed it. A leading Scottish Conservative, David Maxwell Fyfe, played a major part in drafting it. The UK was one of the first states to ratify it.

It is also important to point out that the Human Rights Act in 1998 did not give any new rights to UK citizens, but simply ensured that Convention rights could be interpreted and considered by courts here in Britain. That is perhaps one reason why its introduction was relatively uncontroversial and received cross-party support. That cross-party support makes it somewhat surprising that the Conservative manifesto at the last election said: 'We will scrap *Labour's* Human Rights Act and introduce a British Bill of Rights'.

At this moment, none of us know how this Bill of Rights would work. The UK Government does not seem to have any clear idea, but that is perhaps because their pledge created an unnecessary dilemma. Nobody believes that the UK Government will take this opportunity to strengthen existing human rights protections, which would be opposed bitterly by some in the Conservative party. They must also know, as former and current Tory MPs have warned, that weakening human rights protections will diminish the UK's reputation overseas, damage relations with devolved governments, and impact on the welfare of people in the UK.

It would also cause unnecessary confusion and inconvenience. If we assume, although this might not be a safe assumption, that the real agenda of the Tories does not include withdrawing from the European Convention then, even if the Human Rights Act were to be repealed, the Convention will still apply to UK citizens. Instead of being interpreted by domestic courts, cases could only be heard in Strasbourg and those who need fundamental human rights protections might still be able to obtain them... albeit with longer delays, less convenience and greater expense. Ironically, with less of a role for courts in the UK, given that the Tories' stated objective is the supremacy of the UK courts.

To consider this issue in detail is to quickly reach a conclusion that the UK Government, for reasons of media presentation and party management, finds impossible to acknowledge. The Human Rights Act exists for a reason. It is a sensible way of ensuring that Convention rights, which the UK did so much to define, are taken into account by UK courts. A proportionate, pragmatic, and progressive piece of legislation, its value is greatest for those who are most marginalised and most in need of protection.

That point becomes especially clear when you look at the key rights protected by the European Convention and the Act. They include, and this is not a full list, but it is representative: the right to life... the right not to be tortured... the right not to be enslaved... the right to liberty and the security of the person... the right to a fair trial... the right to marry... the right not to be discriminated against... the right of fair access to education... the right to free elections.

When Lord Bingham spoke at Liberty's 75th anniversary in 2009, he posed these questions: 'Which of these rights would we wish to discard? Are any of them trivial, superfluous, unnecessary?' Questions that have never been answered, and certainly not by the UK Government, rights that matter to all of us, they should be among the founding principles of any civilised society.

Applying human rights is not always easy, and nor should it be, because it should challenge governments. Some of you will remember that, shortly after the Scottish Parliament was established, Scotland's custom of appointing temporary sheriffs was ruled as being incompatible with the right to an independent and impartial tribunal. There was uproar for a time in Scotland but, looking back now, nobody would defend the old system in which members of the judiciary had their tenure renewed every year by the head of the prosecution service. Although that decision was deeply uncomfortable for the government at the time, it was beneficial in the long term, and it improved our system of justice.

That is as it should be. Human rights are not always convenient for governments, but they are not meant to be. Their purpose is to protect the powerless, not to strengthen those in power. If you weaken human rights protections, contrary to how things are sometimes portrayed, you are not striking a blow at judges in Strasbourg, lawyers in London or politicians in Scotland. You are striking at the poor, the vulnerable, and the dispossessed, and I think Shami and Liberty have done a fantastic job of documenting and illustrating that fact.

Article 4 of the Convention prohibits slavery and forced labour. It is startling to many people that such a right should be necessary in modern society, but it has been used, very recently, by victims of modern slavery within the UK. For example, by Patience Asuquo in Snaresbrook in London, who was forced to work without pay and time off for almost three years. Her employer removed her passport and abused her. The police initially chose not to investigate her complaints, but eventually had to because of a human rights case brought by Liberty under Article 4. As a direct result, the law was changed across the UK to criminalise modern slavery. That is a case where a Convention Right did not secure justice for one person; it helped to secure stronger protections for everybody.

In Scotland, we have now introduced a Human Trafficking and Exploitation Bill to further improve the legal safeguards.

Article 3 grants freedom from torture, inhumane and degrading treatment, and has protected residents in care homes from neglect and mistreatment. It has also been used to protect rape victims from being cross-examined by alleged attackers.

There have been numerous other benefits. Improved standards on how people with disabilities are treated in police custody are a consequence of the Human Rights Act. The compensation that was paid to bereaved families affected by mistreatment at Mid-Staffordshire hospital was also a consequence.

The Human Rights Act has real benefits for people in the UK, but there is a wider point. Whatever decision the UK Parliament takes, it will have implications beyond these islands. If they take the wrong decision it will send the wrong message internationally.

I was struck by the testimony of Hossam Bahgat, the director of the Egyptian Initiative for Personal Rights, who was involved in the Tahrir Square uprising four years ago. He said, 'The most important thing that the British can do to support human rights in Egypt is to support human rights in the United Kingdom...It is significantly more difficult for us to fight for universal human rights in our country, if your country publicly walks away from the same universal rights.'

Dominic Grieve, the former Conservative attorney general, has made a similar point by highlighting the facts that (a) Russia is already using the UK's position on human rights to delay implementing European Court judgements, and (b) that the UK is being cited by countries like Venezuela as justification for ignoring obligations under the American Conventions on Human Rights. In Edinburgh, two days ago, he went on to say that the European Convention is, 'arguably the single most important legal and political instrument for promoting human rights on our planet'. He has previously stated that if the UK is 'instrumental in damaging its effectiveness it will sit very strangely with our settled policy of promoting human rights globally'.

I think those words demonstrate the unnecessary difficulty the UK Government has created. Repealing the Human Rights Act meets no pressing need and addresses no obvious problem. Instead, there is a risk that it will create legal confusion, harm people in the UK who need support and protection and give comfort to illiberal governments around the world. No responsible government should contemplate such a step. The question is where do we go from here?

That is a significant question for the Scottish Government and the Scottish Parliament, since this is an issue where we have potentially great influence. The Human Rights Act is reserved legislation. Responsibility for it rests with Westminster but, as most of you know, Convention Rights are embedded into the devolution settlement and human rights is a devolved issue. Any attempt to amend the Human Rights Act is likely, in our view, to require the legislative consent of the Scottish Parliament and it is inconceivable, given the breadth of support which the Act commands across the Scottish Parliament, that such consent would be granted.

Let me make clear that the Scottish Government will advocate that it is not granted by the Scottish Parliament. However, that is not the end of the matter. The Scottish Government will also oppose any weakening of human rights protections, not just in Scotland, but across the whole of the UK.

It has been rumoured that the UK Government will somehow try to carve Scotland out of what they are trying to do, so let me be clear that we would have no interest in doing a deal at Westminster that leaves rights intact in Scotland, but dilutes them in other parts of the country. Or as is perhaps more likely, protects human rights on devolved issues but not on reserved issues.

Human rights are not English, Scottish, Welsh, or Northern Irish rights. They are universal rights.

We believe that this approach will benefit people in Scotland and across the UK. We also believe that it stands a real chance of success. I believe that those who want to see the Human Rights Act retained can ensure that it is retained. After all, it did have cross-party support in 1998. The current UK Government has a small majority, and no guarantee of unanimous support on its own benches.

Repeal of the Human Rights Act is not inevitable. There is still a huge amount to be gained by making its case as strongly and clearly as possible. That is what the Scottish Government intends to do, and we will work with anyone and everyone to achieve it, whether they are from other political parties, other devolved governments, organisations like Liberty, Amnesty International and the Scottish Human Rights Commission, or civic society more widely. Human Rights protect everyone, and we want the broadest possible cross-section of society to support the Act.

The other thing the Scottish Government will do, and this is the final point I wish to make, is use our devolved powers to promote human rights across different areas of policy making. When the Act was passed in 1998, the intention was for the Convention to provide a floor for human rights across the UK and be incorporated within the domestic law of all the nations through the different devolution settlements. But the Convention was always intended to be a floor, not a ceiling. Devolved governments have the flexibility to go further and complying with the Convention should not be the limit of our ambitions.

The key challenge for progressive governments is not finding ways to avoid human rights responsibilities. It is finding ways to embed those responsibilities across different areas of policy.

The clearest possible example of that is the refugee crisis. We are seeing the largest movement of individuals in Europe since the Second World War. All countries should recognise and protect the fundamental rights of those fleeing war and persecution, which is why Scotland has promised to play a full part in offering sanctuary to those who need it. We have been helped hugely by the solidarity we have had from people across Scotland.

We are also putting human rights at the heart of our domestic policy, as we pledged to do in the National Action Plan for

Human Rights, which we launched two years ago. For example, our dementia strategy and standards are based on agreed rights for patients such as the right to be as independent as possible, to have access to a range of treatment, to have the right to be treated with dignity and respect.

Respect for the individual will be a central part of the new social security system we will develop as we gain additional powers[13], and we are looking at how to improve the system for disabled people and carers. A rights-based approach is one reason, although only one of many, why we are opposing the UK Government's Trade Union Bill. In Scotland, we see trade unions as partners, not opponents, and that partnership approach is one reason why the number of days lost in Scotland due to strikes has declined by eighty-four per cent in the last seven years.

The UK Government's approach to trade unions is, in my view, wrong, but it is also going to be counterproductive. It is bad for the rights and conditions of workers and because it encourages conflict with unions, will be harmful to employers. We will oppose it in every way we can.

What these examples demonstrate, the refugee crisis, trade unions, crucial healthcare services, is the point I made at the start. The cause of human rights is also the cause of social justice, which is why diluting the protections of the Human Rights Act will cause harm to those who most need help. It is why, if the UK Government sets out proposals to do that, the Scottish Government will be a vigorous and vociferous opponent.

We also want to move the debate about human rights on by setting an example which goes beyond the Convention rights that were signed more than sixty years ago. We want to embed human rights, including economic and social rights, in the way we make decisions as a nation, in the way public authorities deliver services,

13. After the recommendations of the Smith Commission, set up after the independence referendum of 2014 to deliver more powers to the Scottish Parliament.

and in the way we can empower individuals and communities.

Doing that will, I believe, help to achieve our ambition of a fairer, healthier, happier nation that protects the vulnerable and gives everyone an equal chance to flourish. One which comes closer to the ideals and inspirational example of social pioneers like the great Mary Barbour.

10

SCOTLAND AND ALCOHOL

Given to the Global Alcohol Policy Conference
Edinburgh International Conference Centre 7th October 2015

> Scotland's indulgent attitude to alcohol has for long been a
> byword throughout the world, with the drunken Scot as much
> a popular comic caricature as the miser. The reality has too often
> been tragically different. Endemic health issues and domestic and
> other violence have been all too common and all too routinely
> accepted, although the problem has been recognised in the
> Scottish Parliament, the health service, and supportive charities.
> In this speech, NS outlined how the Scottish Government was
> addressing the problem and the impressive degree of success that
> had been achieved.

Scotland has a distinctive approach to tackling the harms caused
by alcohol, which has been based on international evidence. In our
work on minimum pricing we have looked at Canada's example,
and the Framework for Action (published 2009) is closely aligned
with the ten priorities set out by the World Health Organisation.
As we look to refresh and revise that framework in the coming year,
we are keen not merely to share our knowledge and experience but
to learn lessons from others. So, this is an ideal time for Scotland
to host a conference such as this one, attended by delegates from
more than fifty countries around the world.

I warmly welcome all of you and will give a summary of the
Scottish Government's priorities in relation to alcohol policy,

explain why it is important to us, and set out some of our key approaches. I will also set out our current position on minimum unit pricing, an issue which has attracted international attention. To set the context for our policies...

Scotland is not unique in having a problem in our relationship with alcohol. Unfortunately, we are unusual among other western European countries in its severity and extent. Alcohol consumption in Scotland is almost a fifth higher than in England and Wales, and our rates of liver disease and cirrhosis are the highest in Western Europe.

During the three days of this conference, it is likely that approximately three hundred people in Scotland will be admitted to hospital after alcohol misuse and that approximately ten will die. Those consequences affect some sections of our population more severely than others. People in the most deprived parts of Scotland are six times more likely to die from alcohol misuse than those in the most affluent areas.

The evidence is clear. The extent and nature of alcohol consumption in Scotland damages individuals, families, businesses, and communities, but harms the poorest most of all. No responsible government can ignore an issue which has such devastating consequences. Our Framework for Action (published 2009) set out more than forty proposals to reduce consumption, promote a healthier attitude towards alcohol, and improve treatment and support for people who need it.

We introduced a ban on bulk discounts in shops, which had previously encouraged people to buy alcohol in greater volume, and estimate that it has reduced alcohol sales by 2.6%. We have also increased investment in alcohol treatment and care services, and now deliver around 100,000 alcohol brief interventions every year. Brief, structured conversations which encourage people to think about and change their pattern of alcohol consumption are low-cost with a big impact.

We are now looking at refreshing the Framework and, as we do that, are increasing the ability of health boards to deliver in a wider range of settings. We want to have more alcohol brief interventions in places such as prisons and custody suites. By doing that, we can potentially make further progress in tackling health inequalities and reach more of the people who need it most.

There are two other areas where we are keen to see progress as soon as possible. The first of those is advertising, particularly in relation to children, which I know is an important part of tomorrow's conference proceedings. Broadcast advertising is reserved to the UK Government, so is not something that the Scottish Government has responsibility for. However, we are arguing that the UK Government should protect children from alcohol advertising on television, in the cinema and online, and believe that one way of achieving that would be to prevent alcohol being advertised before the 9.00pm watershed.

There is mounting evidence that alcohol advertising has an impact on children and young people, so we believe their exposure to it should be reduced. This is a case the UK Government has not heeded so far but is one we will make as persistently and persuasively as possible.

The second area, where we have legislated but are now awaiting the outcome of legal proceedings, is minimum unit pricing, an essential part of how we address alcohol harm.

There is good evidence that the other approaches adopted in the Framework are having some effect. We have seen a nine per cent fall in alcohol consumption since 2009, and rates of alcohol-related deaths, which doubled between 1981 and 2003, have fallen by more than a third. It is possible that we are starting to shift individual behaviour and public attitudes and may be starting to develop a healthier relationship with alcohol. However, we also know that much more needs to be done.

Alcohol-related deaths may be significantly lower than in 2003, but they have risen in each of the last two years, which suggests that many of the changes we have seen are heavily influenced by affordability. Our framework has helped to reduce consumption, but so too did the economic downturn. As economic recovery continues, as unemployment falls and living standards rise, the improved affordability of alcohol seems to be causing an increase in consumption.

There is a danger that much of the good work of recent years will be undone, which is why reducing the affordability of alcohol is seen as the best way of reducing the harm it causes.

In our view, minimum unit pricing is more effective than general taxation. It allows us to respond to changes in affordability, especially as a consequence of rising household incomes, and to target the strong-alcohol and low-cost products which are especially associated with damaging drinking patterns. A Sheffield University study which looked at the impact of a 50p minimum unit price indicated that it would save three hundred lives a year after ten years and reduce hospital admissions by more than six thousand.

The case for minimum unit pricing initially met widespread opposition in Scotland but, steadily, hearts and minds have shifted, swayed by the overwhelming fact that we have a major problem and clear evidence, such as the Sheffield study, that minimum unit pricing is an important part of the solution. As a result, in 2012, when the legislation was passed, it received support from four of the five parties in the Scottish Parliament.

Our position is now attracting international endorsement and recognition. A supportive study was published recently by the Organisation for Economic Co-operation and Development, whose *Policy Brief on Tackling Harmful Alcohol Use,* argues that raising prices will lower consumption. It also acknowledges that raising prices where they are cheapest can be the most effective way of reducing harmful drinking.

It was heartening to see that, when the European Union took evidence on court proceedings relating to minimum unit pricing, Scotland's stance received support from five member states and the European Free Trade Association. I am going to touch on those court proceedings very briefly. Not to pre-empt the outcome, but to make two points clear. The first is that I welcome the opinion last month from the EU's Advocate General. He confirmed that minimum unit pricing is not precluded by EU law and stated that it is for domestic courts to take a final decision. He also found that the policy can be implemented if it is shown to be the most effective public health measure available.

The second point is that I can confirm the Scottish Government continues to commit to minimum unit pricing, as you would expect. We believe that it is the best way to reduce the harm caused to our communities by low-cost and high-strength alcohol, and are convinced that it will reduce damaging alcohol consumption, improve health, and save lives more effectively than any alternative measures available.

What Scotland is trying to do, through minimum unit pricing and more than forty other measures, is create a cultural transformation. We want to change Scotland's relationship with alcohol forever, and for the better, but that cannot simply be about government action. Industry and the media have important roles, and individuals need to consider their personal alcohol consumption, as well as their position as parents, role models and friends.

The Scottish Government is determined to take a lead, understanding that by doing so, we will reduce inequality, increase prosperity, and improve the wellbeing of individuals and communities across the country.

11

A VISION FOR THE HIGHLANDS AND ISLANDS

The Sabhal Mòr Ostaig Lecture
Isle of Skye, 21st October 2015

Given annually at the Gaelic College on Skye, the Sabhal Mòr
Ostaig Lecture is a cornerstone event in the island's year. The Sleat
peninsula, where the college is located, is recognised as one of the
most beautiful places in the world, but it is also one of the most
tragic, having suffered from depopulation for centuries. Likewise
Gaelic, one of Europe's oldest living languages, over the same period
suffered decline to the point of extinction. In her lecture, NS took
the opportunity not only to outline their partial recoveries, with the
Gaelic College central to both, but also to widen her commentary
to include the far-sighted activities of the Highlands and Islands
Development Board (now Highlands and Islands Enterprise) and
a developing vision of the region's future that includes language,
industry, housing, and culture. Twenty-five years after the first
Sabhal Mòr Ostaig lecture was given by Dr James Hunter, she
followed in a distinguished tradition that includes three previous
First Ministers and Mary Robinson, then President of Ireland.

Sabhal Mòr Ostaig has gone from strength to strength and been a
real joy to watch over the years. With over two hundred students
enrolled in higher education, and many more taking its shorter
courses, the college is now an integral part of the University of the
Highlands and Islands and much of its research into Gaelic and
Celtic studies has been assessed as internationally excellent. Having a

hugely beneficial effect on the Sleat peninsula, and Skye more generally, it does a great deal to bring in visitors, businesses, and residents.

Today we celebrate the opening of the first stage of the Kilbeg
development, the first new village on Skye in almost a hundred
years. A quite staggering and massive achievement, it is not only
further tangible evidence of these successes but also a testament
to the vision of Sir Iain Noble, the college's founder. It is fitting
that the first new building of the Kilbeg development, which I
have had the privilege of officially opening, should be named after
him and I am delighted that his widow Lucilla is with us today.

When Sir Ian established this college, his vision was partly based
on the view that cultural regeneration would encourage economic
regeneration. That vision really has been vindicated over the last
four decades and provides the underpinning for my message this
morning. I am going to focus on how the Scottish Government
will support the Gaelic language, especially through education and
culture, but also want to talk about how we see that support as just
one element in a wider programme of growth and regeneration.

The establishment of a new village on Skye has special historical
resonances. When this college was founded in 1973, Sabhal Mòr
Ostaig, the Great Barn of Ostaig, was a derelict building dating
from the 1820s, part of a farm established during the 19th century.
These farms had largely taken the place of communities which
had emptied during the Highland Clearances. In the decades after
the barn was built, many people must have passed on their way to
make new lives in lowland Scotland and the new world.

One of the great Gaelic poets of the late 19th century was Mary
Macpherson of Skye. In *Nuair bha mi og,* or *When I was young,* she
reflected on the communities of her youth:

> *These fields and plains under heather and rushes,*
> *Where I often cut a clump and a sheaf of corn,*
> *If I could see them peopled, and houses built there,*
> *I would become joyful, as I was when young.*

It is genuinely joyful to see new people, new buildings, and new development evidencing the importance of this college's work over the last four decades. It also demonstrates the significant opportunities available to encourage Gaelic and develop the Highlands and Islands in the decades to come. My starting point for this lecture is that the Gaelic language in Scotland, for all the challenges it still faces, is in a better position than it was in 1973.

Much of that progress is due to the efforts of individuals and local organisations across Scotland, but another reason is that Gaelic now has stronger political and institutional backing than it has in centuries. We have come a long way since the 1970s, when Sir Ian campaigned to get a single bilingual road sign established on the road to Portree. Support for Gaelic now spans the political spectrum.

The legislation to establish Bord na Gaidhlig, passed under the previous Labour and Liberal Democrat [coalition] Scottish Government, received unanimous support in the Scottish Parliament. Gaelic is also benefiting from a wider change in cultural attitudes, which is something Mary Robinson picked up on in her lecture almost twenty years ago. When she was growing up in Ireland, people often saw Gaelic as a language of the past, not relevant to the modern world, and often seen as somehow holding you back. That is no longer the case. We know that there is no contradiction between traditional heritage and modern culture. Having a distinctive heritage, and being proud of it, is an asset in the modern world.

There are several reasons for that shift in perspective, including modern technology, greater economic confidence and, as Mary Robinson argued, membership of the European Union, because it encourages different nations and cultures to interact as equals. These factors make it easier for people to realise, through real life experience, that Gaelic is part of our future as well as our past and that has big implications for encouraging young people to take up the language.

Because of cultural trends, political backing, and community efforts, the census figures for Gaelic now give grounds for hope. The number of Gaelic speakers under the age of twenty increased between 2001 and 2011. Very moderate, giving no room for complacency, but almost certainly the first time in more than a century that we have seen such an increase.

We have also seen a significant slowing in the overall reduction in Gaelic speakers. Between 2001 and 2011 there was a decline of 1,500 people. In the 1980s, it was 17,000. This is not a cause for celebration, a decline of 1,500 is still 1,500 too many, but major progress has been made. Having slowed the decline, the challenge of the future is to reverse it, with the first and most fundamental way being through the growth of Gaelic medium education. Since 2007, the number of Primary One children starting Gaelic medium education has increased by almost half, and it is now offered in fifty-nine primary schools across Scotland.

That growth is not confined to the north-west. The Gaelic Schools Capital Fund has benefited schools across the country, from Portree to Kilmarnock and from Bowmore to Cumbernauld. In Glasgow Southside, the constituency I represent, a new Gaelic primary school will open in Pollokshields in December, accommodating up to two hundred children.

The Scottish Government introduced the Education Scotland Bill in March and is now preparing amendments to strengthen it. We do not think it would be appropriate to require all local authorities to provide Gaelic medium education. Instead it will give parents a statutory right to ask local authorities to assess whether there is a need for Gaelic medium education in their area. Local authorities must respond to that request. The Bill will be the first time that local authorities have been required to consider local demand for Gaelic in this way and is a landmark in the provision of Gaelic in schools.

In the past, the health of Gaelic has been linked to our education system. The 1872 Education Bill, which made elementary education compulsory but effectively excluded Gaelic, is often seen as a major factor in the language's decline. What we are trying to do now is ensure that our education legislation and schools system helps rather than hinders its development by adopting a proportionate and practical approach that helps to secure its future. In doing that, we are not just emphasising school education. The more we do to support learning from the earliest possible age, the better. If we want to ensure more children learn Gaelic, it makes sense to support it during the early years.

By 2020, the number of hours of pre-school provision to which children are entitled will match primary school provision for all three and four year olds, and the most disadvantaged two year olds. That means that the level of care being made available will almost double from six hundred hours a year to 1150. That doubling of care represents a major investment during an immensely tough financial climate, but it will give our young people the best start in life. It will provide parents and families with the flexibility they need to support their working lives, and children in Gaelic early-years settings will have more opportunities to speak the language.

We want to ensure that Gaelic pre-school providers can take advantage of that opportunity so, today, I am announcing an allocation of just over £100,000 of support for forty-one Gaelic pre-school education providers. Funding that will assist them with day-to-day running costs such as accommodation and more Gaelic speaking leaders. Four of the groups to benefit are based in Broadford, Dunvegan, Kilmuir, and Portree. The grant to each organisation will often be relatively small but can make a significant difference to the sustainability of the services.

This funding is further evidence of our determination to encourage the next generation of Gaelic speakers while, alongside our work to support Gaelic education, we also support Gaelic culture and media.

Broadcasting is an essential part of our plans. Because it is now so well established, it is difficult to remember that BBC Alba started broadcasting as recently as 2008, and only became available on Freeview and Cable in 2011. It now produces almost five hundred hours of original programming a year, supports almost three hundred jobs, and reaches approximately 700,000 viewers weekly. Its services are valued across the country, and its programming, from news and sport, or the drama series Bannan, to special events like last week's Mod coverage, all meet a distinctive and important need. Its website for learning Gaelic received more than a million page views last year, which speaks of the demand from people who want to know about the language.

MG Alba helps many young people to gain important skills in broadcasting and digital technology, and the production facilities it operates here, in partnership with Sabhal Mòr Ostaig, are a major resource for film makers and producers. BBC Alba has become an important part of the creative economy of Skye and the Western Isles, and across Scotland.

That is what we are doing to support Gaelic education and Gaelic media and culture, but such support has much greater impact when accompanied by economic opportunities. Again, there are encouraging signs for the Highlands and Islands, and therefore for Gaelic, notwithstanding the challenges we know lie ahead.

Next week will see the 50th anniversary of the establishment of the Highlands and Islands Development Board, now Highlands and Islands Enterprise. There was considerable gloom about the economic prospects for the Highlands and Islands when the population had been in decline for more than a century. It is important to recognise that times have changed dramatically, that the Highlands and Islands have a stronger, more diverse, and more productive economy than ever.

You can see the consequences in the census returns. The population is now at its highest for more than a century, and accounts for four-fifths of Scotland's total population growth since the 1960s. Prospects look bright too. Looking at our national economic strategy, you will see that in several key economic sectors such as tourism, food and drink, and renewable energy, the Highlands and Islands are well-placed to prosper. The University of the Highlands and Islands has also created new learning opportunities across the north of our country.

Broadband technology will bring new economic opportunities too, although I am aware that, at present, virtually no properties on Skye have access to superfast broadband. This college is an exception but, later this year, the first exchanges in Portree will go live and more will follow in 2016. In 2013 only four per cent of properties across the Highlands had access to Superfast broadband. By the end of next year it will be eighty-four per cent, but we need to do more and Skye is a good example of an area where additional progress must be made. That is why we are funding Community Broadband Scotland to find solutions for communities like Skye, which are not part of the eighty-four per cent. The organization is currently helping Sleat Community Trust with its Skyenet project, bringing superfast broadband to more than a hundred households across this peninsula. In this way government investment can help committed community groups to make a difference.

The broadband programme is part of a much wider investment in infrastructure. Last week we signed a £100m contract for two new ferries, including one for the Tarbert, Lochmaddy and Uig triangle. Last month work began on the dualling of the A9 between Perth and Inverness. The largest road infrastructure project in a generation, it will bring benefits across the north of the country.

We know that economic development requires more than central or local government investment. As Sabhal Mòr Ostaig shows, it is often more about local initiative and enterprise, so we are also seeking to give communities more power to take their own decisions. When the previous First Minister [Alex Salmond] spoke at this college a couple of years ago, he announced our intention to ensure that one million acres of land were in community ownership by 2020. We have set up a group to help us achieve that target, are currently introducing a Land Reform Bill, and trebling the size of the Scottish Land Fund which supports community buy-outs.

The Parliament passed a Community Empowerment Act earlier in the summer that requires public bodies, including the Scottish Government, to consider how to engage with local communities. We are also taking steps to give more powers to island and coastal communities having, last year, set out the most comprehensive package by any government for empowering Scotland's ninety-three island communities. Last month we published a consultation paper seeking views on proposals for an Islands Bill, an important additional step in empowering island communities. I encourage everyone here to respond.

We are also ensuring that, when Crown Estate lands are devolved to the Scottish Parliament, the parliament will not only devolve power to local communities but also consult on the best way of doing so. We have already made it clear that coastal and island communities will benefit from the net revenues from offshore activities within twelve miles of their coast, ensuring that they benefit from their natural resources.

All this is consistent with a vision for Scotland as a nation proud of its past and confident of its future, whose natural resources bring prosperity to every corner of the country. Our support for Gaelic is an integral part of that wider vision. We want more people to learn Gaelic, use it, and see its relevance to their everyday lives and, by doing that, ensure that Gaelic contributes positively to their social and economic wellbeing.

I began this speech by quoting the great poet Mary Macpherson and want to end by quoting another: Sorley MacLean, who was a founding board member of Sabhal Mòr Ostaig. He wrote 'A Waxing Moon Above Sleat' in 1973, about the new college, claiming to see 'a light/sunbeam of the Gael's hope/about its old and new walls'.

That 'Gael's hope' of 1973 has been vindicated. The new walls of the Kilbeg development demonstrate the massive contribution

Sabhal Mòr Ostaig has made to Gaelic learning, the regeneration of the Sleat peninsula, and the culture and economy of the Highlands and Islands. Partly because of the work done here, we have the opportunity in the coming decade to reverse, not just slow down, the decline in Gaelic which for generations has seemed almost inevitable.

The key message I want to give you, as First Minister and leader of the Scottish Government, is that we will do everything we can to seize that opportunity and, in doing so, protect our heritage, enrich our culture, boost our economy, and make this country a better place.

12

FOOD BANKS AND THE HEALTH OF THE NATION

Given to the Scottish Grocers' Federation
Edinburgh 30th October 2015

> In a speech that strongly recognises the place of social respon-
> sibility, NS put on record her recognition that private sector
> success underpins the wellbeing of communities, a sentiment
> unlikely to be expressed by traditionally left-leaning politicians
> in Scotland. In fact, food and its distribution are significant in
> environmental, health, and poverty issues, and the individuals
> and businesses operating between supply and demand meet
> needs far beyond their immediate functions. As so often, she
> stressed the importance of partnership and interdependence
> across the sectors.

The Scottish Grocers' Federation has existed for just under a
hundred years, but its significance to Scotland's society and
economy is as great today as ever. In economic terms alone,
convenience stores directly employ more than 41,000 people, and
support many more jobs among local suppliers, contractors, and
other businesses. More broadly, you help underpin the prosperity,
wellbeing, and sustainability of communities across the country.

At one of the first of these annual conferences, in the 1920s, one
of your early presidents said, 'it should never be forgotten that the
consumer's interest is also our interest'. In the decades since then,
you have frequently demonstrated how you recognise that truth
and have shown a strong sense of social responsibility. So, I am

delighted but not surprised by a very welcome announcement you have just made, that you are signing up to the 50:50 by 2020 pledge, meaning you are committed to working towards your Executive Board having equal male and female representation. I congratulate you warmly on that.

In doing so, you are joining 157 other organisations which have already signed, including Virgin Money, the Alliance Trust, Social Enterprise Scotland and virtually every public sector body in Scotland. I hope that individual businesses, as well as the Federation itself, will also consider making the pledge because, by doing so, you will help us promote a more equal society and live up to the best traditions of the Federation's past.

Today I want to talk about that wider social role the Scottish Grocers' Federation plays, but also want to recognise something else. You can only play that role if your members are successful, profitable and enterprising companies, and I want to say very clearly that the Scottish Government I am proud to lead knows it is the success of the private sector that underpins the wellbeing of every community in our country.

As the government, we are determined to do everything we can to help business, and perhaps the most obvious example is the Small Business Bonus, which benefits almost two thirds of all retail premises in Scotland. We have published statistics this morning, which show that almost 100,000 properties now benefit from the scheme. It as a major factor in giving Scotland the most competitive business taxation system in the UK, and where we implement changes which have an impact on business, we consult widely and work in partnership.

In the last year, we have worked closely with the Scottish Grocers' Federation on issues such as the carrier bag charge, which came into effect last year and has been a huge success. Reducing carrier bag usage by four fifths (that is 650 million bags!) has raised £6.5 million for good causes. That level of success would not have been possible without the co-operation of retailers across the country.

It is important that we work together, and as important to work together on the areas where we disagree as those where we do.

Even on issues where we have not always necessarily agreed, we have established a good working relationship. The Federation helped draw up guidance for retailers for the display ban on tobacco products, which came into force in April, and has played an important role in ensuring we implemented that move as effectively as possible. I am pleased to say, and I hope it will be echoed across the audience here, that we do have a close and positive working relationship.

I also want to look at three areas where we can develop that partnership for the good of the communities you serve, as well as your own benefit. The environment, food poverty and healthy living.

To take the environment first, Scotland has the most ambitious climate change legislation in the world, so meeting our targets to reduce greenhouse gas emissions will take concerted effort across both our economy and society. Therefore, I am delighted about yesterday's announcement that Zero Waste Scotland is making £100,000 available as part of a partnership with the Federation, funding that will help your stores to become more energy efficient. Double-glazed refrigerators, more efficient lighting and heat recovery systems can all help save stores up to a third of their annual energy costs. They can cut your carbon emissions and reduce your bills. Better energy efficiency is good for your businesses, and good for climate change targets, and is an area where it makes sense to work together. In the months and years ahead, I am sure there will be more such opportunities.

The second area is food banks. Anybody who visits a food bank (I know this is what I feel when I visit, or even when I stop to think about them), is struck by two different and contrasting emotions: a deep anger that food banks should be necessary in 21st century Scotland, but also admiration, pride, and respect for the efforts of the volunteers who run them and the generosity of those who donate.

The Scottish Government allocated a million pounds to food poverty programmes last year and is now working closely with providers and funders to look at how we address food poverty in the longer term. We welcome the fact that the Scottish Grocers' Federation is also looking at this issue. Helping people to give to food banks is a valuable way of showing solidarity at a time of serious hardship for many, and in the best traditions of the Scottish Grocers' Federation.

The final area I want to talk about is healthy living and healthy eating. Your healthy living programme currently has 1,600 members across the country, and what is especially significant is that well over ninety per cent are based in the most deprived third of our communities.

We know from the evidence that deprived communities are more likely to have low life expectancy and high incidences of conditions like heart disease, strokes, and cancer. Encouraging people to eat more healthily, particularly in our deprived communities, is one way, just one way, in which we can start to reduce those inequalities, and improve the wellbeing of people right across the country.

We cannot force people to eat more healthily, so what we must do is give consumers the choice. Your programme makes it easier to make healthier selections by making fresh produce and healthy food more widely available in convenience stores. Often, that means stores doing simple things that have a big impact on the choices people make, for example, by placing fruit and vegetables at till points. We know this approach works. Sales of healthy products have consistently increased by one fifth when marketed in that way, and increasing sales is good for you as businesses.

Last year, the Scottish Government set out a strategy to become a 'good food nation'. We already have a global reputation for the quality of our food, but we want to ensure we can take pride in the food we consume at home, as well as the food we export. The Scottish Grocers' Federation became the first organisation to partner the Scottish Government in that good food programme. The Food Commission will work with you to agree joint goals, and this is a further example of how your stores can play a part in making Scotland a healthier nation.

At the outset of my remarks, I mentioned the words of one of the early presidents of the Grocers' Federation: that the consumer's interest is also your interest. That basic principle of serving your consumers and your communities being in your own best interests remains at the heart of so much of what you do. So, I look forward to strengthening the Federation's partnership with the Scottish Government. By working together, we can help make Scotland a greener, fairer, and healthier country, and boost the wellbeing and prosperity of the communities we serve.

13

RESPONDING TO THE PARIS ATTACKS

Given to the Scottish Parliament
Holyrood, Edinburgh, 17th November 2015

On Friday 13th November 2015, a series of terror attacks on Paris took the lives of 130 people, left 413 injured and many others traumatised. Security forces and governments across Europe were galvanised into action and planned responses were quickly adapted and actioned. Four days later, NS reported through the parliament to the Scottish people. Several other attacks occurred in Britain in the period covered by this book, but this response describes national and international action most completely, and demonstrates how a national leader, conscious of the power of division such an attack might have, can anticipate and foster social healing by her words and example.

It is with great sadness that I move this motion. The terrorist attacks in Paris on Friday night have caused shock and grief around the world. Today, we mourn the innocent victims, at least 129 of them, who lost their lives, and hope for the recovery of those who were injured. We send our thoughts, prayers, and condolences to all of those affected and, in doing so, this Chamber and the people of Scotland say, unequivocally, that we stand in solidarity with France and the French people.

On Saturday, I met the French Consul-General, who joins us here today, to convey the message of solidarity that has been echoed many times by people across the country.

Expressions of sympathy have poured into the French consulate and been widely shared on social media. Landmarks across the country have been lit in the colours of the French flag, and yesterday's one-minute silence was observed across Europe. People in Scotland have sent the clearest possible message that we stand as one with France in their condemnation of terror and in their grief for its victims.

As well as making that fundamental statement of solidarity, the Scottish Government has also considered what steps need to be taken after the attacks. Over the last three days, I have chaired three meetings of the Scottish Government's resilience committee. The Scottish Government has also been in regular contact with UK Government Ministers and officials, and I have participated in two COBRA[14] meetings.

An important initial focus has been on ensuring assistance and support to anyone who needs it, and Police Scotland and the Scottish Ambulance Service have been deploying teams to meet flights incoming from Paris.

We have also reflected on security in Scotland. The overall threat level in the UK is classified as severe. However, people in Scotland are safe to go about their day-to-day business and should continue to do so. Police Scotland is advising people to be vigilant and alert but not alarmed.

I can assure the chamber that, working closely with Police Scotland and UK Government colleagues, we will continue to reflect carefully on the position, and take all necessary and proportionate steps to ensure that people and communities here at home are as safe and well protected as possible. An important part of doing that, is to reaffirm this Parliament's commitment to a diverse and multicultural society. I observed the minute's silence yesterday at Glasgow Central Mosque. John Swinney on Sunday attended a service at St Giles. Michael Matheson is meeting the Scottish Council of Jewish Communities this afternoon.

14.   Cabinet Office Briefing Room A.

Reaction to the events in Paris, the shock, sorrow, anger and fear, is shared by those of all faiths and none. Just as it is shared throughout this Chamber, and in every community across Scotland and around the world. The terrorists who committed these atrocities in Paris claim to be Muslims but, in truth, terrorism has no religion. Their evil actions do not speak for Islam. Instead they are a perversion of that faith and a deep insult to the millions across the world who adhere peacefully to its values. The attacks in Paris, like all acts of terrorism, were intended to spread fear and undermine our way of life. They were also meant to be divisive; to drive a wedge into communities and societies and turn neighbour against neighbour.

It is a normal and understandable human instinct to be anxious and fearful after what happened on Friday night. We all feel it. Governments must recognise and address these concerns and I give a commitment today that we will do so but we must also, together, as a society, resist the instinct to retreat or turn on each other. If we are determined, as we must be, that the terrorists will not prevail, difficult and challenging though it undoubtedly is, our response must be one of defiance and solidarity, not fear and division. The actions of the few must not be allowed to undermine the values, freedoms, and way of life of the many.

Today, Scotland is welcoming refugees from Syria. Other parts of the UK will do likewise over the next few weeks. Let me be clear, people have every right to seek and receive assurances from their governments that robust security checks are being carried out and public safety is not being comprised but, here in Scotland and across the UK, we should also feel proud that we are providing refuge for vulnerable individuals fleeing for safety from the type of people who carried out the Paris attacks.

We should be confident that Scotland will benefit from their presence, just as we have benefited so often in the past when we have welcomed people from around the world, and we should reflect once again that diversity is one of modern Scotland's great strengths. Today is an opportunity for this chamber to support that diversity, and to demonstrate a wider solidarity.

We grieve deeply for those in Paris who lost their lives and stand shoulder to shoulder with our friends in France. We remember too those who have been the victims of terror elsewhere, including the 224 people who died when a Russian airliner was brought down in Egypt last month, and reaffirm our commitment to a peaceful, secure, multicultural and tolerant Scotland. The kind of society that the terrorists want to destroy but which we are determined to uphold, cherish, and protect.

14

THE IMPORTANCE OF NATURAL CAPITAL

Given to the Second World Forum on Natural Capital
Edinburgh International Conference Centre, 23rd November 2015

> As a consistent part of her messaging, NS emphasises the interdependence of progressive policies and economic development. The concept of natural capital, meaning the world's stock of natural resources from which the human population withdraws not only its basic requirements for living but also resources its industry and leisure, fits this outlook precisely. In this speech she confirms acceptance of its finite nature and sketches out the Scottish Government's actions and intentions. A peripherally significant point is that Scottish venues, such as the Edinburgh International Conference Centre, were by now becoming increasingly popular for international events such as this well-attended forum.

Scotland hosted the first ever World Forum on Natural Capital two years ago, and we are delighted to be hosting the second. I congratulate the Scottish Wildlife Trust on organising this event and thank their associate partners: the United Nations Environment Programme; the International Union for Conservation of Nature; the World Business Council for Sustainable Development; the Natural Capital Coalition; and The Wildlife Trusts.

There are around five hundred people here, from more than forty countries, demonstrating the scale of international interest in this subject, and I am aware that they hold a range of views about the valuation of natural capital and the involvement of business.

Having an opportunity to consider and debate such issues is hugely important, and one reason why this forum is so valuable.

It is not surprising that there is such growing interest in the concept of natural capital. This year, perhaps more than any other, exemplifies why it is of such profound importance. Over the summer, Scotland became one of the first countries to pledge to implement the Sustainable Development Goals. As you know, the Goals set out a plan of action for people and the planet, starting from the premise that eradicating poverty in all its forms, including extreme poverty, is an indispensable requirement for sustainable development.

Protecting the resources we depend on is crucial, and why many of the sustainable development goals are directly relevant to natural capital. In less than two weeks' time, world leaders will travel to Paris for global talks on climate change and reducing greenhouse gas emissions. Protecting ecosystems and enhancing our natural capital will be an important element in those discussions. The basic concept behind natural capital, the idea that economic growth cannot be sustained if it comes at a continuing and unsustainable cost to our natural resources, is urgent and more important than ever. In Scotland we are determined to play a leading role in developing the thinking about the concept and its application.

Our Biodiversity Strategy, the 2020 Challenge for Scotland's Biodiversity, has a chapter on natural capital that recognises how our rich and diverse natural environment is a national asset which contributes to our economy and our wider sense of wellbeing. In 2011 we became the first country in the world to establish a natural capital asset index, which demonstrates the extent to which our natural capital declined between 1950 and 2000, although it also provides evidence of stability since then, partly as a result of cleaner rivers and lochs, and cleaner coastlines.

Studies suggest that the elements that can be given a monetary value are worth more than £20 billion each year to our economy. They directly support more than 60,000 jobs and are indirectly responsible for many more. Our tourism sector, which employs 200,000 people, benefits hugely from our scenery, habitats, and wildlife.

Not all benefits of natural capital can be quantified. You cannot place a value on the feeling of wellbeing you get from a beautiful landscape, but it is important to recognise that damaging our environment has a cost. We are more likely to treat it with care if we appreciate its value, and recognise that natural capital has a role to play in our policy making. When we published our revised economic strategy in March, it stated explicitly that 'protecting and enhancing our stock of natural capital... is fundamental to a healthy and resilient economy'. You can see some of the implications in the draft Land Use Strategy we released for consultation on Friday, making clear our determination to protect ecosystems and enhance our natural capital.

An obvious example in Scotland is our peatland, which is not land with obvious financial value by conventional accounting measures, but the peatlands store over 1,500 million tonnes of carbon, more than is held in all the trees and vegetation across the whole of the UK. It is a good example of the fact that loss of ecosystems is a major contributor to climate change, just as climate change is a threat to ecosystems. Losing just one per cent would release the same amount of carbon as an entire year of human activity. So, instead of reducing our peatland, we are restoring it. Last year we restored just over twenty square miles and spent approximately £5m on doing so. Such spending makes no sense using conventional accounting methods, but when focussing on climate change and using natural capital as a guide it is one of the best investments we can make as a society.

Another example is forestry. Trees also help to absorb carbon dioxide and store it as carbon. In recent years, Scotland has been responsible for almost three quarters of the UK's new tree planting, approximately sixteen million trees every year, and is committed to increase planting rates until we plant 100,000 hectares of trees in the decade to 2022. That would be equivalent to 200 million new trees, just under forty for every person living in Scotland.

Alongside the environmental importance of protecting and enhancing our natural capital, we believe it will help create a fairer society. There is an obvious issue of fairness between generations; we should not reduce natural capital for our own temporary benefit, at the expense of future generations. However, there is also an issue of fairness within each generation. Preserving natural capital often involves enhancing common assets, our environment, woodlands, and natural resources, which everybody benefits from.

The Central Scotland Green Network aims to transform central Scotland over the next three decades, an area of 3½ million people, the largest greenspace project in Europe and one of fourteen national developments listed in our latest National Planning Framework. Ranked alongside projects such as national broadband infrastructure, its projects range from transforming derelict land at Irvine Bay on our west coast, to improving the Castlemilk Woodlands in Glasgow, to establishing a community orchard in Kirkcaldy in Fife.

It also has major environmental benefits, which in themselves make it worthwhile, but it will also help us tackle inequality. The network prioritises action in disadvantaged areas. Its projects provide employment, training, and volunteering opportunities, while also promoting walking and cycling. The John Muir Way, a cross-Scotland walking route named in honour of the great environmentalist, runs through the area, passing within half a mile of this conference centre. It links Muir's birthplace in Dunbar on the east coast with Helensburgh in the west.

We know from Forestry Commission research that people are more likely to exercise if they live in areas with lots of greenery. We also know that Scotland is scarred by serious health inequalities, which the green network can contribute towards reducing. Green spaces enhance our natural capital, improve the wellbeing of our communities, and play a part in reducing health inequalities. The

Scottish Government recognises that natural capital contributes to a fairer society, a more sustainable economy, and a healthier environment. What we are now looking to do is make further progress.

Two years ago, at the first World Forum, the Scottish Forum on Natural Capital was established. The Scottish Government is a member. The Forum has already done much to raise the profile of natural capital by bringing together public sector bodies, landowners, non-governmental organisations, and businesses. The presence of the private sector is an important element and the forum, like this conference, helps spread best practice about how companies can take account of natural capital.

We are also working to encourage an awareness of natural capital among young people by encouraging ideas for our junior climate challenge fund, where young people can lead local projects to tackle climate change. Scottish Natural Heritage has joined forces with Young Scot, our national youth information and citizenship charity, to establish a youth panel on biodiversity.

The 2050 Climate Group in Scotland, which is our youth climate group, recently launched a Young Leaders Development Programme to ensure that future public, private and third sector leaders think about the challenges of natural capital, the circular economy and climate change. This development programme is a world first and another mark of our determination to ensure that Scotland continues to be at the forefront of progress towards a truly sustainable model of economic growth.

I mentioned earlier that the John Muir Way passes close to this conference centre. Also within a mile of here is the grave of Adam Smith, who practically invented the modern study of economics. What we need to do now, more than ever, is combine the preoccupations of those two great men, and it seems fitting that we play a leading role in doing that.

We intend to ensure that our approach to economic development takes account of the custodianship of our natural resources.

The Scottish Government is determined to lead by example by measuring and enhancing our own natural capital and, by doing so, benefit the ecosystems and people not only of our own country but also the environment and wellbeing of the wider world.

15

WORKERS' RIGHTS ARE HUMAN RIGHTS

Given to the Jimmy Reid Foundation and guests
Glasgow University, 24th November 2015

Jimmy Reid was a working-class hero whose reputation and popularity outgrew his original trade union base. One of the organisers of, but also principal spokesperson for, the famous Work-In at Upper Clyde Shipbuilders, he became an inspirational figure thanks to his eloquence, idealism, and strength of character. In 1971 he was elected Rector of Glasgow University and the acceptance speech he gave went down in history. Describing it as 'the greatest speech since President Lincoln's Gettysburg Address' the New York Times printed the text in full. After the Work-In he stood for Parliament as a representative first of the Communist party, and later the Labour party, on neither occasion with success. After he died in 2010 the Jimmy Reid Foundation was founded in his memory as an independent think tank. He was a great reader, a fine writer, and the author of several books as well as much journalism. NS gave the third Jimmy Reid Memorial Lecture after she and an audience of over a thousand had viewed the famous speech on screen.

You know, I sat quite a few university exams in this room, but I do not think I have ever been set a bigger test than to follow what we have just seen. To give a lecture in Jimmy Reid's honour on the very spot he delivered the finest political speech in Scotland's post-war history is a daunting challenge. I was privileged to know

Jimmy, and it is an honour to speak in the presence of his family. I am grateful to them, and to all of you, for coming here and to the Jimmy Reid Foundation for organising tonight's event.

I am going to start with the rectorial address we have just listened to, partly because it is magnificent, but partly also because it is directly relevant to what I want to talk about tonight. The reason that speech has endured is that Jimmy was making a moral case, articulating the values he exemplified throughout his life. He argued that humans are essentially social beings. We flourish through contact, conversation, the contribution we make to each other and to wider society, and not when we sign up to the values of a rat race, when we allow ourselves to be blinded to the misfortunes of others.

When things are done to people, when they are told they are expendable, or feel excluded from decision-making, it does not simply cut their income. It corrodes their soul and diminishes their sense of self. The basic principle of empowerment through respect for individual dignity, and encouragement of individual potential, is at the core of what I want to talk about tonight.

The title of this speech is that workers' rights are human rights. I will spend some time looking at the UK Government's Trade Union Bill since it is such an extraordinary and unwarranted assault on some of the social and economic rights we value and have come to take for granted. I will then make a broader case about rights; about our duty to recognise and cherish the value, dignity and potential of every individual in our society and the fact that when we fail to do so, we do not just harm those individuals, but diminish our society as well.

I want to start with some immediate context. Tomorrow, the Chancellor of the Exchequer[15] will announce the results of the UK Government's spending review. He has a chance, possibly the final chance, to accept that austerity is not a necessity, to change course on some potentially catastrophic decisions. For example, if all the

15. George Osborne, Conservative MP for Tatton 2001–2017.

UK Government's proposed tax credit changes are implemented, around 200,000 families with children in Scotland stand to lose an average of approximately £3000 a year. More than three quarters of the families who receive tax credits have at least one person who works. The cuts are directly targeted at working people on low incomes and their children, and hurt many of the people we most need to help.

I call again, tonight, on the Chancellor to reverse his decision to cut tax credits when he has the opportunity tomorrow. If he does not do so, the Scottish Government will set out proposals to protect the incomes of low-paid families in our budget in December. Obviously, the substance of his proposals on tax credits is of greatest concern, but the process is deeply damaging too.

There was no consultation before he announced these cuts in June and no mention of them in the Conservative manifesto. The decision was taken behind closed doors with no opportunity to vote against, and the full implications will be made clear to families in letters around Christmas time. This is something which is being done to people, to working families and their children, with no opportunity for meaningful debate or discussion, or for them to influence their own destiny.

If you reflect on the opening of Jimmy Reid's rectorial address, its evocation of 'the despair and hopelessness that pervades people who feel with justification that they have no real say in shaping or determining their own destinies', it is hard to avoid the conclusion that UK Government policy is not tackling alienation, it is breeding alienation.

The tax credit cuts; the bedroom tax; the way in which budgets in recent years have impacted most negatively on women, those on low incomes and people with disabilities. These are things which are being done to the least powerful in our society, by a government which too often seems oblivious to the consequences.

They are now being accompanied by other measures which seem set to strike at basic and fundamental rights: protections which are most valuable, for people who are at their most vulnerable. The proposal to abolish the Human Rights Act is one deeply regressive step; the Trade Union Bill is another.

When Jimmy Reid spoke here in April 1972, it was towards the end of the Upper Clyde Shipworkers dispute. The work-in Jimmy helped to organise was arguably, in my view unarguably, the greatest achievement of the post-war union movement in Scotland. It asserted the fundamental right of individuals to work. It did so through a peaceful, positive, optimistic, uplifting protest which captured the imagination of people at home and around the world. It stands as an enduring example of how trade unions empower people; of how they provide a voice for those who might otherwise go unheard.

The right to strike is an essential part of that, but the real value of trade unions goes much further. They help employers to create the safe, humane, productive working conditions which head off industrial disputes and which build better businesses. Because of that, trade unions are a force for good in modern society.

That has certainly been our experience in Scotland. Industrial relations here are strong. The number of working days lost due to strikes has declined by 84% since 2007, the highest reduction anywhere in the UK. Last year, fewer days were lost in Scotland, relative to our working population, than in any other part of the UK.

The UK Government's proposed Trade Union Bill is based on a world-view we simply do not recognise. It sees the relationship between employers and unions as one of conflict rather than co-operation. It does not reflect public opinion here, or the reality of industrial relations either. It offers illiberal solutions to a problem which simply does not exist in Scotland.

It makes an overwhelming case, which both the Scottish Government and the STUC [Scottish Trade Union Congress] put last year, for trade union law to be devolved to our own democratically elected parliament. After all, that Bill does not contain a single proposal which would be passed by the current Scottish Parliament. In a debate two weeks ago, the Scottish Parliament disagreed with the bill by 104 votes to fourteen.

It is worth looking at some of the measures. The UK Government wants the right to restrict facility time. Facility time means that employees can spend time carrying out union duties: helping employees at disciplinary hearings, offering training, or meeting employers. It is a vital part of partnership working, the embodiment of how we do industrial relations, not an abuse which needs to be controlled. The UK Government also advocates a ban on public sector employers using 'check-off' facilities. That is the payroll mechanism which enables union membership subscriptions to be deducted at source.

The Scottish Government, as an employer, has been operating a check-off facility for years. The costs are so minimal that we have never charged unions for it. The UK Government intends to make our actions illegal. It is worth repeating that. The UK Government does not want to stop using check-off procedures themselves but wants to make them illegal for the Scottish Government. It is an extraordinary and completely unacceptable attempt to control how we act as an employer. It demonstrates that, fundamentally, the UK Government wants to discourage union membership. The provision has no other conceivable purpose.

The UK Government also wants the power to call in agency workers to take over the duties of people who go on strike and has consulted on the proposal that picket leaders should wear armbands or identification tags. A proposal that quite frankly borders on the sinister. Liberty has pointed out that this provision increases the chances of blacklisting. Something which has been a very real and recent danger for union members.

In fact, Liberty has stated that the Bill 'represents a severe unnecessary and unjustified intrusion by the state into the freedom of association and assembly of trade union members.'

The UK Government's own Regulatory Policy Committee

has pointed out that key consultation proposals are not backed by any supporting data. The entire Bill is driven by dogma and ideology rather than being underpinned by evidence, which is why the Scottish Government is part of a broad coalition among the devolved administrations, the trade unions and wider civic society. We are and will continue to be vigorously opposing the Bill.

We have argued for it to be voted down at Westminster. We have proposed that Scotland should be exempted from its provisions. Since the Bill will have a significant impact on Scotland, including on how the Scottish Government as an employer carries out devolved functions, we will argue that it should only apply to Scotland if legislative consent is given by the Scottish Parliament. It is almost impossible to imagine that such consent would ever be granted.

We will do everything in our power to frustrate this Bill. Finally, if it is passed, and its provisions do apply to Scotland, the Scottish Government will not willingly co-operate. We will seek to do everything we can to continue the good workplace practices that the Bill attacks. Indeed, I can pledge categorically tonight that we would never employ agency workers in the event of industrial action in the Scottish Government.

In addition to opposing this Bill, we want to do something more positive. We want to exemplify that there is a better way of conducting industrial relations, one which is based on a different vision of society. There is a fundamental contradiction in the UK Government's approach. The UK Government claims to want a high-wage/high-productivity economy, but, if you genuinely want to bring that about, hostility to union membership makes no sense.

It is worth looking at West Germany after the war, which developed what became known as Rhine capitalism based on a strong sense of partnership between workers, trade unions, businesses, and the public sector. Rhine capitalism encouraged competitive markets but combined them with strong social protections. As a result, the German economy has been characterised by innovation, high productivity, and strong exports.

That approach to the economy was based on a distinct vision of society. Article 1 of post-war Germany's constitution places human dignity as the underpinning principle of the entire state. That feeds into concepts such as the constitutional principle of the 'social state', a state which strives for social justice.

What we are aiming to create in Scotland is not identical, we are in a different time with different contexts, but the core principles are similar. They are based on human dignity, value, and potential. We have put a commitment to inclusive growth at the heart of our economic strategy. We reject the idea that a strong economy and a fair society are competing objectives. Instead, we recognise them as mutually supportive.

Of course, we need a strong economy to fund the public services we value so highly, but it is just as true that a more equal society, where everyone can participate to their full potential, will lead to a stronger and more sustainable economy. Workers who are well-educated and trained, well-paid and highly valued and supported, will be more productive than those who are not. That is the principle driving our Fair Work Convention that was established earlier this year. It is a partnership between government, unions, employers, and employees. It aims to promote productivity in a way that ensures that companies and employees all benefit.

We have also established the Scottish Business Pledge for companies that openly embrace those values to show public leadership and commitment. More than a hundred and fifty companies in Scotland have signed up. We are championing the real living wage. Last year there were only thirty-four living wage-accredited employers in Scotland, now there are four hundred, and that number is growing. We have also published new procurement guidance, which explicitly recognises fair work, including payment of the living wage, as important considerations when we decide how public sector contracts are awarded.

These are just beginnings, but they are important beginnings. We are starting to use the influence and purchasing power of government to send a clear signal. Progressive employment practices are something to be celebrated, not simply because they are good in themselves, though they are, but also because they contribute to long-term economic and business success.

The basic principle that applies to businesses, that they prosper when their people are valued and empowered, also applies to society as a whole.

Many of you will remember Jimmy Reid's memorial service. Billy Connolly, who was one of the speakers, told a story about going for walks with Jimmy in Govan when they were young. This was probably in the late 1950s or early 1960s. It resonated particularly strongly with me because many of the streets they walked are streets I now represent in parliament.

Jimmy would point to a tower block and say: 'Behind that window is a guy who could win Formula One. And behind that one there's a winner of the round-the-world yacht race. And behind the next one... And none of them will ever get the chance to sit at the wheel of a racing car or in the cockpit of a yacht.'

Jimmy put the same sentiment even more poignantly when he spoke in this hall. 'I am convinced that the great mass of our people go through life without even a glimmer of what they could have contributed to their fellow beings.' Getting people to see that glimmer and kindling it into a spark or fire of ambition, and then enabling them to realise that ambition, is one of the key challenges today for government and for wider society.

If you were to ask me to sum up what I consider to be my mission as First Minister, assuming I am re-elected next May, it would be that: the mission of making real progress towards genuine equality of opportunity. It will require sustained work to tackle intergenerational poverty, so I have appointed an independent adviser on poverty. To advise and, more importantly, challenge my government to subject all our policies to the test of whether they help tackle poverty.

It is also why our commitment to transformative, high-quality and universally available childcare; and our determination to close the attainment gap at school; and our work to ensure that more children from deprived areas get to university are such important priorities for this government. Helping everyone to realise their potential, creating a society in which the determinants of an individual's success are their own talents and capacity for hard work, not the accident of their birth or family background, will also require sustained work to overturn stereotypes and challenge assumptions.

Last week I went to two events, one after another, one relating to digital skills, and another relating to childcare. Both are hugely important. We will need thousands more digital specialists in our workforce every year for the next decade, and we will also need many more childcare workers, but ... if we proceed as we always have done eighty per cent of the new digital workers will be men, and more than ninety per cent of childcare workers will be women. It would be wrong to proceed as we have done, which is why I put such emphasis on gender equality and the need to tackle gender stereotypes.

Similarly, we know we need many more doctors over the coming years, but ... if we proceed as we have in the past only one in twenty will come from the most disadvantaged areas, rather than the one in five that equality of opportunity would demand. That is why the work I have put in train through the Commission on Widening Access to university is so important.

The facts that I have just cited do not reflect the real talents of people in Scotland. Instead, they reflect social circumstance and entrenched assumption and, the truth is, we simply cannot afford as a society, morally or economically, to squander so much of our talent. The price is too high.

I was incredibly fortunate when I was growing up, to have parents who instilled an absolute belief that if I wanted to, had the ability and worked hard enough, I could go to university and achieve my dreams. I am all too aware that many people still, more than thirty years later, are not that fortunate.

There is a responsibility on all of us to encourage each other's ambitions, and also to vigorously challenge society's barriers and stereotypes, and there is a particular obligation for government in everything we have responsibility for: support for pregnant mothers, or care for older people; tackling the inequities in our education system; reducing reoffending, or developing a new welfare system; promoting equal marriage rights, or resettling refugees.

There is a fundamental human right and an obligation to demonstrate that we value the dignity and recognise the potential of every individual. It is an important part of empowering our people and our communities.

One of the things which came to define the referendum debate last year was not just a desire, but a yearning for a better society. Not just a more prosperous society, but a fairer one as well, and it was not confined to those who voted Yes. It was shared across the entire country. Another thing that changed was that we got to see that alternative futures for Scotland are possible. As a nation we could see what every individual would ideally know from birth: that we control our own fate; that with hard work, the sky is the limit. I see it as my job, and the job of my government, to take that sense of possibility, and help people experience it in their day-to-day lives. Our great challenge and opportunity is to ensure that schoolchildren thinking about their future know that if they work hard, they can achieve their dreams; workers have a real voice in how their employers operate; their rights are not expendable; welfare recipients are spoken to as human beings, not scrutinised as cheats; people who run small businesses get encouragement to grow; citizens have a say in the future of their communities; older people receive the support and care they need to live with security and dignity. That is the society we should be striving for.

Jimmy Reid rejected a society where human beings are told

they are expendable; where ordinary people are excluded from the forces of decision-making, where people feel themselves to be victims of forces beyond their control. We must reject a society where workers' rights are derided and inequality is unchecked, where working families wait to get letters telling them their income is being cut by thousands of pounds. Instead, we must build a better society based on respecting rights, recognising dignity, encouraging and, crucially, enabling each other's potential.

Near the beginning of my speech I quoted some of the opening words of Jimmy Reid's rectorial address. I want to end with the final verse of the final song which was played at his memorial service. It was Paul Robeson's wonderful version of 'Ode to Joy', which speaks of a society where:

None shall push aside another
None shall let another fall.
March beside me, sisters and brothers
All for one and one for all.

The verse represents the antithesis of the rat race Jimmy Reid rejected. Its vision, of individuals making progress through solidarity, is the one which he worked towards throughout his life. My hope is that we in Scotland can make much more progress towards it in the years ahead. If we do, we will live in a wealthier, fairer, better nation, and we will have built a fitting memorial to the wonderful, inspiring, and challenging legacy of the great and irreplaceable Jimmy Reid.

16

THE IMPORTANCE OF THE EUROPEAN UNION

Given to the Resolution Foundation
St John's Smith Square, Westminster 29th February 2016

> With the referendum on membership of the European Union less than four months away, NS was invited by the Resolution Foundation[16] to give a keynote speech on the benefits of membership for living and working standards. Addressing an audience of guests, she described her preference that all the United Kingdom countries continue to benefit and share sovereignty within the larger union. She also pointed to the irony of Scotland possibly being removed from the European Union when that very possibility had been used in the argument against independence in the 2014 referendum.

Thank you very much indeed, Torsten [Torsten Bell, chief executive of the Resolution Foundation], for that introduction and to the Resolution Foundation for hosting today's event. As Torsten has just said, February 29th is a rare occasion to speak to you all. In Scotland at any rate, we seem to have more frequent referendum days than leap years. It is interesting, I have to say, to hear many of the same arguments that we heard during the Scottish referendum repeated, albeit in a different context.

There are lessons emerging from the Scottish referendum that all of us should pay heed to in the weeks and months ahead. One

---

16. The Resolution Foundation is an independent think tank focussed on raising living standards for those on low to middle incomes.

of them is that if people are given the opportunity to engage with the issues, and realise the potential impact, good or bad, on their own day-to-day lives, it is possible to generate a democratic debate that leaves a positive legacy. I hope some of that happens with this referendum and, I have to say, seeing so many people gathered on a Monday morning to discuss the issues is a thoroughly good start.

I also hope, and this is the second lesson I would take, that the debate we engage in over the next few months is uplifting, positive, and focused on the issues Torsten spoke about. If that happens, not only do I believe it will lead to what I consider to be the right outcome, a vote to remain in the EU, it will also be an experience that people across the UK benefit from. The opportunity to have a fundamental debate about the future of your country is good.

I am going to look forward to June's referendum day in a moment, but want to start by looking backwards because yesterday, February 28th, marked a significant anniversary that had relevance to this morning's subject matter. Yesterday was the thirtieth anniversary of the final signing at the Hague of the Single European Act, a noteworthy occasion because so many consequences that flowed from it are still with us today. It was a major move towards the creation of the European single market.

It encouraged further pooling of sovereignty, for example by removing national vetoes in some areas, and intensified efforts, notably by Jacques Delors, the then Commission President, to ensure that social values were part of the single market. The Commission wanted to ensure improvements in living and working conditions.

For many people, and I am one as this speech will make clear, social protections are a significant part of what makes membership of the European Union good and worthwhile. I do not see a tension between the economic elements and the social side. On the contrary they should, and must, go hand in hand, so I am going to talk about that social and economic case for Europe later.

Before I do, because this comes up quite frequently when I

talk about the European referendum, I will address two misconceptions that sometimes arise when people ask me my view on Europe. The first is something which is not questioned much in Scotland, where it is easily understood, but is sometimes seen as curious outside of Scotland. It is the idea that there is somehow a contradiction in believing in independence for Scotland, while also supporting membership of the European Union. This ignores the obvious point that all twenty-eight members of the European Union are independent countries. Nine of them have smaller populations than Scotland.

The fundamental principle that independent nations work together for the common good appeals to me, as it appeals to many people across Scotland. There is nothing at all contradictory about independent nations recognising their interdependence and choosing to pool some sovereignty for mutual advantage. On the contrary, that is the way of the modern world.

Scotland has been pooling sovereignty, in one form or another, for many years. We have always had to look outwards to the rest of the UK, Europe, and the wider world. That is true now, and would be true should Scotland become an independent nation, and might help to explain why opinion polls consistently show that support for the European Union in Scotland seems to be significantly higher than in the rest of the UK.

This raises a further issue, which has been widely discussed in Scotland. If we were to vote in favour of EU membership, and the rest of the UK voted to leave, in other words if Scotland was to be out-voted, there is a real chance that it could lead to a second referendum on Scottish independence. That should not be surprising as a key plank of the No campaign was that if Scotland voted for independence, our membership of the European Union would be at risk. That argument was always (to use the technical terminology) complete rubbish, but it was made repeatedly and forcefully. If, less than two years later, we were to find ourselves taken out of the European Union against our will, because we had chosen to stay in the United Kingdom, it is not hard to foresee a growing clamour for a further referendum.

I have made that point frequently because it strikes me as an honest assessment of what could happen but, and here is the second misconception, it is not what I want to happen. Yes, I want Scotland to be independent, but I do not want Scotland to become independent because the UK chooses to leave the European Union. I want the United Kingdom to choose to stay in the EU. That option will be better for the rest of the UK and the EU and, should Scotland become independent, which I believe will happen, better for us too. If you think about it for a second, with Ireland's stance on the UK referendum as good evidence, why would we not want our closest neighbour also to be a fellow member?

Let me be clear. I want the vote on 23 June to result in an overwhelming victory, across all parts of the UK, for remaining in the European Union and will campaign wholeheartedly to achieve that result. The main argument I will stress is a simple one. The European Union is good for the prosperity and wellbeing of individuals, families, and communities across our country. Some of the benefits are so basic that we take them for granted, whether it is the ability to travel freely across the continent or the reciprocal right to free medical treatment in other EU countries.

The debate around free movement usually tends to focus, sometimes exclusively, on those who chose to come and live in the UK, but let us not forget the right to live, work and study across the continent has created opportunities for two million UK citizens who have chosen to live in other EU countries. Free movement has helped to turn London into perhaps the most cosmopolitan city on the planet, and the 170,000 EU nationals who live in Scotland enrich our culture, strengthen our society, and boost our economy.

The volume of immigration in England is greater than that in Scotland, which inevitably and understandably means it is a bigger part of the debate but, fundamentally, all parts of the UK benefit from people choosing to come here to work and study.

They contribute significantly to economic growth, and the answer to the concerns that some harbour is not to clamp down on free movement. It is to ensure that the economy works more effectively for those who are currently unemployed, or on low wages, or struggling to access housing or offer services. It is to generate hope rather than play on fear.

In some respects, the European Union can be and is part of the solution, and it is worth looking at some of the social protections it has established which benefit everyone in the UK, but often are not attributed to it.

The right not to be discriminated against on the basis of age, gender, religion, disability, sexual orientation, race or ethnicity; maternity and paternity leave entitlement; the right to paid holidays; the right to work for no more than forty-eight hours each week. All enshrined in EU directives and regulations.

It is open to governments to provide better rights and protections if they wish, but it is not inevitable that they will. In 2013, the UK only increased the minimum entitlement to parental leave as a direct result of European directives, and there are cases where the UK complies with the European minimum and no more. Which begs the question: without European regulations, would minimum standards be met at all?

Looking at some of the UK Government's other policies, we should be thankful that the European Union sets some basic social standards. There are some who see these rules as burdens on business rather than statements of basic human decency. None will be at a Resolution Foundation event, but they do exist! Even for those who hold that view, leaving the EU does not resolve the issue.

Presumably, although taking the UK out of the European Union, we would still want to access the single market. We need only look at countries like Norway and Switzerland who comply with these directives, without being able to shape or influence them, because compliance is a requirement of access.

There are sound reasons for these rules and regulations. They prevent a race to the bottom, where the single market is undermined by exploitative working practices. More fundamentally, they set minimum civilised standards for what workplace rights should look like in an advanced economy, which is as good for workers in London and Glasgow as it is for those in Bucharest or Berlin. These directives are not a burden on business, and not simply statements of principle. They are real achievements, which make a real difference to millions of people's lives.

Beyond those benefits for individuals, now woven so deeply into the fabric of our lives that we hardly register them, there are also big economic and environmental advantages. The EU gives us open access to a market of 500 million people. In Scotland, annual exports to EU countries outside the UK are worth more than £2,000 per person and help to support 300,000 jobs.

Trade deals are easier to negotiate as part of a block. Harmonised regulations help businesses to export, and all of us benefit as customers. For example, the abolition of roaming charges next year results from the move to a single market in digital products and services. It is possible to get some of those economic benefits without being part of the EU but, as Norway and Switzerland demonstrate, that involves being bound by EU rules without having the ability to influence them.

It is also worth considering the environment. European decisions helped us to reduce sulphur dioxide emissions by almost nine tenths in the last four decades. Nitrogen oxide levels have decreased by two thirds in Scotland since 1990. Again, decisions on these issues could have been taken separately by twelve, fifteen or twenty-eight individual nations but, because air quality and the environment are international issues, and pollution knows no boundaries, it makes sense to develop common goals and targets. A major reason for the drive to reduce sulphur dioxide emissions was the impact that UK pollution was having on West German forests. There is more that Europe can and should do, but joint action in this area has almost certainly saved tens of thousands of lives.

If you look at climate change, the biggest environmental, economic, and moral challenge facing the planet, the EU was the first major economy block to make its plans for reducing emissions known before last year's Paris summit. Active in working with developed and developing nations it was able to talk as an equal with China, India, and the USA. It could negotiate more effectively than twenty-eight individual member states would have been able to do on their own.

None of this is to say that the European Union is perfect. No international organisation is. No national government is, for that matter. The EU is and always will be capable of improvement. Last year, for example, the Scottish Government proposed ideas on reform on issues ranging from the integrated energy market to more discretion for domestic governments on public health measures (which was shaped by our experience of minimum pricing for alcohol).

Many people, including many who consider themselves social democrats, have deep-seated concerns about the EU. The handling of the Greek crisis troubled many and I share some of those concerns. I have also heard an argument from people on the left that we should not support the EU because of the proposed trade deal with the USA: TTIP [Transatlantic Trade and Investment Partnership].

I share some of the concerns about TTIP, and cannot and would not support a trade agreement that put at risk our public NHS, but the blame for that lies not with Europe and the EU but the current UK Government that, so far, refuses to insist that it is specifically and expressly protected.

Of course, the single biggest issue facing Europe at present, the area where the need for action is greatest, is the refugee crisis. Even if we wanted to, we would not be able to solve this crisis by building walls or erecting barbed wire fences. Jean-Claude Juncker put this well in September. He pointed out that, if you just imagined for a moment that you were a refugee, 'there is no price you would not pay, there is no wall you would not climb, no sea you would not sail, no border you would not cross' to flee from the horrors of war, and the barbarism of Daesh[17].

Burying our heads in the sand or turning inwards will not make the refugee crisis go away. It will simply make the management of it more chaotic. In my view, the most effective solution must be through a fair and humane processing of asylum claims, contributed to by all EU members, and the relocation of refugees among all EU nations and other willing partners. The reluctance of so many governments to help is, I think, a genuine failure of leadership. This is an area where I would like to see the UK do more.

Scotland has taken nearly forty per cent of the refugees to arrive in the UK so far under the Syrian resettlement programme. In all the preparatory work, we have engaged constructively and well with the UK Government, and it has to be said that the UK Government has done some genuinely positive things. For example, it has made significant aid contributions to help refugees in Syria, Turkey, and Lebanon. All to be applauded, but...

I am going to put this next comment gently. Two weeks ago at the European Council, the heads of government and the heads of state broke off from discussing the refugee crisis, one of the most defining issues of our times, to negotiate the taper rate at which the UK is allowed to cut benefits for working EU citizens. I cannot be the only person who wondered whether the UK's standing in the world was enhanced at that moment.

My hope, although in the short term it may be forlorn, is that when the referendum is over, preferably before, the UK will focus more on working with partners to help with the refugee crisis, because it is the most significant of the issues currently facing the EU. For all its shortcomings on this issue, the solution is more co-operation between different countries, not less.

We need a collective response, not closed minds or isolationist actions, and the European Union, for all its flaws and imperfections,

17. Also known as Islamic State in Iraq and the Levant, or ISIL.

is better placed to provide than anyone else. My point is that the European Union is inevitably an imperfect organisation, but we should work in good faith with our partners to make it better. We should help to create the Europe we want.

I started this speech by looking at a 30th anniversary. Now I want to end it by looking at a 75th. In 1941 this church was largely destroyed by an incendiary bomb on the last night of the London Blitz. There is a handwritten account of the fire, which is displayed at the back of this room. For more than two decades afterwards, this space we are in was left open to the skies. It is difficult to imagine now, as we look around this hall, and maybe hard for this generation to appreciate the place the European project had in the hearts of so many who lived through those times. It is also hard not to be inspired by the determination of the EU's founders to avoid war and build something better. It is impossible not to be impressed by the extent to which they succeeded.

Free trade, free movement, environmental protections, and employment rights, all of these are substantial achievements of the European Union. They make hundreds of millions of people wealthier, healthier, happier, freer, and that is to be celebrated not renounced.

There is something inherently noble about twenty-eight independent sovereign democracies choosing to work together to promote peace and mutual prosperity. Not just a noble principle; it brings us real and meaningful benefits. Of course, it is not surprising that the European Union sometimes falls short of its own ideals, or that it is often bureaucratic, frustrating, and messy. What is more surprising is how well it has lasted and how much it has achieved.

For all its imperfections, the European Union is a force for good in the world and I would much prefer Scotland to be one of its independent states. I believe that, in the future, we will be. Independent or not though, we are better off in than out, working with our neighbours to create a wealthier, fairer, happier continent.

17

STEP IT UP FOR GENDER EQUALITY

Given to the Scottish Women's Convention
Holyrood, 5th March 2016

Established in 2013 by the Scottish Government (then termed 'Executive'), led by First Minister Jack McConnell and depute Jim Wallace, the Scottish Women's Convention brings women's views, opinions and concerns to the attention of policy makers working in key areas. Their website says: 'Women have a right to be heard. Decision-makers have a right to listen.' Speaking just two months before the Scottish Parliament election, NS spoke in detail of her government's increasingly active approach to violence against women both at home and overseas. In May her party won another resounding victory and she returned as First Minister of a minority government that was frequently supported by the independence-seeking Scottish Green Party.

Since it was established, the Scottish Women's Convention has played a hugely valuable role in ensuring that women's voices are heard on key policy issues. The election hustings that you are hosting in two weeks' time is just one example. This annual convention is another and, since it is just three days before we mark International Women's Day, it is highly appropriate that there is an international dimension to the programme.

The theme for International Women's Day is 'Planet 50-50 by 2030: Step It Up for Gender Equality'.

The slogan which is frequently used is 'pledge for parity',

motivated in part by a recent report from the World Economic Forum after it looked at women's progress around the world towards health, educational, economic, and political equality. It found that at the current rate of progress, women will achieve full equality not in 2030, but in 2133, a stark reminder of the fact that, although progress is being made, the rate of change is often far too slow. It is unacceptable to think that women in three or four generations' time could still be living in a world of gender inequality. All of us, women and men, need to ensure that does not happen, and work to achieve change more quickly. I have been determined to see rapid, significant, and lasting progress towards gender equality during my time as first minister.

In my remarks today, I will speak about the national and international elements, but talk first about how we are tackling domestic abuse and promoting economic opportunities within Scotland. I will also speak about some of our international development work and what we are doing to advance gender equality across the globe but, since we are in the Chamber of the Scottish Parliament, and just two months from the next Scottish elections, I will start by talking about women's representation in politics.

The creation of this parliament resulted in a step forward for women's representation in Scotland, when forty-eight were elected in the first election of 1999. More than had ever been elected to Scottish constituencies in all previous Westminster elections put together.

The very existence of this convention is an indication of how the parliament has enabled women to play a more prominent role in public life. There is a gender-balanced Cabinet, and the three largest parties are all led by women[18]. Even so, we cannot ignore the fact that only thirty-six per cent of MSPs are women. A bit better than Westminster, where thirty per cent of MPs are women, it is not nearly good enough, and I am acutely aware that as a party leader I must play my part in achieving change.

18.   Kezia Dugdale MSP led the Scottish Labour Party and Ruth Davidson MSP led the Scottish Conservatives.

All parties are looking at local government, as well as this parliament. In just over a week, organisations promoting more diversity in politics, whether on gender, race, or disability, will be gathering in this parliament with all political parties to discuss how we improve the proportion of councillors who are women. I look forward to the outcome of those discussions, while hoping and expecting to see more women MSPs sitting here after May. All parties need to keep making progress after that. Half of this chamber should be women. The parliament, which represents Scotland, should be representative of Scotland.

It is even more important that the parliament pursues policies which promote gender equality, as they can improve the lives of women across the country. A good example of an area we have prioritised in recent years is addressing violence against women, which, as all of us know, is both a symptom and a cause of gender inequality.

We cannot have true equality in Scotland while violence remains so widespread in our society. So, we are providing record levels of funding to tackle it. Over £20 million in this year alone. Funding that has helped the Scottish Courts and Tribunals Service and Crown Office to ensure that domestic abuse cases are heard in court more quickly. It has allowed us to invest in prevention support, as well as specialist advocacy services for victims of abuse.

Alongside additional funding, we are taking legislative action. The Abusive Behaviour and Sexual Harm Bill was introduced into parliament in October and includes provisions to ensure that courts take domestic abuse into account as an aggravating factor when sentencing. It also creates a new offence for sharing private intimate images without consent, helping to address cases where an ex-partner seeks revenge by sharing images never intended to be seen more widely.

We are in the final month of a consultation on the exact wording of a new specific offence, dealing with people who subject their partner to coercive and controlling behaviour, something that has been difficult for the current law to deal with. Our aim in all of this is clear. We are determined to prevent and eradicate all forms of violence against women, and are acting at all levels: legislation, prevention, better support for victims, and more effective prosecution of those who abuse.

Domestic abuse is a symptom and a cause of inequality. We need to address domestic violence to live in an equal society, but those actions are part of a much wider set of policies to promote true equality. Gender equality is an overwhelming moral imperative, and increasingly recognised as a significant economic opportunity.

The IMF has conducted studies on some major Western economies, and estimate that increasing female participation in the labour market to the same level as men's would increase the size of the economy by five per cent in the USA and nine per cent in Japan. In Scotland we have made good progress in recent years in promoting female participation. The gender gap between male and female employment rates has reduced by almost a third in the last three years and is now six percentage points. Across the UK it is ten percentage points.

The gender pay gap has also decreased in Scotland in recent years. In 2014 it was nine per cent, whereas last year it was seven. There are other encouraging signs. For example, women made up one in four modern apprenticeship starts in 2008–09. That figure is now four in ten, but all of us know there is more to do to create true equality of opportunity.

Our work to promote childcare is an essential part of that. We have promised to almost double the level of free childcare available for three and four year olds, and some two year olds, from six hundred hours a year to 1140 by the end of the next parliament, and intend to ensure that this care is delivered flexibly, in a way which meets parents' needs and the needs of children. It is an investment which gives children the best possible start and helps parents, especially mothers, into work. By doing so, it will help to make Scotland a wealthier and fairer country.

We are acting on other issues, too. I mentioned earlier that we had made progress on low-pay knowing, of course, that any pay gap is too big. That is why we are increasing transparency about pay rates. Two months ago, we laid regulations to ensure that all public authorities with more than twenty employees need to publish information about their pay, which means we will know whether there is a gender pay gap in those organisations, and how big it is. This will be an important step in ensuring that the public sector leads by example.

We are promoting the living wage because women are disproportionately more likely to be in low-paid jobs. Getting employers to sign up to the living wage is not merely a good thing, it also promotes equality. We are tackling gender segregation in careers by helping employers to address this issue in modern apprenticeships. We are funding work experience programmes for female undergraduates in subjects such as science and engineering. We want to ensure that more girls and young women study those subjects, and that they take up careers in those areas.

There is an important point here in terms of our economic future. Women are currently underrepresented in sectors with major growth opportunities for Scotland such as digital technology, engineering, renewable energy, and life sciences. We know those areas will need highly skilled new workers in the years and decades ahead, and it is simply not economically sustainable to underuse the talent and potential of half of our population. Not affordable for our economy and not acceptable for our society.

These actions will help ensure that women are better represented across all sectors of our economy. However, we also need to ensure that women are represented at all levels of the economy. Women currently only account for a quarter of private sector board members among the UK's largest companies, which is why the Scottish Government has established our 50:50 by 2020 pledge, to speed up the process at which we achieve equality. In total, more than 170 organisations are signatories, ranging from third sector groups to major firms such as Virgin Money and the Alliance Trust.

The public sector is leading by example. Last year, fifty-four per cent of regulated public sector board appointees were women, the first time that women have made up more than half of the new members of regulated public sector boards. There is a huge amount more to do in both public and private sectors. Progress has been made but we must keep moving forward.

I have concentrated so far on Scotland but, of course, there is an international dimension. All over the world, women suffer systematic discrimination in relation to healthcare, educational opportunity, and employment rights. According to some estimates, women represent seventy per cent of the world's poor, their unequal status shaped by the interlocking factors of general poverty, discriminatory treatment in the family and public life, and a vulnerability to HIV. For those reasons, gender equality is a vital element of our international development and climate justice work.

The Scottish Government's Climate Justice Fund includes help for projects which prepare women to speak out and take a leading role in their communities. That is a recognition that women are often the main victims of the negative impact of climate change. Empowering them must be part of the solution.

For the last three years the Scottish Government has been supporting women's education in Pakistan. Our Scottish scholarships scheme has already enabled more than two hundred young women from disadvantaged backgrounds to study Masters courses in Pakistani universities. I can confirm today that we have allocated a further £150,000 for the programme, which means that two hundred more students will start their studies later this year.

This programme is already making a huge difference. One of last year's graduates, for example, had been unable to find employment after being forced to move from her hometown to Lahore. She is now working as a primary teacher, helping other young boys and girls to achieve their dreams. She is a good example of how the programme is transforming the lives and futures of individual women, and by doing so can play some part, not a major one, but still an important one, in making Pakistan a more equal, peaceful and prosperous nation.

Last summer, Scotland became one of the first countries to pledge to implement the Sustainable Development Goals, and in doing that, we made a dual commitment. We pledged to tackle poverty and inequality in Scotland, and we also promised to help developing countries to grow in a fair and sustainable manner. Gender equality is fundamental to that. As UN Secretary General Ban Ki-Moon has said, 'Removing the barriers that keep women and girls on the margins of economic, social, cultural and political life must be a top priority for us all: businesses, governments, the United Nations and civil society'.

I believe we can and must make rapid progress towards that goal in Scotland. We can also, by our example and through our international development work, be a positive influence for change across the world. We can help to ensure that gender equality is not something that has to wait until 2133, and work instead to achieve planet 50-50 by 2030. We can secure lasting change, for the benefit of those who are girls and young women today.

18

REFLECTIONS ON THE EU REFERENDUM

Given to the Institute for Public Policy Research
Edinburgh, 25th July 2016

On Friday 24th June, all Europe woke to the news that 52% of a 72% UK turnout had voted to leave the European Union, a result that defied most expectations. Prime Minister David Cameron resigned immediately and was succeeded by Theresa May who, although the referendum was advisory, pledged her Conservative Government to implementing the decision. As would soon become apparent, there was no real appreciation of the implications and no vestige of a plan. Neither was there any clear idea of how new relationships could develop with the European Union, other nations, or indeed within the United Kingdom. In Scotland, the vote was dramatically different. As NS had suggested was possible to the Resolution Foundation, a large majority (62%) had opted to remain, the largest for either side, by a considerable margin, among the four British nations. In addition, the result was consistent across the country, with every local authority reporting a remain majority. A month later NS gave this considered and remarkably frank appraisal to a nation still in shock.

We are now exactly one month on from the EU referendum, which seems, in some ways, no time at all. In others, a lifetime. Many of you will feel the same way. Today, I will reflect on the result, how it felt, what some of the lessons might be, and give an insight into my own feelings and how my thinking developed in the early hours of 24th June. Then I will consider where we are now and what lies ahead, rooting this firmly in Scotland's interests and values, why they matter and how we will seek to protect them in a way that, as far as possible, unites us.

Scotland's place in the EU, just like Scotland's place in the UK, is not some constitutional abstraction or distraction. It is fundamentally about how we best equip ourselves to deal with the complex, interdependent challenges facing governments, businesses, and individuals in the 21st century. It is about jobs and the economy. It is about living standards, fairness, equality, and our place in and contribution to the world. It matters for, and to, all of us and, as we navigate our way through the difficult weeks, months, and years ahead, that is what we must bear in mind.

Firstly though, let me take you back to the result, to the morning of Friday 24th June.

Every generation has its 'do you remember where you were when . . .' moments, and I suspect this will be one of ours. We will all remember exactly where we were and how we felt when we heard the result of the EU referendum. Some of you will have woken to the news, having gone to bed a few hours earlier assured that the polls, the bookies, and the markets were all pointing firmly in the direction of a Remain vote. Others, like me, will have watched events unfold through the night and many, again like me, will have experienced a horrible, sinking feeling as the early results came in.

I told the Scottish Parliament a few days later that I was 'disappointed and concerned' by the result but must admit that was parliamentary language for a much stronger feeling. I felt angry that Scotland faced the prospect of being taken out of the EU against our will, with all the damaging consequences that would entail.

I felt, and still feel, contempt for a Leave campaign that lied and gave succour to the racism and intolerance of the far right. I felt frustration, on behalf of people across the UK, at the political irresponsibility that had brought us to this point. I am the last person you will hear criticising the principle of referenda but proposing one when you believe in the constitutional change it offers is one thing. Proposing, as David Cameron did, a referendum even though he opposed the change on offer, is quite another. To do so, not because of any public appetite, but to appease UKIP and the Eurosceptic voices within the Tory party was worse. It was reckless.

I also felt my share of responsibility, as a senior politician on the Remain side, for our collective failure to convince a majority across the UK of the case for staying part of the EU, imperfect though it may be.

These were the feelings I was experiencing in the early hours of the 24th June, although tempered by a sense of pride in Scotland and how Scotland had voted. More than sixty per cent, with a majority in every one of our thirty-two local authority areas, had said clearly that they wanted Scotland to stay in the EU. So, at around 4.00am, when I started to write the statement that I would give later that morning in Bute House, there were several thoughts crystallising in my mind.

Firstly, it seemed abundantly clear that people, even many of those who had voted Leave, were going to wake up feeling very anxious and uncertain. It was therefore the job of politicians not to pretend that we instantly had all the answers, but to give a sense of direction. To create some order out of the chaos, which is what I was determined to try to do for Scotland. I assumed that UK politicians would do likewise, but I was wrong. Indeed, the absence of any leadership and the lack of any advance planning, either from the politicians who had proposed the referendum or those who had campaigned for a Leave vote, must count as one of the most shameful abdications of responsibility in modern political history.

Secondly, although it was clear that the result would impact on all our lives, it seemed obvious that the anxiety it would cause would be felt more immediately and acutely by one particular group: nationals of other EU member states who had chosen to make their homes in the UK. I felt then, and still feel very strongly today, that we must give them as much reassurance as possible. It is wrong that the UK Government has not yet given a guarantee of continued residence to those who have built lives, careers, and families here.

Thirdly, given how Scotland voted and the consequences for our economy, society and culture of being removed from the EU, I felt strongly, and still do, that my job as First Minister is to explore every option to protect Scotland's interests. That last point, protecting Scotland's interests, is the one I will dwell on today. I will look at what they are and how the Scottish Government will seek to protect them.

Before I do that, though, let me briefly touch on another thought that was in my mind then and has developed and strengthened since; the need to learn the lessons of this referendum, both the campaign and the result. The lessons of the campaign will no doubt be talked about by politicians and political commentators for years to come. Some were the subject of advance warnings to David Cameron that I suspect he now wishes he had listened to more carefully. I do not have time to discuss these in detail, but there are three I will mention in passing.

First, the limitations and dangers of negative, fear-based campaigning, particularly in the social-media age where people have access to information from all different sources.

Second, the need to understand that campaigns are not Year Zero affairs. You tend to reap what you have sown over many years. It should not have come as a surprise to politicians who have spent years denigrating the EU and pandering to the myths about free movement, that some voters did not believe them when they started extolling the virtues of both.

Third, the mistake of excluding certain groups of the population from the vote. I think it was wrong in principle to deny EU nationals, and sixteen and seventeen year olds, the right to vote.

As well as being wrong in principle, it was tactically foolish. These were precisely the groups most likely to be positive about the EU.

Mistakes were made and there will be plenty of time in the months and years ahead to mull over the lessons. What is perhaps more urgent, and certainly more important, is that we learn the lessons of the result. To do that, we must make sure that we properly understand it. Leave campaigners may have played the anti-immigration card to the point, at times, of overt racism, but seventeen million Leave voters were not racist. Nor even anti-immigration. So why, despite all the warnings about the economic and financial consequences, did they choose to vote to leave the European Union?

That is a question we must address and, let me be clear, it is important to ask and to answer that question here in Scotland too. The country may have voted overwhelmingly to Remain, but one million of us voted to Leave and we must not lose sight of that. As First Minister, I have a duty to listen and respond to the concerns behind that vote. Academic theses will be written on this subject for years to come but I am a politician, not a Doctor of Philosophy, so what follows are just my observations.

I do not doubt that many people voted Leave, simply and straightforwardly, because of what they think about the European Union. The EU is not perfect, far from it. Its institutions too often seem remote and its regulations unnecessary and interfering and, as I said earlier, UK politicians have spent years blaming it for all our ills and denying its achievements. It is hardly surprising that many took the opportunity to vote against it.

For many though, I suspect that the real roots of their Leave vote lay closer to home. The referendum was a chance to send a message, consciously or unconsciously, about how they are governed, and the effect government policies have on their day-to-day lives. This vote was about Europe but, in my view, also reflected a loss of confidence and trust in UK institutions that have become remote and detached.

We should not be complacent in Scotland, but there is at least a partial explanation to be found for the different result here in the statistics measuring trust in the Scottish and UK Governments. Since devolution, people here have trusted the Scottish Government more than the UK Government to act in Scotland's interests, and that has been true under all governments since 1999. It is not a party-political point. Trust in the Scottish Government to act in Scotland's long-term interests is higher today (73%) than it has been at any time since the establishment of the Scottish Parliament in 1999 (81%), and it is more than three times higher than trust in the UK Government (23%).

Trust in institutions, or lack of it, is in my view a factor, but a bigger factor is policy. There is little doubt that many voted to leave the EU (voted against the status quo, in other words) out of a feeling that they were being left behind.

Marianna Mazucatto, a member of my Council of Economic Advisers, has said that many Leave voters were protesting about the effects of austerity and an economic system that does not work for them. However, she also said that 'If the Leave campaigners were right about how many felt about life and work in Britain today, they were wrong about the causes, and wrong about the solutions. Blaming the EU was a category error. In truth, the blame lies closer to home' ... and that is the hard truth.

Much of the blame for what happened on 23rd June lies with the UK Government's ideological obsession with austerity, with its decision to make ordinary people pay the price of a financial crash they did not cause and with its cynical collusion in the myth that cuts and public service pressures are the fault of migrants rather than deliberate economic policy. This referendum result, if the right lessons are being learned, must put tackling inequality and democratic renewal at the top of the political agenda. A good start, which I say more in hope than expectation, would be for the new Prime Minister and Chancellor to abandon the austerity economics pursued by their predecessors.

Those are my reflections one month on, but the present and future matter more than the past. However much we might like to, we cannot turn the clock back. So, how do things stand today?

First and most obviously, we have a new Prime Minister[19] and government, but not yet any clear explanation of what a Leave vote means in practice. If we can read anything from the early signs, whether from government appointments or initial pronouncements it is, though I hope I am wrong, that the UK is heading towards a hard rather than a soft Brexit. A future outside the single market, with only limited access, and significant restrictions on free movement.

'Brexit means Brexit' is intended to sound like a strong statement of intent but is, in truth, just a soundbite that masks a lack of any clear sense of direction. There is also a sense of calm before storm. The initial shock might have worn off, but we do not have to look far for warning signs of what is to come.

Last week, the IMF cut its growth forecast for the UK by almost half and, on Friday, the Purchasing Managers' survey (in recent years a very strong indicator of GDP growth or, indeed, contraction) plunged heavily into negative territory. These are just two of a plethora of warnings and are surely a sign of things to come.

At a time when we were dealing with real fragility in our economy, because of global trends and, here at home, the impact of the oil price, this is bad news indeed. It will impact on jobs, investment, living standards and public services. Will a UK Government facing shrinking tax revenues be willing to protect the funding that currently comes from the EU, let alone deliver the increased NHS spending that the Leave campaign promised? Nor will the impacts be only economic. Already there is evidence, initially anecdotal but becoming firmer, of UK universities being shut out of research partnerships.

---

19. Theresa May MP, Conservative member for Maidenhead and former Home Secretary, succeeded David Cameron as prime minister of the United Kingdom on 13th July 2016.

It is against this backdrop that I am determined to protect Scotland's interests. Let me turn then to what those interests are and why they matter. Protecting our place in, and relationship with, the EU is not just an article of faith. It is about our vital interests and really matters to the lives of people across our country.

There is our democratic interest. To put it simply, we did not vote to leave. We voted to remain. To be told that we must leave, regardless, is tantamount to being told that our voice as a nation does not matter. Some will say that we also voted to stay in the UK, so we must accept the UK-wide verdict but, in 2014, we voted to stay part of a UK that was a member of the EU. Indeed, we were told then that protecting our EU membership was one of the main reasons to vote against independence.

Our democratic interest is, in my view, a strong one, but it is not the only interest at stake.

For a country that sends almost half of its international exports to other EU countries, retaining membership of a single market of 500 million people matters. For a nation that has a strong financial services sector, the system referred to as 'passporting' matters. With a significant rural economy, retaining access to CAP payments matters. With a reputation for punching above our weight in research, ensuring access to competitive research funding and the global collaborations that flow from it, matters. For a country that needs to grow its population to help address skills gaps and deal with an ageing demographic, free movement of people matters. All of that is now at risk, and people will pay the price if jobs, investment and living standards suffer.

Then there is our interest in social protection. The EU guarantees core rights and protections for workers. The right to paid holidays and maternity leave, limits to working hours, the right not to be discriminated against, health and safety protections, all matter to workers the length and breadth of our country. I genuinely fear that a UK Government outside the single market will seek economic competitiveness through de-regulation and a race to the bottom. That would be devastating for the rights and protections that we have come to take for granted.

We also have an interest in solidarity, in independent countries coming together for mutual protection against the threat of crime and terrorism and working together to address big global challenges. The European Arrest Warrant, intelligence sharing, the cross border enforcement of civil rights, collective action to tackle climate change, initiatives like Erasmus that give our young people the chance to study in other countries and deepen their understanding of different cultures, all these matter to our collective peace and security and the future of our planet.

Lastly, it is in our interests to have influence. To end up in a position where we have to abide by the rules of the single market and pay to be part of it, but have no say in what the rules are, would not be taking back control (to coin a phrase we've heard more than once). It would be giving up control. Having influence in the world we live in matters for all of us.

Democracy, economic prosperity, social protection, solidarity, and influence are the vital interests at stake that we must now seek to safeguard. They are not abstract. They are real and matter to every individual and business in the country. What then are our options?

Simply and in summary, we can seek to find or create a solution that enables Scotland's distinctive voice to be heard and our interests to be protected within the UK…or we can consider again the option of independence. I said the morning after the referendum, and I repeat again today that, at this stage, we must keep all our options open.

That means exploring in the first instance, in this crucial period before the triggering of Article 50, as the UK Government develops its negotiating position, options that would allow different parts of this multi-national UK to pursue different outcomes. It means the nations that voted Leave can start figuring out what Brexit means while others, like Scotland, can focus on how to retain ties and keep open channels we do not want to dismantle.

I do not underestimate the challenge of finding such a solution. Even if we can agree a position at UK level, we would face the task of persuading the EU to agree. The barriers are substantial, but to those who want to rule out the possibility of success before we even try, I would say two things.

Firstly, we live in unprecedented times. When Article 50 of the Lisbon Treaty was drafted, it would have been considered inconceivable that any country would ever vote to exercise it. You only have to read it to know it was not drafted to be executed, but that has now happened, and beyond a few lines of text, there are no rules for what happens next. The territory is uncharted and the page blank, giving us an opportunity to be innovative and creative. An opportunity to shape the future.

Already, ideas are being floated. Terms like 'reverse Greenland' and the 'Norway model' have entered our lexicon and some academics and experts have started to sketch out other possibilities. Some may prove impractical or undesirable but, in a union where the relationships between our nations are evolving, there is no black and white. Let us consider all the options with an open mind and work to develop the right outcome for Scotland.

The second point I would make to those, particularly in the UK Government, who are at pains to say how highly they value the United Kingdom, is this. Now is the time to do more than just assert, against evidence to the contrary, that the Union works for Scotland. It is surely time to demonstrate that Scotland's voice can be heard, our wishes accommodated, and our interests protected within the UK. It seems to me that the UK Government now has a responsibility, indeed a vested interest, in doing so. For our part, the Scottish Government has already started work, advised by the Standing Council of Experts appointed in the days following the referendum, to develop such options.

I welcomed the Prime Minister's commitment in Edinburgh, just over a week ago, that different options would be considered and that Article 50 would not be invoked until there was agreement on an overall UK position. My government is now working with the UK Government to establish exactly what these commitments mean. We need to set out in detail the manner in which the Scottish Government will be involved in the development of the UK position ahead of Article 50 being triggered, and the mechanism for ensuring meaningful assessment of the options we bring forward.

We must also be clear what our involvement, and that of the other UK administrations and parliaments, will be in the political decision to invoke Article 50. Not just in the evidence gathering and consultation to inform that decision, but in the actual decision itself. I know other administrations are equally anxious and at the British–Irish Council meeting in Cardiff on Friday Carwyn Jones, First Minister of Wales, put forward a suggestion about the involvement of all four parliaments across the UK. This is the work we are doing to turn the commitments that have been given into practical reality.

I hope to be able to update the Scottish Parliament on the progress of these discussions, and the implications for the organisation of the Scottish Government's work, over the course of the summer.

As we do all of this, we will continue our engagement with Europe, with the institutions and other member states, to build understanding of, and support for, Scotland's position. The response so far has been warm and welcoming. Many across Europe can see that it would also be in Europe's interest to allow those who do not want to sever their ties to find a way of not doing so.

That brings me, of course, to the question of independence. I am a lifelong Nationalist, but I said in the immediate aftermath of the EU referendum that, in seeking to chart a way forward, independence was not my starting point. That remains the case. Protecting Scotland's interests is my starting point and I will explore all options, but I am equally clear about this. If we find that our interests cannot be protected in a UK context, independence must be one of those options and Scotland must have the right to consider it. That is why we will take the preparatory steps to ensure that this option is open if the Scottish Parliament considers it necessary. I do not pretend that the option of independence would be straightforward. It would bring its own challenges as well as opportunities but consider this...

The UK we voted to stay part of in 2014, a UK within the EU, is fundamentally changing. The outlook is one of uncertainty, upheaval, and unpredictability. In these circumstances, it may be that the option offering the greatest certainty, stability, and maximum control over our own destiny, is that of independence.

These are my reflections on the past month and my thoughts at this stage on the way forward.

Just as the past few weeks have been the most tumultuous in my memory, so too will the period ahead be difficult and uncertain. Standing here today, I do not claim to have a clear line of sight to the future, nor do I have all the answers to the many questions we face. What I do know is this. Scotland did not choose to be in this situation. I also know that our vital interests are at stake, with potential consequences that will affect us all. As First Minister, I have duty to do all I can to protect those interests and to do so, as far as I can, in a way that unites us a country.

19

THE DEFINING CHALLENGE OF OUR TIME

Given to the Arctic Circle Assembly, Reykjavik, Iceland
Reykjavik, Iceland 7th October 2016

Speaking to the Arctic Circle Assembly provided NS with the opportunity not only to confirm alignment with neighbouring nations but also to reiterate the seriousness with which her government viewed the climate emergency. Although still denied by vested interests and governments afraid to grasp the nettle of change, rising global temperatures caused by greenhouse emissions were apparent in an increasing number of weather incidents across the world. Implicit in her message is an absolute requirement for international empathy and co-operation.

Scotland and Iceland share ties of trade, culture and kinship, which go back for centuries. The early history of the Orkney Islands was chronicled in the Icelandic sagas more than eight hundred years ago. More recently, in 1874, the national anthem of Iceland was composed in central Edinburgh. Even more recently than that, Scotland gave Iceland another anthem. Your football supporters' 'Viking Chant', which attracted worldwide attention at Euro 2016, was reportedly inspired by a similar chant by fans of a Scottish football team, Motherwell. I bring that up because it was nice to have any Scottish presence at Euro 2016!

Iceland and Scotland co-operate on areas ranging from energy policy to marine science to sustainable tourism. In fact, our tourism agencies are today signing a memorandum of understanding.

Our ties with Iceland are mirrored in connections to many other countries represented here today. For example, our ancestral ties to Canada and our trading links with nations such as South Korea and Japan. We often learn from your countries in our social and economic policy and are aiming to adopt Finland's policy of giving expectant parents a baby box containing vital items to help them look after their babies in the earliest days.

Scotland may be not quite, geographically, part of the Arctic Circle, but in our heritage, culture, policy approach (and sometimes our weather!) there is much that we share, and those shared interests are actually the theme of a Scottish art installation, Prospect North, which I am opening today on the first level of this venue[20]. I hope that as many of you as possible will visit and enjoy it.

Scotland and Iceland, like so many delegates to this forum, share a strong commitment to tackling climate change, which President Grimsson and I discussed during the Paris Climate Change summit last December. It is the reason he invited me to speak here today, and I am going to concentrate on the steps Scotland is taking not only on climate change but also in promoting climate justice. In doing so, I hope to send out a wider message about our positive contribution and confirm our desire for even stronger partnerships with our northern neighbours.

The Paris Agreement[21] is the most significant step yet towards tackling climate change, and I am sure all of us welcome Wednesday's announcement that the agreement will come into force on 4th November. It is a remarkable achievement, not least for Ban-Ki Moon, who will address this forum tomorrow, and who has prioritised climate change throughout his time as Secretary General of the United Nations.

However, Paris is a milestone, not a destination. A global

---

20. The Harpa Conference Centre and Concert Hall.
21. The agreement on greenhouse gas emissions within the United Nations Framework Convention on Climate Change.

temperature increase of one degree Celsius, which is what we saw in 2015, is already melting glaciers and ice-sheets in the Arctic and creating drought and extreme weather incidents around the world. The consequences of a two degree increase would be deeply damaging for all nations, and catastrophic for some. It would induce rising ocean levels, an increased number of famines and, almost certainly, a displacement of populations beyond even those arising from recent and current conflicts. When Ban-Ki Moon spoke in Paris last year, he called climate change 'the defining challenge of our time'.

It is essential that the world meets the overall target set in Paris, of limiting global temperature increases to below 2 degrees Celsius and making serious efforts to keep them below 1.5 degrees. That, let me be clear, will mean going beyond the specific pledges made last year, which would still lead to warming of more than two degrees Celsius. We cannot simply applaud ourselves for agreeing in Paris, important though that is. We need to deliver and exceed the specific commitments.

Scotland will play its part. As the video showed, in 2009 our parliament unanimously passed its Climate Change Act. Using the year 1990 as a starting point, the Act committed us to a 42% reduction in greenhouse gas emissions by 2020, and an 80% reduction by 2050. At that time, a 42% reduction by 2020 was the most ambitious legal target anywhere in the world, but we deliberately set a goal we thought would be difficult.

However, we achieved our 2020 target in 2014, six years ahead of schedule, and now are looking to do even better. We aim to more than halve our 1990 emissions by 2020, which means looking at a huge range of issues. Scotland has reduced energy use by almost a sixth since 1990, but we know we need to do more. We recently made energy efficiency a national infrastructure priority and see big opportunities in areas such as renewable heat and the circular economy.

We are expanding renewable energy supply. When our Climate

Change Act was passed seven years ago, 28% of Scotland's electricity demand was met by renewable power. Last year, the figure was 57%. That still leaves us a long way behind countries such as Iceland and Norway, but it is a big increase, largely caused by onshore wind production. We aim to do better in the years and decades ahead and are increasingly looking at offshore resources. Our European Marine Energy Centre in Orkney is a global leader, and more wave and tidal power companies have demonstrated their technologies there than at any other site in the world.

Last month I launched the first stage of the Meygen tidal array project. When it is fully deployed in the Pentland Firth, it will produce enough electricity to power approximately 175,000 homes, making it the largest planned tidal stream project in the world. There are also hugely significant projects in offshore wind. The largest floating wind farm in the world is being developed by Statoil, the Norwegian energy company, off the North Sea coast of Scotland. Potentially, it is an important step in making offshore wind economically viable in deep waters.

Scotland's northern seas were central to the Norse culture that so many countries here share, but they can sometimes seem peripheral to the wider world, so it is wonderful that they are now at the cutting edge of global energy innovation. Technologies being tried and developed will play their part in providing the renewable energy the world will need in future, not simply bringing environmental gains but also creating economic benefits. In Scotland, the low-carbon and renewable energy sector already supports more than 21,000 jobs with potential for many more. Other low-carbon advances, such as better energy efficiency, will make our businesses more competitive.

The need to tackle climate change is an overwhelming moral imperative, but it is also a significant economic opportunity, and one we should aim to seize.

Scotland's approach to climate change is part of a deeper desire to be a good international citizen. We want to set a good example through our domestic policy and to learn from other countries. However, we also want to recognise our international responsibilities and today have announced a one million pound contribution to the Capacity Building Initiative for Transparency, the fund established by the United Nations after Paris, recognising that many developing nations lack the capacity to measure their greenhouse gas emissions accurately. Our contribution comes from our Climate Justice fund.

One key point about climate change is that its worst effects are often felt in developing nations, although those nations have not been major emitters of greenhouse gases. In addition, the individuals affected by climate change are often the young, the old, the ill, and the poor. Women are suffering disproportionately, since they are often the main providers of food, fuel, and water.

The countries which have done least to cause climate change, and the people who are least equipped to cope with its consequences, are hit hardest.

In 2012, Scotland became the first national government in the world to establish a climate justice fund. We increased our support this year and, so far, it has supported eleven projects in four sub-Saharan African countries. The fund is small in terms of the scale of the problem. Tiny, in fact, but it makes a significant difference to the communities in which it operates and is a powerful statement from a country which is determined to do the right thing.

That motivation also lies behind Scotland's increasing role in international development. We were one of the first national governments to confirm we would adopt the new sustainable development goals. In doing so, we committed ourselves to tackling poverty and supporting sustainable growth within Scotland. We also pledged to promote international development overseas, a growing priority for us. We have development partnerships with Pakistan, Malawi, Zambia, and Rwanda, in which we work closely and well with the UK Government while also looking to learn from other countries.

The annual Contribution to Development Index suggests that four of the five most effective countries in the world, in terms of the impact of their policies on international development, are Denmark, Sweden, Norway and Finland, and Scotland is now pursuing approaches which they have pioneered... such as the idea that all government policies, not just aid policies, should be consistent with international development goals. It is a good example of how the exchange of ideas among Arctic Circle countries can have a positive impact across the world.

Scotland's commitment to internationalism is relevant to one final issue I want to talk about this morning. Earlier this year the Scottish Government argued strongly for the UK to remain a member of the European Union. We welcome the EU's practical benefits of free trade, free movement, social and environmental protections but, for all its imperfections, we also admire the principle behind it. We like the idea of independent countries working together for a common good and believe that on some issues twenty-eight independent nations working together can have greater impact than one on its own. In Paris last year, the European Union was plausibly able to negotiate with the United States and China as an equal and played an influential role in achieving a successful conclusion.

People in Scotland voted by 62% to 38% to remain in the EU, and the Scottish Government is currently looking to find ways that enable us to retain the benefits of membership. We are also arguing strongly for the United Kingdom to retain membership of the single market, even as it leaves the EU. The Nordic countries have taken different views on membership but all, including Norway and Iceland, have chosen to be within the single market.

Scotland will do everything possible to remain an open, inclusive, and welcoming nation working with our neighbours, playing a positive role in the world, and strengthening (rather than weakening) our partnerships. Our friendships with the countries around us matter deeply and we will not allow them to be damaged by Brexit. That, of course, is why we welcome the chance to contribute to this Arctic Circle gathering.

When insularity and protectionism seem to be gaining ground, Iceland should be praised for establishing an important new forum for international co-operation. Scotland will support it in any way we can and, in doing so, recognise that the principles behind this Arctic Circle resonate with significance from Iceland's recent past.

Tuesday will see the 30th anniversary of the Reykjavik summit between President Reagan and General Secretary Gorbachev less than a mile from here. The summit did not see any immediate agreement, but General Secretary Gorbachev subsequently referred to it as a 'turning point' in the Cold War. Within fourteen months, the USA and the USSR had negotiated reductions in missile stocks, inconceivable in previous decades. Just three years later, the Berlin Wall fell, as the Cold War came to an end and barriers across Europe came down. Before he departed for Reykjavik, President Reagan remarked on Iceland's willingness to act as host. He said: 'There could be no better testimony to the enduring commitment of the Icelandic people and government to the search for a just peace.'

The fears of the Cold War have been replaced by other issues, including rising isolationism and international security concerns, but the defining challenge of our generation, as Ban-Ki Moon said last year, is climate change. It is therefore fitting that Iceland is again demonstrating its enduring commitment to a just and peaceful world, bringing people together to help find solutions to the interrelated challenges and opportunities that Arctic Circle countries share.

Scotland, a country proud of our Nordic connections, committed to our European neighbours, and keen to work with our friends from around the world, is an obvious and willing partner.

20

A SPECIAL AND UNBREAKABLE BOND

Given to the Seanaid
Leinster House, Dublin, 29th November 2016

> In a winter visit to Ireland, NS was made an honorary patron
> of Dublin University's Philosophical Society, an honour shared
> with German Chancellor Angela Merkel, then Vice President
> Joe Biden, Nancy Pelosi and Weird Al Yankovic (as she said, 'an
> impressive and eclectic list') and the following day addressed
> the Seanaid, the upper house of the Irish legislature. In this
> amicable speech she noted that both Ireland and Scotland have
> within their long histories painful experience of both forced
> and voluntary emigration and, in a logical connection that had
> evaded many, therefore had a moral responsibility towards refu-
> gees in the present era. The complex challenge presented by the
> EU referendum result was her main topic, together with a firm
> reassurance of continued friendship and co-operation.

I understand that I am the first serving head of government to
address the Seanad, so this is truly a historic day and I thank you
warmly for the opportunity. It is wonderful to join you in these
beautiful surroundings

Last night in Dublin I had the pleasure of visiting Trinity
College and viewing for the first time the Book of Kells, a moving
reminder of how deeply and inextricably linked the peoples
and cultures of Ireland and Scotland have always been. When
Colmcille travelled from Ireland to Iona in 563 he helped shape

Scotland and when, more than two hundred years later, monks made the corresponding journey from Iona back to Ireland they bequeathed to this country, in the Book of Kells, one of the great masterpieces of European civilisation.

These exchanges have continued ever since and have helped create a special and unbreakable bond between us. As a student, a lawyer, and most recently a Member of the Scottish Parliament in the city of Glasgow, I have seen evidence of that bond every day of my adult life, and know it has enhanced both Glasgow and Scotland. One of our great Gaelic poets, Sorley MacLean, described it as 'the humanity/that the ocean could not break/that a thousand years has not severed', but its strength is not only defined by the people who have moved between our two countries. Much of our modern history has been shaped by emigration beyond these islands and, as a result, for all the regret we feel about its historic causes, both of our countries can take great pride in what Scottish and Irish people have achieved overseas.

We are unusually blessed with ambassadors and supporters in every corner of the globe. Indeed, when Ireland's rugby team beat New Zealand three weeks ago, a result I thought it politic to mention (not least because it gives hope to us all), you had the good fortune of being able to play at home[22] in the great city of Chicago!

There are two points I want to make today about our shared history and experiences.

Europe, now, is facing its greatest refugee crisis since the end of World War II. Scotland and Ireland both know that, in other times and different circumstances, the peoples of our nations were also driven by self-preservation and the desire for a better life to seek a future far away from the lands of their birth. Perhaps that helps to explain why both Scotland and Ireland have responded with such open hearts to today's crisis.

Today, Scotland is home to almost a third of the Syrian refugees

22.   Chicago is home to many Americans with Irish ancestry.

that have been resettled in the UK, and Ireland too is playing her full part. Of course, both of us are making the case for a co-ordinated European response. Given our own national experiences, for Scotland and Ireland to turn away from this crisis would not simply be a failure of compassion, it would be a denial of our own identity. By assisting people who so desperately need help today we are, in some senses, repaying the obligations of our past.

The second point I want to make is perhaps more straightforward. Although we share more than a thousand years of history, relations between Scotland and Ireland are stronger, warmer, and more harmonious than ever. I have been immensely touched by your hospitality since I arrived in Dublin yesterday, and hope that your President, whom I had the honour of spending time with yesterday, felt the same warmth when he did us the honour of visiting Scotland in June.

In terms of political co-operation, Ireland has recently increased its diplomatic representation in Scotland, and we have this year established a new government office here in Dublin. Ireland is one of our biggest export markets and I discussed with your business community earlier this morning how we can further strengthen and deepen those links. As well as healthy business relationships, we share and enjoy strong cultural ties. The Abbey Theatre is now directed by two people who were previously based in Glasgow, while a Dubliner runs the Edinburgh International Festival.

These political, economic, and cultural links draw strength from, and reinforce, the most important connection of all: the friendship, indeed the kinship, shared by millions of Scottish and Irish people across these islands and around the world. I believe passionately that these ties will be strengthened even further, to our mutual benefit, in the years ahead.

Throughout the last four decades, an important context for our co-operation has been our shared place in the European Union. Last year I gave a lecture at Sabhal Mòr Ostaig, the Gaelic language college on the Isle of Skye. Your former President, Mary Robinson, delivered the same lecture eighteen years previously and I was struck that she attributed the revival of traditional Irish culture in part to your membership of the EU. She said that 'The experience of interaction with other European states, on a basis of equality, has helped our national self-confidence and heightened our awareness of the value of our distinctive contribution to European culture and civilisation.'

Scotland's experiences in Europe have not been identical. We are not an independent member state... yet... but much of what President Robinson said holds true for us as well. The sense that small countries can be equals in a partnership of many is something that appeals to us. The basic principle of membership, that independent countries co-operate for the common good, has generally seemed praiseworthy rather than problematic.

That perspective may explain why Scotland voted so convincingly to remain within the European Union. It is not just that we value the practical benefits membership brings, although we do. It is also that, for many people in Scotland, as in Ireland, being European has become a positive part of who we are and how we contribute to the world. The UK-wide vote to leave was deeply unwelcome and for Scotland, as for Ireland, creates a challenge which is not of our making or choosing.

Last week I had the pleasure of meeting the Taoiseach at the British–Irish Council in Cardiff and yesterday I also met your Foreign Minister, Charlie Flanagan. It was clear from both of those discussions that Brexit is the greatest foreign policy challenge Ireland has faced since it joined the EU. In Scotland too, we know that how we, and the UK, respond to June's vote will define us for generations.

It might be helpful to set out some of the principles that are guiding the Scottish Government as we confront the consequences and seek to navigate the best way forward. The first is straightforward. Scotland believes that the UK should now seek continued membership of the single market and the European Customs Union.

48% of voters in the UK chose to remain in the EU, as did two of the four nations. Many who campaigned to leave were clear in their view that doing so need not involve leaving the single market. I accept that there is a mandate for the UK Government to take England and Wales out of the European Union. However, I do not accept that there is a mandate to take any part of the UK out of the single market, especially when we consider the economic consequences.

Secondly, to guard against the possibility that the UK does decide to leave not just the EU, but also the single market, we are exploring options that would respect the vote in Scotland by remaining within it. Not instead of free trade across the UK, but in addition to it, and we will publish proposals before the end of this year setting out further detail.

These proposals will focus on Scotland within the UK, but there is also the option of Scotland considering again the question of becoming an independent country. That remains firmly on the table. If the path that the UK chooses to take turns out to be damaging to our economic, social, cultural, and international interests the people of Scotland must have the right to choose a different future. We understand that none of what lies ahead will be easy, but nothing about Brexit is going to be easy. We are living in unprecedented times, which require imagination, open minds, and fresh thinking.

The third point I want to make relates specifically to Ireland. The Scottish Government knows and understands how vitally important it is to maintain an open border on the island of Ireland and will unequivocally support an open border. For reasons of geography, history and the simple preservation of peace, Ireland's circumstances demand close attention.

The final theme I want to address today is more general. It is about cohesion, social justice, and solidarity. When President Higgins spoke to the Scottish Parliament in June, he talked about the 'consequences of unsustainable economic models, which have fomented instability and widening inequalities.'

In my view, Brexit is one of those consequences. There are many different causes of the UK's vote and we will no doubt be analysing and debating them for many years to come. For a lot of people, they will include legitimate concerns. The EU is, no doubt, an imperfect organisation, but there seems little doubt that the Brexit vote was a product of inequality, of disillusionment with the established order and a sense of alienation and disenfranchisement.

If people do not feel they are benefiting from the status quo we cannot be surprised if they choose not to vote for it and, although every single region in Scotland voted to Remain I cannot ignore the fact that one million of our fellow citizens voted Leave. Therefore, one consequence of the referendum, for us, is an even sharper focus on social justice.

That crystalizes the challenge, and the choice, that the Brexit result poses for all who support free trade and value the economic, social, and cultural benefits of immigration. We can choose to turn inwards, or we can choose to stand strong for the principles of an open economy and a progressive, liberal democracy. I choose the latter but recognise that we must not simply assert the benefits of these values. We must be able to demonstrate them.

Ireland provides an interesting example. The decisions you took, after 1958, to open your economy to the world were transformational. You are a wealthier, more open, and more diverse society as a result, but recent years have demonstrated that all open, trading nations, including Ireland, and certainly including Scotland, need to ensure that growth is truly sustainable. All parts of society must have a fair chance to contribute, and everyone must fairly share the benefits.

There need be no contradiction between an open, dynamic, and competitive economy, and a fair, inclusive, and welcoming society. Evidence from around the world demonstrates that the two must go together. A fair society is essential if we are to sustain support for an open economy and that is why, in Scotland, our economic strategy prioritises fairness together with economic competitiveness.

It is also why Scotland, like Ireland, was an early supporter of the UN's Sustainable Development Goals. We believe they provide a framework for all countries to follow, encouraging us to exemplify fair and sustainable development at home, while promoting it overseas. While doing this there are many areas where Scotland and Ireland can work with, and learn from, each other.

I had talks yesterday that touched on how our governments and businesses are co-operating to promote renewable energy and tackle climate change. Our ban on smoking in public places was influenced by Ireland's example, and is already improving the health of our people... and Ireland is currently considering Scotland's legislation on minimum unit pricing of alcohol. I wish you well as you do so.

Both of our nations have travelled a long way on issues such as same-sex marriage. It was legalised in Scotland at the end of 2014, while Ireland, to your great credit, became the first state to enshrine that right in its constitution.

Finally, I know that President Higgins recently called for small countries to work together on conflict resolution and sustainable development. I welcome that call and believe that we, as individual nations but also as partners, are well placed to play our part. In overseas development co-operation, Scotland is committed to learning from other small countries, including Ireland.

In 2012, it was partly the influence of Mary Robinson that led Scotland to become the first country in the world to establish a climate justice fund, recognising that the people affected most by climate change are those who have done the least to cause it. The fund is further evidence of our determination to show leadership on climate change, the biggest environmental, economic, and moral issue facing the planet, and demonstrates our desire to lead by example at home while exerting a positive influence overseas.

In all of this, and so much more, Scotland and Ireland are living examples of the positive impact that small, open, outward-looking countries can have on the world. The need to safeguard and enhance our reputations as such is perhaps greater now than for decades, and I hope that we can and will support each other as we seek to do so.

I began this speech by referring to the Book of Kells. The first line of the first page is widely believed to have been from St Jerome, setting out his intention 'to make a new work from the old'. My hope is that Scotland and Ireland, sharing as we do an open heart for newcomers and faith in dialogue's power to move minds, will work even more closely together in the years ahead. We will make new works, new meanings, new impacts from our ancient ties and shared values and, by doing so, ensure that our small nations send a powerful signal to others across the world.

21

THE UNDERPINNING PRINCIPLE OF THE STATE

Given to the Freeman Spogli Institute for International Studies
Stanford University, California, 4th April 2017

With the United States now under the presidency of Donald Trump, NS made two major speeches on successive days. The first was given at Stanford University in California, the second to the United Nations in New York. At Stanford, she ranged across many international issues including climate change, the refugee crisis and, with the eyes of the world on Scotland, in what fashion the UK might achieve its withdrawal from the European Union. It was an occasion for a statesperson of stature to which she rose comfortably. Beginning in light-hearted fashion on Scotland's many connections with California she proceeded through the expected list until she reached gender equality. At this point, followed by her reference to post-war Germany and its constitution, she took her speech to a different level.

It is a pleasure and privilege to be here at one of, if not the, most beautiful campuses in the world. It was President [George W.] Bush in, I think, 2008 who proclaimed 6th April as Tartan Day, the key event in Scotland Week, so Thursday of this week is Tartan Day. Scotland Week and Tartan Day are intended to celebrate the contribution of Scottish people to the United States down the generations, as well as the many links and relationships between our two nations. Most importantly, we are looking at how we strengthen those links.

One thing that strikes me every year is how various surveys suggest that almost thirty million people in the United States claim Scots or Scots–Irish ancestry. However, the official census figures show there are only around ten million. What that means is there are twenty million people in the USA who are not actually Scottish but want to be! I think that is a great compliment, but also an opportunity and, let me tell you, one we are determined to take. As far as I am concerned, if you want to be Scottish, nobody, least of all me, is going to stop you.

There is a more serious point here. Scotland's modern identity, much like that of the US, is an inclusive one. We take the approach that, if you want to be Scottish, you can be, and that is relevant to some of the points I will make later.

Many of the ties between us are evident here in Palo Alto and the surrounding area. There is a hill called Ben Lomond twenty miles south of here, close to a town called Bonny Doon, which was named by a Scottish settler, John McLaren, a Scottish emigrant from Bannockburn. Everyone here will have heard of the famous Battle of Bannockburn. John worked on Leland Stanford's[23] estate here in Palo Alto, and was instrumental in establishing San Francisco's Golden Gate Park.

The ties between our two countries are longstanding, and it has been clear during the two days I have spent here that the connections between Scotland and California, of culture and history, trade and commerce, family and friendship, continue to flourish. That is something that means a lot to Scotland... and to Californians as well. Those international ties are part of what I want to talk about today. The desire we have in Scotland is not just to create a fairer and more prosperous country but also, as a relatively small one, to play a big part and make a positive contribution to the world we live in.

I will start by looking at some of the events of the last year and, indeed, the last week. It is fair to say that 2016 was a tumultuous

23.   Joint founder of Stanford University with his wife, Jane.

year in politics at home in Scotland, across the United Kingdom, and here in the US. The decisions taken will have ramifications for many years to come. Ten days ago, for example, twenty-seven of the twenty-eight governments across the European Union came together to celebrate the 60th anniversary of the signing of the Treaty of Rome. The Treaty being, of course, the foundation treaty of the European Economic Community [EEC].

Scotland has been a member of the EEC, which is now the European Union, for more than forty years, bringing us significant economic, environmental, social benefits, and the fundamental principle of independent nations working together on equal terms for the common good. To tackle the problems and seize the opportunities that few countries can do alone, appeals to me and to many people across Scotland. As a result, EU membership has become an important part of our identity. It speaks to our sense of who we are.

That is why in 2014, when Scotland had a referendum on whether to become an independent country, our membership was an important issue. Nobody really argued or debated about whether Scotland should be part of the EU, the debate was about whether we would be if we were independent. Many of those who opposed Scotland becoming independent, including the UK Government, argued that leaving the United Kingdom was a risk that would threaten Scotland's membership. So, it is ironic that the opposite has turned out to be true.

When the UK held its referendum on EU membership last year, a large majority in Scotland chose to remain as part of the EU but were outvoted by the rest of the UK, and the UK was the only member state not represented at the 60th anniversary celebrations. Instead, the UK Government, last week, notified the European Commission of its intention to leave and Scotland, despite the arguments of 2014 and how we voted in 2016, will be forced to leave as well. What is even worse is that the UK is not just leaving the EU. There is a real danger developing that it will leave the EU in the most damaging way possible.

Scotland and the Scottish Government have proposed, over the past few months, different ways in which the UK could retain membership of the single market. Several other countries, such as Norway, have such an arrangement, but those proposals have been disregarded by the UK Government, and this could potentially have a wide range of impacts.

It could mean tariffs for farmers who export, higher regulatory barriers for trade with Europe, and is already causing deep uncertainty and anxiety for people from other parts of the EU who have chosen to live and work in Scotland. I take a very simple view of anybody who comes to live and work and study in Scotland. You do us a great honour, a great privilege and pay a great compliment, and we want you to consider Scotland as your home. The vote to leave and the implications for those who have chosen to live in Scotland or other parts of the UK are serious.

It is worth looking in detail at what that might mean for Scotland's universities. For Scotland, as for California, our universities are incredible cultural, social, and economic assets. When the Times Higher Education Supplement published its rankings of the best universities in the world last year, it showed Scotland had more world-class universities per head of population than any other country in the world, with the sole exception of Switzerland... but we are determined to beat Switzerland to the top spot sometime soon!

I have just attended an event highlighting the research partnership which Stanford has established with five of our universities, Edinburgh, Glasgow, Heriot Watt, St Andrews and Strathclyde, and have welcomed Heriot Watt's decision to launch a new economics scholarship for US students, based at Panmure House in Edinburgh. Panmure House is significant because it is where Adam Smith lived and worked in the final years of his life.

Those examples demonstrate that our universities have a reach which extends beyond the European Union. That said, membership of the European Union has been fundamental to Scotland's academic success. One sixth of our academic staff are EU citizens from outside the UK. So are one sixth of our postgraduate students. These EU students are disproportionately likely to be studying subjects such as science and technology, hugely important areas for any country in the modern world.

Scotland significantly benefits from the opportunities for collaboration provided by European programmes available only to countries inside the single market, or which are applying to join the European Union. At the end of last year, the Principal of Edinburgh University (not someone who is known for exaggeration), told a House of Commons Select Committee that the impact of Brexit on higher education 'ranges from bad, to awful, to catastrophic'. It is a significant and a serious risk to a sector that is fundamental to Scotland's future.

The reason for running these risks, for leaving the single market as well as the European Union, is that the UK Government has prioritised control of immigration over everything else, a policy likely to be damaging to Scotland. We benefit hugely from the contribution made by people who choose to work or study in our country, whether from the rest of the UK, from the European Union or, of course, from the USA. Historically, our population growth has been lower than other parts of the UK, and lower than many other parts of Europe. So, for the sake of our economic prosperity we need to see more people choosing to come and live and work in Scotland. There are two points which perhaps follow from that.

The first is that, if any of you are uncertain what to do after you leave Stanford, you are very welcome to come to Scotland! We offer a warm welcome and fantastic quality of life. The whisky is rather good, in moderation, and our weather is more . . . shall we say interesting than the constant sunshine you get here in California every day?

The second point is more fundamental and more serious. In my view, it is counterproductive for the UK to prioritise control of immigration over any other Brexit outcome, but especially damaging for a country like Scotland. It is interesting that, at a time when debates about immigration rage in many parts of the world, there is no major political party in Scotland arguing for constraints, because we know they would be damaging to our interests. This is a good example of how Brexit is forcing upon Scotland a policy agenda which is not of our choosing and not in our national interest.

Brexit, and the way in which the UK Government is choosing to impose it, presents Scotland with a dilemma. We had, as I have already mentioned, a referendum on independence less than three years ago and some are understandably reluctant to have another in the next two years. However, if we do not give people a choice, we will have to accept a course of action determined by a UK Government that most did not vote for. A course which may be damaging to our economy and our society for decades and possibly generations to come.

That is democratically unacceptable, and is why the Scottish Parliament, last week, agreed to seek consent from the UK Government for a further referendum on independence, once the final terms of the Brexit deal are known. This will mean that, rather than having Brexit and a future direction imposed upon us, we will have the opportunity to choose our own future, to choose the direction we want to take. We will be considering issues that go beyond membership of the EU, such as what kind of country we want to be, and how we can best achieve that. How we can build a better society at home and make a positive contribution to the wider world.

One of the things I encountered time and time again during the campaign in 2014 was an overwhelming desire to create a fairer society, as well as a more prosperous one. That desire came from many people who voted against independence, as well as those who voted for it, and is a desire we seek to respond to under Scotland's current devolved powers.

Shortly after I became First Minister, the Scottish Government revised our economic strategy. One of the biggest changes we made was to promote equality alongside economic competitiveness. That focus is a matter of basic morality. Everyone in any society should have a fair chance to fulfil their potential. It is also an issue of economic efficiency. There is strong and growing evidence that inequality in western economies has harmed growth, and the UK is a good example. The Organisation for Economic Co-operation and Development has estimated that, between 1990 and 2010, rising inequality reduced growth by nine percentage points.

Professor Joseph Stiglitz, who taught here at Stanford for more than a decade, is one of the Nobel Laureates who serves on my Council of Economic Advisers. He said at the time that 'Tackling inequality is the foremost challenge that many governments face. Scotland's Economic Strategy leads the way in identifying the challenges and provides a strong vision for change'. He recognised that a more equal society, where everyone can participate to their full potential, will lead to a stronger and a more sustainable economy in the longer term. Workers who are well educated and trained, well-paid, highly valued and supported, will be more productive than those who are not.

Two weeks ago, research was published on the happiest countries in the world. As you might expect, countries in developed nations ranked highest. The USA, I can tell you, was 13th, and the UK was 19th. It was striking that the five highest spots were taken by small European countries: Norway, Denmark, Iceland, Finland, and Switzerland. Two of those countries are EU members, the others are members of the European single market. All score highly on measures of income equality and do considerably better than the UK.

There is strong evidence for the Scottish Government's prioritisation of inclusion, but there is an important political point to be made as well, which I think is relevant here in the US. Policies such as free trade and the free movement of people will bring benefits to the economy, but also have the potential to disadvantage, or be seen as disadvantaging, particular groups. Therefore, their sustainability depends on ensuring they benefit not just the few, but the many in our society. The vote to leave the European Union had many causes, but we know that people on low incomes were more likely to vote to leave. So too were areas with relatively low rates of employment (after allowing for student numbers).

The EU referendum also posed a challenge for those of us who support free trade, welcome immigration, and believe that the benefits of globalisation managed properly (an important caveat) should outweigh the costs. It demonstrated that we can only sustain support for a dynamic and open economy if we do more to build a fairer and inclusive society and that, in Scotland, is what we are determined to do. One of the most pressing challenges that most developed societies face, it requires leadership. No country has all the answers, but I believe that in Scotland we are at least asking some of the right questions.

Scotland voted by a big margin to remain in the EU, and it is at least possible that our referendum result was so different because the Scottish Parliament often adopts policies with fairness and inclusion at their heart. We have taken action to mitigate some of the brutal cuts to social security provision that the UK Government has implemented so, maybe, there was less of a sense of people being left behind and disenfranchised.

That emphasis on inclusion, important for economic reasons, will also be important politically as we navigate through the circumstances that lie ahead, but it is also applicable to another issue that is very close to my heart: gender equality. I was quite struck, when I read about Stanford University, to see that women were admitted on equal terms as men from the very beginning, at the insistence of the founders. Leland Stanford pointed out that, 'if vocations were thrown open to women, there would be 25% increase in the nation's production'.

It is a simple and overwhelmingly obvious point. Nations

impoverish themselves if they underuse the talents of half of the population, and yet that challenge is one which no nation has fully risen to. Scotland is trying to take the lead.

We have launched major initiatives in early years care, primarily because we believe it is an essential part of ensuring that all children regardless of background get a fair chance to realise their potential. It also recognises the importance of childcare in encouraging parents to return to work and in supporting parents, women in particular, to pursue careers. We work closely with trade unions and employers to boost productivity and encourage fair work practices, a partnership approach different to that taken by many other governments.

Our system is closer, although this is not an exact comparison, to the German economic model developed after the war. Rhine capitalism was based on a strong sense of partnership between workers, trade unions, businesses, and the public sector. It encouraged competitive markets but combined them with strong social protections, and resulted in high levels of innovation, high productivity, and strong exports. That approach was based on a very distinct vision of society.

Article 1 of post-war Germany's constitution states that human dignity is the underpinning principle of the state, which helps to establish the constitutional principle of the 'social state, a state which strives for social justice.

What we are trying to create in Scotland is not identical, but there are similarities. As with most countries, our concern for human dignity and social justice is not confined to our own boundaries. We also want to make a positive contribution to the wider world. Later today I will fly from California to New York and tomorrow I will attend meetings at the United Nations. Scotland was one of the first countries, back in 2015, to sign up to the UN's Sustainable Development Goals. That means we seek to build a fair, prosperous, and sustainable society at home and around the world.

As a relatively small country, we must focus our contributions on the world stage. So, it is maybe worth talking about two specific areas where we are trying to make a difference. One of my meetings is with the Office of the Special Envoy for Syria at the United Nations when we have seen today another stark reminder of the horrific impact of the Syrian conflict[24] and noted the pressing need to find a route to peace.

We will discuss Scotland's Women in Conflict programme, which prepares fifty women every year to play a part in mediation and conflict resolution. Last year, it trained women from seven countries in North Africa and the Middle East. The programme is Scotland's way of acting on UN Security Council Resolution 1325, which recognises that women bear many of the worst consequences of civil war and conflict but are too often excluded from efforts at finding peace and reconciliation.

Another area of priority is tackling climate change. In 2012 Scotland became the first country to establish a climate justice fund for developing countries, recognising that the people affected most by climate change are often those who have done the least to cause it. In addition to helping other countries mitigate climate change, we are also determined to be at the forefront of tackling it.

I mentioned earlier that Scotland and Stanford are working together on new technologies in photonics and healthcare. Scotland has a long and proud history of innovation and we want to apply our innovation and engineering expertise to help lead the world into the low-carbon age. In 2009 the Scottish Parliament passed what at that time were the most ambitious statutory climate change targets in the world. We have met the first of them five years early and are now looking to go further.

We produce more than 50% of our net electricity demand through renewable sources and are an important development site for some of the renewable technologies of the future. The world's largest tidal power array is being developed in our Pentland Firth.

24.   A chemical attack perpetrated on the city of Idlib by the Assad regime.

The world's largest floating offshore wind farm is due to be built off our north-eastern coast.

I had the opportunity to discuss this with Governor Brown yesterday. When he gave his inaugural address two years ago, or should I say his latest inaugural address, he pointed out that 'taking significant amounts of carbon out of our economy without harming its vibrancy is exactly the sort of challenge at which California excels'. He was referring, of course, to California's astonishing track record of innovation, much of it linked to work done here at Stanford. For both California and Scotland, innovation is part of our history, as well as part of our modern identity. We discussed ways in which Scotland and California could together apply our capacity for innovation to the biggest environmental, economic, and moral issue facing the world.

There is one final point about the issues I have talked about in this speech: climate change, peacekeeping, inequality and immigration, the flows of people and talent. All of them are interrelated. Drought exacerbated by climate change may have been an initial cause of the Syrian civil war, and the refugee crisis caused by that war directly impacted the debate on the UK's membership of the European Union.

Immigration is a major topic of debate in the USA as well as in Europe. We know that the displacement of populations which will be caused by climate change, especially if global warming exceeds 1.5 degrees Celsius, is likely to dwarf the scale of migration that Europe has seen from the Syria crisis, demonstrating that no nation is or can be insulated from our reliance on, and obligations to, the wider world. All independent nations must accept interdependence and that it is not only our own national interests that matter but the interests of the wider world.

The best balance between independence and interdependence is, of course, the question that Scotland once again faces. Over the past sixty years, the European Union has built a single market and encouraged economic co-operation while developing common social standards for workers and shared environmental standards. It has enabled independent neighbours to trade and travel freely while respecting the environment and protecting living standards. It has enabled us to work together on some of the world's biggest challenges like climate change.

Brexit puts all of that at risk and forces Scotland to ask itself a fundamental question. Do we remain as we are? Facing exit from the EU, where we are able to participate in all of that collaboration, at the hands of a UK Government determined to curb immigration at the expense of so many other things? Or choose to become an independent country with opportunities and challenges, but freedom to be an equal partner with other countries across our British Isles, Europe, and the wider world?

My view, as a supporter of independence, is that we will choose the second course. Independence, combined with interdependence and equal partnership, is the best way to build a fairer society at home and make that positive contribution. These things will be debated and discussed across Scotland as we move forward and, as we do so, there will again be debate and disagreement about how we can best contribute. I am also sure that there will be no disagreement about whether we want to make that positive contribution.

Our modern identity will remain open, outward-looking, and inclusive. People from around the world will always be welcome to call themselves Scottish if they so wish, whether they are or are not, and Scotland will continue to build partnerships with governments, businesses, and universities in California and across the United States.

22

WOMEN IN CONFLICT RESOLUTION

Given to the United Nations
United Nations Building, New York, 5th April 2017

In the second of her American speeches NS was more specific in
her subject. Again addressing a full house, she first identified her
gender-balanced cabinet as one of only three in the world when it
was formed, and then the importance of example by, and visibility
of, female leaders. She went on to describe her government's role,
in partnership with the UN's Mediation Support Unit and
Beyond Borders, in the training of women for involvement in the
Syrian peace process. On this occasion, as at Stanford University,
she aimed to leave a strong and positive impression of the sort of
international citizen that Scotland intends to be.

Earlier this afternoon, I had the pleasure of meeting the Executive
Director of UN Women and the Assistant Secretary General for
Human Rights. I am grateful to both for their time, and for the
opportunity to discuss how the Scottish Government can further
support the vital work of the United Nations in both those areas. It
is good to see so many here today for this discussion about the role
of women in conflict resolution, an issue of obvious international
significance, and an area where I hope that Scotland can make a
distinct and positive contribution.

Before I came to New York last night, I was in California, at
Stanford University. While preparing for my speech I read up on
some of the history of that university and was interested to learn

that the founders, Leland and Jane Stanford, at the very establishment of the university, insisted that women were admitted on completely equal terms to men. In a letter of 1893 Leland Stanford said this: 'If vocations were thrown open to women, there would be a 25% increase in the nation's production'.

I thought that was striking in a letter written 124 years ago, because it makes a simple, overwhelmingly obvious point that is still relevant. Any nation that underuses the potential of women, that underuses half its population, is needlessly impoverishing itself. Yet last year, the World Economic Forum predicted that, at our current rate of progress, it would take 170 years for the world to reach genuine gender equality. I do not think any of us can afford to wait and, even if we could, it would not be acceptable.

I am determined, as the First Minister of Scotland, that my country will take a lead in driving progress not only within Scotland, but also by helping to promote gender equality beyond our own borders.

When I took office as the first woman First Minister of Scotland, I was moved by the number of girls and women who contacted me to say how much it meant to see a woman in the most senior political role in the country. It underlined the importance of two things. Firstly, the importance of role models for girls. Secondly, the importance of genuinely leading by example, and I am determined to do that ... lead by example and use my time as First Minister to improve opportunities for women.

The government I lead is committed to tackling violence against women, closing the gender pay gap, and ensuring that more women work in careers traditionally seen as for men. Along the way, we would like to encourage men to work in careers that have been traditionally seen as for women.

I was also determined to lead by example in my appointments, and appointed a cabinet that was, and remains, gender-balanced. We learned from the UN that we were one of only three such cabinets in the developed world. There are now five. So, in two and a half years we have gone from three to five. I suppose we should celebrate all progress, but that really does tell us how much work we still have to do.

Commitment to gender equality at home I hope can be extended to our work overseas. A good example is our work on climate justice, where we have very much been influenced by the work of Mary Robinson. So many of our climate justice projects (we were the first country in the world to establish a climate justice fund) help to empower women, which is an outcome we ask all our partner organisations to measure.

We all know that the worst impacts of climate change are disproportionately felt by women. Women are more likely to be subsistence farmers or affected when crops fail. Women are usually the people who get water and have to walk further in areas of drought. It is girls who are more likely to stop going to school when tough times force families to work harder.

That basic logic applies beyond the context of climate change. Women's rights have to be the concern of everybody, not just women but, to advance women's rights, we need to make sure that women work in key areas and hold key positions of influence. Which brings me, of course, to Security Council Resolution 1325, because that principle applies directly and powerfully to conflict resolution.

Conflicts that target civilians, as so many civil wars do, like climate change, often have a disproportionate effect on women. Yet women are too often excluded from having a voice or a say in resolving conflict. That needs to change, and the new Secretary General of the UN himself has set a powerful example in how he intends to progress.

Last year, Staffan de Mistura, the UN Special Envoy for Syria, invited the Scottish Government to fund a project to train women for involvement in the Syrian peace process. We had already committed to accepting refugees from Syria, and Scotland is home to almost a quarter of all who have come to the United Kingdom under the resettlement programme. We were delighted to help with a project which will play a part in establishing peace, rather than simply coping with the consequences of war. I am grateful to the UN for giving us the opportunity, to the Mediation Support Unit for helping, and of course to Beyond Borders who organised the training programme.

The first ten participants were all from the Syrian Women's Advisory Board, but we took the decision to broaden the programme and last year trained fifty women from Iraq, Lebanon, Libya, Palestine, Syria, Turkey, and Yemen. We are able to provide them with a safe space to discuss issues freely and securely, away from the peace process itself, and the programme is widely regarded as a success.

The determination of these women is incredible; to make a difference in circumstances that are difficult to appreciate or comprehend. They attended an event at the Scottish Parliament on, by coincidence, the morning after our own elections in 2016. So, they were able to engage with sleep-deprived Members of Parliament who had just participated in a robust election campaign and immediately gathered to accept the outcome of the democratic process. There is cross-party support in Scotland, and every party leader was represented.

I am really delighted to confirm that we will train fifty more Fellows every year until 2021 and are committing to extending the remit to include South Asia, South and Central America, and sub-Saharan Africa. All of this is in line with our determination to be a good global citizen.

We were one of the first countries to sign up to the UN's Sustainable Development Goals, wanting to be a model of fair sustainable development at home, and also to promote prosperity, equality, and peace overseas. We want to put economic and social rights, as well as human rights, at the heart of all our policymaking and, in doing that, of course, we find the framework that the UN provides so helpful.

We contribute in a range of ways to the work of the UN, but part of the reason for being so delighted to be here today is that I want us to explore ways in which the Scottish Government can further support the work that the UN, in its various different forms, is doing. One of my great heroes, I am sure in common with many people in this room, was Eleanor Roosevelt, and she was very clear that 'alone, none of us can keep peace in the world, but if we cooperate together, then we can achieve that longed-for security'.

My message today, to all of you doing vital work across the world, is that Scotland wants to play our part. We are a relatively small country, but one that potentially can have a big, positive, and powerful voice. In the work we are doing in peacekeeping and reconciliation, hopefully we demonstrate that.

23

THE IMPORTANCE OF TRUTH

Given to the Political Studies Association[25]
University of Strathclyde, Glasgow 12th April 2017

A common factor between the EU referendum of 2016 and the US presidential election of the same year was the sheer quantity of organised disinformation disbursed by one side, and the steady lowering of the standard of debate from reasoned, evidence-based argument into prejudice, partisan insecurities, and fear of difference. In this speech, NS compared the independence referendum of 2014, largely a positive experience, with these other democratic exercises and made what would in different circumstances be a banal observation: 'it is important that people can make an informed choice'. In this she anticipated the following year's release by Tim Duggan Books, in America, of Michiko Kakutani's seminal text, *The Death of Truth*[26] and Alan Rusbridger's *Breaking News*[27] from Canongate in Great Britain.

Scottish universities have been involved with the Political Studies Association from its foundation in 1950, and Scotland has hosted this annual conference on several occasions, most recently in 2010

---

25. Founded as a Trust in 1950 to 'promote the development of political studies and encourage education and the advancement of learning in the art and science of government and in other branches of the political sciences.'
26. Published in Great Britain in the same year by William Collins.
27. Published in Great Britain by Canongate Books in 2018.

during your 60th anniversary year. I am really delighted that you have returned, and it is, sincerely, a huge pleasure to welcome you all to Glasgow.

The scale and reach of this conference are impressive. You have been discussing issues from environmentalism to gender in politics (a subject close to my heart), to the design of parliaments and how they affect politics. Sessions are being held on political developments in different regions across the world from North America to South East Asia.

I am sorry not to have been able to attend some of them, because you are addressing issues of direct relevance to politicians across the world. More importantly, you have been addressing issues that are hugely important to citizens right across our work.

One of the truths demonstrated, as we reflect on a tumultuous twelve months, is that the work of political studies specialists is more important and valuable than ever, and it is important to stress that point because, in the last year, I am not sure you will have felt appreciated by all politicians.

One of the most notorious comments of the EU referendum was that the public 'have had enough of experts'. There has been a sense, fuelled by that referendum and by the US election, that evidence-based arguments have stopped being important in political campaigns and public discourse. Actually, experts do make important and positive differences not only to the academic understanding of political issues, but also to wider public debate and the health of our democracy.

Scotland, in recent years, provides a good example, with high-profile examples of teams who have made it their mission to help the public, and the media, understand issues better. For example, the Centre on Constitutional Change[28], the work on polling at

---

28. Established in August 2013 to research the UK's changing constitutional relationships.

Strathclyde University and through What Scotland Thinks[29], have all had a real public impact. I often think that Professor John Curtice[30] appears on television more often than I. Actually... Professor John Curtice does appear on television more often than I!

There is excellence in all the political studies teams in Scotland, as has been reflected in their contributions to this conference. Their work does not simply meet rigorous academic standards. It also makes a real difference to the quality of our public discourse, which is important and encouraging when we think about our current constitutional position. The prospect of another referendum on Scottish independence, of course, is of interest much further afield.

In 2014, the European Union was a significant issue in the independence debate, and many who opposed Scotland becoming an independent country argued that leaving the UK was a risk. They said it would threaten our place in the European Union, and it is somewhat ironic that the opposite has turned out to be true. Despite the arguments that were made and how we voted in 2016 (62% of those who voted opted to Remain) we now face being forced to leave the EU against our will. Not just forced to leave, but in a deeply damaging manner by a UK Government determined to prioritise control of migration over membership of the free market. Thereby making a hard Brexit all but inevitable which, of course, presents Scotland with something of a dilemma.

Some people are understandably reluctant to have another referendum on independence in the next two years. However, if we do not give the people a choice, we will be accepting not only a course of action determined by a UK Government that most

---

29. The What Scotland Thinks website provides impartial, up-to-date information on public attitudes towards how the constituent parts of the UK should and are being governed.
30. Professor of Politics at the University of Strathclyde and Senior Research Fellow at the National Centre for Social Research. Now Sir John Curtice.

people in Scotland did not vote for, but also one which may be deeply damaging to our economy and society for decades, possibly generations to come. In my view, that is democratically unacceptable, and that is why the Scottish Parliament agreed to seek consent from the UK Government for a further referendum on independence once the final terms of Brexit are known. To ensure that our future as a country is decided by us and not for us, we once again face a time of intense political debate. There are two points that I want to make about that this evening.

Although I make these points in a Scottish context, they are applicable to elections and referendums the world over and, given the climate we currently live in, fuelled by a polarising social media, where opinions often matter more than facts, these points are worth underlining.

The first is this. It is important that people can make an informed choice. Comparing the 2014 referendum on independence with the 2016 referendum on EU membership, a key difference was that, in 2014, the Scottish Government set out a detailed prospectus to be scrutinised, analysed, and often criticised by political opponents, the media, business groups, wider civic society, and academics. Their analysis was not always comfortable for the government, or for those of us advocating independence, but it was incredibly valuable. It fed into a much wider public debate about what kind of country Scotland wanted to be, a debate that became extremely well-informed.

In the summer of 2014, genuinely detailed issues, such as who would be the lender of last resort for financial institutions in an independent Scotland, were not being debated only in the chamber of our parliament or on television. They were discussed and debated in detail in pubs and cafes, hairdressers and bus stops, workplaces, and homes in every part of the country. The Scottish population became engaged, educated, and informed as never before, and that included young people, a legacy that lives on today, given the lowering of the voting age in the referendum to sixteen. In passing I would say that, if it had happened in the EU referendum, the result would have gone the other way.

In 2016, on the other hand, people were asked to vote for a change without really being told what it involved. A slogan on the side of a bus was as detailed as it ever got, and that slogan should not be confused with the truth. Nobody who wanted (and I think this is a key point of difference with the Scottish referendum) to leave the EU had any real responsibility for setting out how it might be achieved, or what the implications were. Many big issues, including the difference between single market membership, customs union membership and World Trade Organisation rules, are only being discussed and debated widely now. They should have been at the heart of public discussion before the vote took place.

I do not pretend that the 2014 referendum was perfect, but I do think it was a better process than the 2016 vote on the EU.

We want to ensure that the next referendum on independence again gives people the information they need to come to an informed and considered judgement. That is why no one wants the referendum to take place immediately. Instead, it should happen when the details of the final Brexit agreement are known. Based on what the Prime Minister says currently, that is likely to be in late 2018 or early 2019.

Well before the debate, the Scottish Government will also set out our proposals for what an independent Scotland would look like. We will address issues such as the currency, our plans for fiscal stability, the process of securing our relationship with Europe, and all with as much detail and clarity as possible.

The second point I want to make relates to the tone of the debate. Again, I make this point in the context of a Scottish referendum, but it has wider applicability. By and large, the 2014 referendum was a positive experience for Scotland, but did not feel that way for everyone. In my view, a referendum is the only way of resolving Scotland's future constitutional status. However, one facet is that it requires a binary choice, Yes or No, from people who often have nuanced or even conflicting views about something that matters very deeply to them.

Everyone in Scotland knows, although this is a point that is usually lost, that there was often very little difference between a No voter tempted by a new path, but with anxieties about the future, and a Yes voter who felt solidarity with the rest of the UK but felt that we would be better taking decisions for ourselves.

The polarisation that exists between politicians rarely exists within the public at large. Fundamentally, all voters want the best for their families, communities and countries and come to their own conclusions. The campaign around Scottish independence needs always to respect that fact, and recognise the honesty and validity of people's anxieties, doubts, and differences of opinion. As First Minister, I have a responsibility to lead by example, and the Scottish Government has a responsibility to build consensus where we can. Therefore, I will do my best to ensure that we make our case not only with passion and conviction but also courtesy, empathy and respect. I hope that all other politicians do the same.

There is a lot of talk in Scotland about how an independence referendum would be divisive. As the Church of Scotland said a couple of weeks ago, there is nothing inevitable about this campaign, or any campaign, being divisive. Campaigns and politics are only divisive if we make them so. We should be determined not to make it so and welcome rather than dismiss the contributions of experts.

Independent academic expertise, along with a free and vigorous media and strong civic institutions, form the lifeblood of a strong political community and a healthy, vibrant democracy. All politicians should cherish and support, rather than denigrate it, even when it is not comfortable for us. Uncertain and challenging times demand the best from politicians. We do not always live up to that, but we have a duty to strive to do so. Times like ours demand the best from those whose job it is to understand and explain. That is true for the media, but also for academics.

This must be a fascinating and invigorating time to work in political studies, but I am sure it is also challenging. I hope this conference has played some part in helping you rise to the challenges and will help you scrutinise, analyse, inform, and enlighten because, when you do that, you enrich public life and strengthen democratic debate.

24

DIVERSITY IN THE MEDIA

Given to the Edinburgh International Television Festival
Edinburgh International Conference Centre 17th August 2017

The furore that followed the BBC's publication of its higher paid
presenter salaries was initially focussed on what appeared to be
astronomic amounts with inexplicable step differences. Second
and third looks though, revealed more deeply set injustices in
gender, race, and social class. These points were brought out by
NS in a wide-ranging speech that included media coverage of
these same issues, in which she mined her own experience as a
high-profile woman in public life.

Edinburgh is a great place to be, but particularly at this time of
year. In August, when Edinburgh and Scotland are the cultural
capitals of the world, we also, albeit quite fleetingly, become the
media centre of the UK as well. It is particularly appropriate this
year.

As you probably already know, we are celebrating the 70th
anniversary of the Edinburgh Festivals, and both the BBC and
STV have expanded their coverage. Particularly relevant to this
gathering today, is that we celebrate an important anniversary in
Scottish broadcasting. Next week marks sixty years since Scottish
Television, as it was then known, first broadcast. It was the first
competition in Scottish broadcasting[31]. Before the channel

31. Competition with the BBC. There were now two channels to choose
between.

launched, Roy Thomson, then chair of Scottish Television, promised viewers 'an infinite variety of programmes'.

Sixty years on, viewers in Scotland and around the world have access to an infinite variety, or at least an infinite number, of programmes. Whether diversity has been achieved is a more open question, which is the theme linking the two things I have been asked to talk about this morning: women in broadcasting, and how we develop production in Scotland.

Diversity links both those issues because, for all its variety of programmes, television still does not fully reflect the diversity of audiences either in Scotland or within these islands. The publication of the BBC's pay figures has exposed the gender pay gap more dramatically than anticipated. However, it is important to be clear that the UK Government did not push for greater transparency from any great desire to expose a gender pay gap. More cynically, they expected to flush out high salaries paid to some presenters and provoke licence fee payers into questioning what was being done with public money by a public institution.

It certainly succeeded in provoking female licence fee payers, by exposing the gross disparity between men and women in screen positions. Perhaps the most obvious and least acceptable element was to see male and female presenters of the same programme, whether BBC Breakfast or the Today Programme, doing the same job for grossly different salaries.

When I was here two years ago, I spoke about how the viewing public was increasingly challenging the lack of women in major onscreen roles. Given that women make up 52% of the population, it seemed odd that men occupied twice as many presenting roles. I think it is fair to say that progress was made with the announcement that Sarah Smith would take over from Andrew Neil on Sunday Politics, but it seems the BBC forgot that there should be equal pay for equal work.

Kirsty [Wark][32] was one of more than forty leading female

32.   A senior broadcast journalist.

presenters who wrote an open letter to Tony Hall, making clear how unacceptable that was and challenging the BBC to accelerate progress. Importantly, the letter pointed out that it is not just an issue for those 'at the top', in the high-profile, high-visibility roles. This is an issue that goes right through the organisation.

As you would expect, I wholeheartedly agree with the contents of that letter and hope the BBC takes action quickly, but it is also important to reflect that it will not be the only media organisation with a gender pay gap. The BBC experience exemplifies the case for greater transparency in the reporting of pay policies, in not just the media but more generally. I am not arguing for the revelation of every single contract, but we must have the information that tells us where gender pay gaps exist and how big they are. We can only call out unacceptable practices when we know they exist. The BBC experience provides lessons not only here but also for society.

It would be difficult to talk about women in the media without reflecting on how women are portrayed by the media, and I am fairly well qualified in the subject, although I cannot promise to be objective, as my day-to-day experience suggests that women's portrayal, perhaps more by the print media than by broadcast media, has a long way still to go. Almost every week I read something about myself, commenting on what I wear or how I look. During the general election, in the Daily Mail there was a double page spread on how I had worn the same suit five times over a two-year period. What really annoyed me was that it was not even the same suit. One was pink, the other red, but the pictures made it look as if it were the same . . . they did not even get that right!

More serious was when the Prime Minister[33] and I met in Edinburgh a matter of months ago to talk about Brexit, and the front page of the Daily Mail next day reduced us to pairs of legs and who won the battle of the legs. You can laugh at that, indeed you have to, but there is a serious issue in terms of how women are portrayed and how that feeds women's sense of themselves and

33. Theresa May MP.

their willingness to enter high-profile or senior roles. These are serious issues. Yes, we have made progress, but there is still a long way to go.

I have talked about gender so far, as it is close to my heart, but these issues are not confined to gender. The BBC's pay data revealed that only one of its twenty-five best-paid stars was from a black or minority ethnic background: George Alagiah[34]. Last month Lenny Henry highlighted research from the Directors Association showing that no talk shows, period dramas, game shows, sketch shows, celebrity TV shows or children's entertainment shows had producers from black and ethnic minority backgrounds. He pointed out that, although Ofcom does now plan to ask the BBC to monitor its onscreen racial diversity, their plans do not apply to roles behind the camera.

These things are no longer acceptable.

The media also faces issues in relation to socio-economic diversity. Alan Milburn's social mobility commission last year criticised the 'increasing reliance on unpaid work as a point of entry to the profession'. Not surprising when the National Council for the Training of Journalists found that three quarters of new entrants had done an unpaid internship. If that is the entry into journalism, it does not take long to work out that young people whose parents cannot support them find that access to journalism is more difficult.

This week's provisional report from the Diamond project[35] demonstrates that disabled people and people over the age of fifty are significantly underrepresented in broadcasting. To be fair, the Diamond project was set up by major broadcasters to monitor diversity, and gives hope that change might be possible. Change, and this is a point that should not be lost, is in the interests of

---

34. Senior broadcast journalist.
35. Diamond is a single online system used by the BBC, ITV, Channel 4, Channel 5 and Sky to obtain consistent diversity data on programmes they commission.

the media, as well as the viewing public. Jon Snow[36], commenting here on Wednesday night, pointed to the serious problem that 'the echelons from whom our media are drawn do not, for the most part, fully reflect the population among whom we live and to whom we seek to transmit information and ideas'.

Doing more to protect and promote diversity is not only a good thing, representing the demographics of your viewers, benefiting from their broad range of experiences, ideas, and stories, is also good for business.

These are fundamental issues, and touch on basic principles. Television needs to do more to represent the diversity of modern life, and that relates to the second issue I want to talk about today, which is how the television production sector in Scotland, and the media in general, reflects the nations and regions of the UK.

Again, it is important to be fair and recognise that things are better now than they have been. It is now just over a decade since my predecessor, Alex Salmond, established the Scottish Broadcasting Commission to address concerns from the public, and across all political parties, about the state of Scottish broadcasting. It is fair to say that there has been significant progress. In 2008 BBC Alba was launched and has been a huge success in its viewing figures and impact on Scotland's production sector.

UK network expenditure has increased as well. In 2006 Scotland's share of UK network commissions had sunk as low as 2.5%. Last year it was 6%, and it seems almost certain to grow further. The BBC has promised to invest an additional £20 million in network content from Scotland.

The last year has also seen two other positive developments. STV has joined its local television stations to create a second channel, STV2, which includes an integrated news bulletin at 7.00 pm, proving it is possible to have an integrated bulletin in Scotland. Coincidentally, I happened to be in the studio on the night the first programme aired and was impressed by what was

36. Senior broadcast journalist.

achieved with fewer resources than the major broadcasters.

Even more importantly, the BBC has announced plans for a new Scottish channel, which will launch next year. I called for that to happen two years ago so, clearly, I warmly welcome it, but I think there is more to be done. There are still legitimate concerns about how some network spending is classified, whether some productions labelled as 'Scottish' really contribute anything to our production sector and our wider creative economy. So, I welcome the fact that Ofcom is reviewing that. It is not an abstract issue. Under current definitions, Scotland's production sector loses business as each year passes.

In addition, the proposed BBC channel is set to have a budget of £30 million, but there are questions about whether that will be sufficient. A decade ago the Broadcasting Commission proposed an annual budget of £75 million for a new network in Scotland, and the new channel only broadcasting in standard definition could limit its appeal. Viewers increasingly expect high definition for drama. At the very least, that must be kept under review.

At present, approximately 72% of the licence fee raised in Scotland will be spent in Scotland. In Wales and Northern Ireland, it is 98%. Even with the BBC's new commitment, we will not have parity with those countries. The BBC has come a long way in improving choice for our viewers and boosting our production sector, but it is hard to escape the conclusion that Scottish broadcasting is still being short-changed. These are issues to be addressed on an ongoing basis, but another issue that has been discussed a lot over the last few days is the possibility of Channel 4 relocating. I know that Channel 4 has reservations, and I understand some of them, but I think the idea has merit. The Scottish Government has made it clear that if Channel 4 moves out of London, Glasgow would be an obvious base. It already has offices there, and Glasgow is a major creative industries hub and home to two other national broadcasters.

There is a broader point about what relocation is intended to achieve. Clearly I would be in favour of Channel 4 moving to Glasgow, apart from anything else it would be moving into my constituency if it went to Pacific Quay, but the point is that basing Channel 4 in Glasgow brings no more benefit to independent producers in Wales or Birmingham, than basing it in Birmingham would bring to Scotland. So, relocation will not be an answer on its own. The key issue is to ensure that commissioning power is decentralised through the United Kingdom, and that is what the Scottish Government has proposed.

As part of that process, we have suggested the establishment of a centre of excellence for factual programming in Glasgow, and that Channel 4's quota for Scottish programming should be closer to our share of the population. We want to see all public service broadcasters do more to commission programmes from the UK's nations and regions.

Wales has benefited in recent years from Doctor Who and other drama commissions and, as a result, people sometimes unfavourably compare the drama base in Wales to the industry here in Scotland. I can understand why, but the television production industry in Wales has benefited from more than thirty years of high-level public funding for [Welsh channel] S4C. There has been nothing comparable to that in Scotland, and that matters.

We are now in a golden age of television content production, especially television drama production. It is impossible to know whether this trend will continue, level off, or whether we are at a peak. What seems certain is that opportunities for attracting investment in drama in the next ten years will be greater than we could have predicted ten years ago. We have already benefited, perhaps most prominently through *Outlander*. Since 2012, the value of film and television production in Scotland has almost doubled, but there are opportunities to do more.

One reason we have consistently asked for public service broadcasters to commission more in Scotland is that investment can sustain and develop the skills base and infrastructure we need, but I am also aware that the Scottish Government cannot simply ask more of broadcasters, or indeed the UK Government, without looking to ourselves and considering the public sector's role. So, that is what we are doing.

We have already increased sector support through the production growth fund, and the first £1.75 million we invested secured £17.5 million worth of productions. Therefore, we will continue to increase the support we are giving. We know that there is a major opportunity here and are determined to seize it. We are addressing concerns that different agencies have overlapping remits by setting up a screen unit based in Creative Scotland to support the economic and the cultural development of the sector.

We are making progress in film studio facilities, which has been a running issue for decades, but are now seeing promising developments. We have said that we are minded to grant planning permission for a development, including a purpose-built studio, at Straiton, just outside this city. The makers of *Outlander* film at Wardpark, and films such as Marvel's *Avengers* and *T2: Trainspotting* have used facilities at Pelamis in Leith and Pyramids in Bathgate. In terms of investment and infrastructure we are making progress in ensuring that we retain programmes and films for significant periods of time, rather than being a base for location shoots.

We are also working to ensure that people can gain and update the skills they need to work in the television and film sector, which is why I am delighted to announce that the National Film and Television School will set up a new base in Scotland. The BBC is giving significant support to the venture, to be based at Pacific Quay where it will use the BBC's studio facilities.

As many of you know, the National Film and Television School is the most renowned school of its type in Europe. Its Glasgow base will be its first anywhere outside of London, so today's news is not only good for the Film and Television School, but also for hundreds of people who want to make a career in screen. It is also a major vote of confidence in Scotland's film and television sector.

We expect approximately four hundred people a year to use the school, including more than a hundred full-time students. The Scottish Government is providing start-up funding for the project, and a significant proportion of that will be used for bursaries. We intend to ensure that the new centre encourages true diversity and gives young people from all backgrounds a chance to develop a career in broadcasting, which takes me back to where I started.

Nobody in Edinburgh in August can doubt the diversity and vitality of Scotland's creative talent but, sixty years from the advent of multi-channel broadcasting in this country, we still wait to see that diversity and vitality fully reflected both on and behind our screens. My belief is that there is a genuine chance to change that. With greater commitment from our public service broadcasters, and strong support from the public sector, we will see significant continued growth in Scotland's television production sector, and the infinite variety of programming available to us will better reflect the infinite diversity of these islands.

25

THE ROLE OF INCOME TAX

Given to The Royal Society of Edinburgh
Edinburgh, 2nd November 2017

> With the Scottish Parliament's powers over taxation still
> extremely limited, and borrowing impossible, questions inevi-
> tably arise on the funding of public expenditure. Introducing
> a consultation paper on prospective income tax changes, NS
> provided this illuminating discourse that covers not only the role
> of taxation in government but also its morality and what these
> choices say about national identity and character.

One of the founding members of this Society, Adam Smith, whose
thoughts on this subject are always worth attention, observed
that: 'The subjects of every state ought to contribute towards the
support of the government, as nearly as possible, in proportion to
their respective abilities...'

A statement of the obvious, it goes to the heart of the discussion
about fair and proportionate taxation and how, particularly in a
time of austerity, we can make the vital investments that enable our
economy to grow and our public services to deliver the support we
rely on.

Scotland's tax powers remain limited. More than 60% of
our spending power is still dependent on decisions taken at
Westminster. However, we now have a greater measure of fiscal
control than at any time since the start of devolution, and by far
the biggest fiscal lever we have is income tax with 30% of Scotland's

budget now coming from income tax receipts. With greater ability to levy tax, comes a duty to do so responsibly and in a balanced fashion, and my government will do exactly that.

In our recent Programme for Government, I expressed the view that the time is right to consider afresh the role of tax in our budget decisions, and committed to publish a discussion paper ahead of the draft budget in December. Today, we meet that commitment with the publication of 'The role of income tax in Scotland's budget' but, before I talk about the paper in more detail, it is worth reflecting on the financial context and wider backdrop to the decisions we face.

The UK Government has imposed almost a decade of cuts to Scotland's budget. The cut to the Scottish Government's discretionary budget between 2010 and 2020 will amount to £2.9 billion in real terms. As well as continued austerity, we face the damaging impact of Brexit. Previous analysis indicates that it could cost 80,000 Scottish jobs over a decade, with more than £11 billion a year wiped off our economy by 2030.

Brexit, coupled with austerity, will make the job of properly funding our public services more difficult, and this comes when an ageing population is placing ever-greater demands on services like the NHS, social care, and housing.

Over the past few years, we have worked hard, with significant success, to balance these pressures. Despite cuts to our budget, we have protected NHS funding and shielded local services as best we can. We have continued to invest in the small business bonus and the infrastructure and business development support that the economy needs. We have mitigated the worst impact of Tory welfare cuts, and safeguarded the social contract, delivering public service provision and a range of social benefits that far exceeds what is available anywhere else in the UK.

The value of university tuition, personal care, prescriptions, and eye tests far outweighs the impact of any of the four alternative approaches discussed in Chapter 7 of this paper. I am proud of what we have delivered in the most difficult of circumstances, but progress has involved sacrifices on the part of some, and it is important to remember that. Our public sector workers have had years of pay restraint.

As the impact of austerity, Brexit and changing demographics bears down ever harder, it is time to ask ourselves some tough questions. None of us want to see our cherished public services constrained. Very few people will want to see the social contract eroded, young people paying thousands of pounds a year to go to university, or older people paying for personal care. It would not be in the country's best interests to scale back our vital ambitions, such as increasing the NHS budget to meet the demand of an ageing population, expanding childcare, giving headteachers more money for our classrooms, extending broadband, building more affordable houses, giving public sector workers a fair pay rise, investing in the transport infrastructure, research and development, and support for entrepreneurs.

It is crucial to protect the next steps in creating that better future for our nation. With the pressures we face, we must consider whether the time has come for those who earn the most to pay a modest amount more and it is to aid and inform that discussion that this consultation paper is published today.

The paper explains the composition of the Scottish budget and how it is changing. It looks at the fiscal framework and sets our high-level expectations of the UK budget later this month. It provides detail about the income tax base in Scotland, who pays what and how much each group contributes to the overall budget. It looks at the scale and scope of our income tax powers, the limitations on them and how they interact with reserved powers. It also sets out some international comparisons.

Most importantly of all, it sets out the four key tests we believe any responsible and progressive use of Scotland's tax powers must meet. Any alterations to tax rates will need to maintain and promote the level of public services the people of Scotland expect … ensure that lowest earning taxpayers are protected and do not see their taxes increase … make the tax system more progressive and reduce inequality … together with our corresponding decisions on spending, support the economy.

I believe that these tests reflect the views of the majority of people in Scotland. That we want world-class public services; that we should not ask the lowest earners to shoulder more of the burden; we should do all we can to make the system fairer and reduce inequality; and that supporting the economy and sustainable growth should be central to our approach.

This paper analyses and applies these four key tests to the tax policies of each of the main parties in last year's Scottish election. In Chapter Seven, it applies them to four possible alternative approaches, which consider a range of alterations to both tax rates and tax bands.

Let me stress that these alternative approaches are not firm policy proposals. That will come in the budget. Nor do they form an exhaustive list. They simply illustrate some of the options open to us. We do, however, believe that the alternatives outlined in Chapter Seven better meet the four key tests than any of the parties' manifesto commitments from last year, and provide a starting point for discussion. We go into these discussions with an open mind and a willingness to listen, but the four key tests are the criteria that will now guide our decisions.

In respect of the first test, all of the alternative proposals in Chapter Seven raise additional revenue for investment in public services and the economy. That is also true, to varying degrees, of all the parties' manifesto proposals, with the exception of the Tories who would cut the money available for public spending.

Looking at the second test, all the alternative approaches protect those earning less than the median income, which is £24,000. With the increase to the personal allowance included, none would see anyone earning up to £31,000 pay a penny more than they do now.

In all four approaches, more than 70% of all adults would continue to pay no tax, or no more than they do today. All the alternatives would also satisfy the third test by making the tax system more progressive and tackling inequality.

The fourth test relates to our duty to support the economy through our tax and spending decisions. This government is committed to supporting sustainable growth and giving businesses the best opportunity to contribute to that growth. We have delivered substantial savings through initiatives like the Small Business Bonus, invested heavily in the infrastructure business needs to thrive, and taken a range of actions to support employment.

Too often, the relationship between growth and tax is mischaracterised. Debates about tax become falsely polarised between the needs of the economy on the one hand and the needs of our public services on the other. I think that is the wrong approach. The taxes we pay fund support for business and the economy, as well as our public services, but competitiveness is about more than just tax rates. It also depends on the strength of our public services, the skills of our people and the quality of our infrastructure.

Everybody knows that a good society needs a strong economy, but it is equally true that no economy will reach its full potential without a strong, fair, inclusive society, prompting the question that should drive this debate and unite us all. What kind of country do we want Scotland to be?

As a government, we will not propose alterations to income tax lightly but, after rigorous, careful, and considered discussion, bring forward policy proposals in the interests of the country as a whole.

My final point is this. In publishing this paper today, I acknowledge that we are a minority administration that must look to build consensus. If all parties stick doggedly and rigidly to their manifesto positions, our parliament will not be able to pass a budget, and we will fail in our duty to the Scottish people. I am making clear our willingness to compromise and my hope is that other parties will do likewise. Together, we can work to build consensus around a fair and balanced tax policy and a budget that works for all the people of Scotland.

26

HISTORICAL SEXUAL OFFENCES: AN APOLOGY

Given to the Scottish Parliament
Holyrood, Edinburgh 7th November 2017

On the 12th March 2014, the Marriage and Civil Partnership (Scotland) Act 2014 received Royal assent, having been introduced as a bill to the Scottish Parliament by Alex Neil MSP in June of the previous year. The bill was carried by an overwhelming majority, after which the MSPs turned to applaud the equal marriage activists in the galleries above. Recognised as an immense step forward there was still the question of the historical prosecutions of gay men for their (at the time illegal) sexual relations. The Historical Sexual Offences (Pardons and Disregards) (Scotland) Bill provided a blanket legal pardon, but this was not enough. Over many decades the law had been upheld but justice denied. NS gave her apology on behalf of the nation.

I am grateful for the opportunity to address the chamber. Today marks an important milestone in achieving true equality for Scotland's LGBTI community. This morning, the Historical Sexual Offences (Pardons and Disregards) (Scotland) Bill was published.

It is shocking to recall that, as recently as 1980, well within my lifetime, consenting sexual activity between men was classed as a criminal activity in this country, and the age of consent lowered to sixteen only in 2001, two years after this parliament came into being. Before then, hundreds of people in Scotland were liable to be convicted simply for loving another adult.

Presiding Officer, the words inscribed on this parliament's Mace set out the values which we seek to uphold and promote: wisdom, justice, compassion, and integrity. Yet within the lifetime of this parliament our nation's laws created suffering and perpetrated injustice. The legislation published today addresses that injustice, providing an automatic pardon to men convicted of same-sex sexual activity that would now be legal. In addition, the Bill establishes that people can now apply to the police for their offence to be disregarded from criminal records. This means it will never appear on a disclosure certificate.

The legislation therefore has both symbolic and practical value. The pardon sends an unequivocal message to everybody so convicted. The law should not have treated them as criminals, and they should not now be considered criminals. This parliament recognises that a wrong was done to them.

The disregard has an important practical consequence, allowing people to ensure that their past will no longer impact on their day-to-day life. That will change people's lives. At present, as the Equality Network has highlighted, people convicted merely of showing love and affection to their partner still have to explain their criminal record every time they change their job or apply for an internal promotion. That is unacceptable, and we are determined that it will end.

The Bill we are publishing today rights a historic wrong. However, I want to go further and do something that legislation on its own cannot. A pardon is, of course, the correct legal remedy to apply to convictions, but the term 'pardon' might still imply that parliament sees them as having done something wrong. That is a common context in which a pardon might be granted but, as all of us know, that is not the case here.

For people convicted of same-sex sexual activity, which is now legal, the wrong has been committed by the state, not by the individuals, and they deserve an unqualified apology as well as a pardon. That apology can only come from the government and from parliament, not from the justice system as courts, prosecutors and police were enforcing the law of the time.

The simple fact is that parliamentarians in Scotland, over many decades, supported or accepted laws which we now recognise to have been unjust, criminalising the act of loving another adult. They deterred people from being honest about their identity to family, friends, neighbours, and colleagues and, by sending a message from parliament that homosexuality was wrong, encouraged rather than deterred homophobia. So today, categorically and wholeheartedly, as First Minister, I apologise for those laws and for the hurt and harm they caused.

Nothing this parliament does can erase those injustices but I hope this apology, alongside our new legislation, will provide comfort to those who endured them, and I hope it provides evidence of this parliament's determination to address the harm that has been done.

The final point I would make is that although today's legislation marks an important milestone in Scotland's progress towards LGBTI equality, our journey is not yet complete. Considering how recently the laws I have just discussed were in force, it is remarkable and inspiring that Scotland is now considered to be one of the most progressive countries in Europe when it comes to LGBTI equality. One of the proudest moments of my eighteen years as an MSP and, I know, one of the proudest moments for many MSPs across this chamber, was in February 2014 when people from all parties came together to support equal marriage.

As all of us know, until we live in a country, in fact, until we live in a world, where no young person suffers hate or fear or discrimination or prejudice because of their sexual orientation or gender identity, we still have work to do. That is why we have promised to improve our gender recognition legislation to reflect the experiences and needs of transgender and intersex people. It is also why I attach such importance to the Scottish Government's work with the TIE campaign[37], ensuring that our young people do not have to fear bullying in school, and reviewing hate crime legislation to ensure that our laws provide the right protections against bigotry and hatred. It is why I hope that today's apology, in addition to its specific significance for gay men, sends out a wider signal to the LGBTI community.

The Scottish Government and the Scottish Parliament are committed to delivering true equality for LGBTI people in Scotland. Wherever there are societal, cultural, legislative, or regulatory barriers to achieving that, we will seek to remove them. We will never again accept laws or behaviours which discriminate against you and hurt you. Although today is a day for looking back and apologising, it is also a day which points to a better future. It is a day when this chamber promotes, and lives up to, our shared values of wisdom, justice, compassion, and integrity.

---

37.   A volunteer charity combating homophobia, biphobia and transphobia in schools with LGBT-inclusive education.

27

THE BEST POSSIBLE PLACE TO BE

Given to the Disabled People's Annual Summit
Verity House, Edinburgh, 16th January 2018

> The austerity policies of the Westminster government under prime ministers David Cameron and Theresa May disproportionately affected disabled people and other minorities. In response, the Scottish Government put many mitigating policies in place. In a speech that was largely about inclusion and consultation, NS listed these policies and actions with an anger that is difficult to gloss over. Not only did she assure disabled people in Scotland of their valued place in society, but also that they would be regarded with dignity and respect.

Events like these are good opportunities to highlight and discuss the issues that matter most to disabled people. They are also a good opportunity to recognise the role that Inclusion Scotland[38] plays in ensuring that the views of disabled people are heard and inform and help develop the policies that affect them.

The Scottish Government highly values the work of Inclusion Scotland. Our partnership over the past few years has made a real difference to the lives of disabled people. We have more work to do but can be proud of what we have achieved together.

---

38. Inclusion Scotland is a registered charity governed by a board made up of a majority of disabled people. Its mission is to achieve positive changes to policy and practice, so that disabled people are fully included throughout all Scottish society as equal citizens.

We have identified and gone some way to mitigating the UK Government's welfare reform programme, particularly its impact on people with disabilities. The Chair of the UN Convention on the Rights of Persons with Disabilities described these welfare changes as 'a human catastrophe', and that is not something we are prepared to do nothing about. We know that the 'bedroom tax' legislation[39] (that we will overturn as soon as we have the ability) disproportionately affects disabled people in Scotland, so we invest almost £50 million every year to ensure that nobody has to pay it, and that is just one example of our mitigation efforts.

In addition, we have established our own Independent Living Fund to replace the one that was shut down by the UK Government. Over several years, we redefined social care by implementing self-directed support and, by doing so, given disabled people, their carers and families, more choice and control over their own lives. We have also created a comprehensive Delivery Plan to help us meet the requirements of the UN Convention on the Rights of Persons with Disabilities.

It should be a source of pride and satisfaction that in its most recent report, the UN Convention recognised Scotland's distinctive approach to protecting the rights, and improving the lives, of people with disabilities. I think it is reasonable to say that, by working together, we have taken important steps to be proud of but the main topic of discussion, and the substance of my remarks, is what more we need to do. Our discussions should be focussed on how we go further to bring fundamental change.

As all of you know, around 43% of disabled people in Scotland are in work. For the rest of the population that figure stands at around 80%, illustrating what we have to overcome. Due to

39. From April 2013, the UK Government limited Housing Benefit and the housing element of Universal Credit for working-age council or housing association tenants if they were considered to be under-occupying their homes. This was widely known as the 'bedroom tax'.

individual circumstance work is not always a possibility, or always a desirable option, but too many disabled people are being denied a route into work, or lack support to accept employment opportunities. That is what we have a duty to tackle.

There are many underlying reasons. As a society we too often focus on what disabled people cannot do rather than on what they can. As a result, some disabled people can lack the confidence they need to pursue employment. We also know that some employers, consciously or perhaps more often, subconsciously, can be biased against having disabled people working for them. Even when disabled people are in employment, they can find it hard to declare their impairment due to a fear of stigma or rejection. Getting a job, holding down a job, thriving and progressing at work, can be more difficult for people with disabilities than it is for others.

The consequences are clear. First and foremost, too many disabled people are unable to fully contribute their talents and their abilities, and all of us lose out. This is an important point. If we have a society or economy where some people face barriers, we all lose out. Not just the individuals who face those barriers. People with disabilities miss the economic benefits as well as the boost work brings to our independence and sense of self-esteem.

All of that is unacceptable from a moral perspective, but it also has implications for our economy and society. No country can afford to neglect or underuse the talents of so many of its people. Increasing the number of disabled people in work, and therefore expanding our labour market, will help to support greater economic growth and output overall, and help to ensure that our prosperity is shared more equally, reducing inequality, exclusion and social deprivation.

What we are talking about today is important for individuals, important for you and others across Scotland, but the important collective point I want to make is this. It is important for all of us. This is a shared responsibility because it is for the good of society if we ensure that those with disabilities have the same opportunities as the rest of the population.

For those reasons, and I am sure many more, halving the employment gap between disabled and non-disabled people is a key commitment of the Delivery Plan, alongside consulting with disabled people's organisations and the public sector on targets to redress the imbalance in our public sector workforce. We have set out a range of actions to help achieve this. In the past year, the proportion of disabled people or people with a long-term health condition who started a modern apprenticeship has doubled. We have also provided Inclusion Scotland with funding to build on their own internship programme. By 2021 that programme alone will deliver 120 placements at public and third sector organisations, including the Scottish Government and the Scottish Parliament.

Alongside that, our Access to Elected Office Fund has supported thirty disabled candidates in running for public office. Fifteen were elected, proving that politics and government should be open to anyone who has the dedication, talent, and determination. This is an important point in principle, whether it is equality for women, equality for the LGBTI community, or equality for those with disabilities, we are more likely to achieve it faster if the councils, governments, and other bodies taking decisions are reflective of the population they serve. Initiatives like the Elected Office Fund are important in bringing that about.

Another initiative I wanted to mention was our new devolved employability service which, from April of this year, will go live: Fair Start Scotland. We understand the impact of empowering people rather than threatening them with sanctions, so those participating will do so by choice and not through fear for their existing benefits. I am opposed to the punitive sanctions regime that characterises the welfare system and, as we build our own employability and welfare services, I do not want that approach to play any part.

The views of disabled people's organisations have played an

important role in shaping Fair Start Scotland through engagement events; the formal consultation exercise; and forums like the Devolved Employment Services Advisory Group which I am pleased to say Sally from Inclusion Scotland is part of. The scheme will offer a personalised, tailored service, including pre-employment support, and opportunities for in-work support.

We recognise that the people who know best how to improve services are those with direct experience. That does not just apply to people with disabilities, but across the board. You will get a better outcome from any process if you involve from the start those who have direct experience. That principle underpins our approach to building our new social security system. We are determined to create services that help people; that value and account for individual needs and circumstances; and which treat them with dignity and respect.

I have spoken about some of the ways in which we are looking to support disabled people into work. However, your theme for today, 'employer-ability', identifies another key challenge that we need to address. Support for disabled people is important, but we need to ensure that employers can play their part, which means ensuring they have the understanding, information and support they need.

Last July, the Scottish Government launched a four-week engagement and marketing campaign aimed at highlighting the benefits of disabled staff. The campaign also involved providing advice and support, particularly to small and medium-sized companies. I think that was a good start, but we readily acknowledge the need to do more and, in this area, a lot more. In March we will hold a major Congress on disability, employment, and the workplace. To help shape the agenda for the Congress, we have held events in Glasgow, Dundee, and Inverness, involving representatives from disabled people's organisations, local government and the third sector.

Today's Summit, and your discussions, will play a part in setting the agenda for that Congress, and it is really helpful and welcome that today's seminars cover each stage of the employment process from getting ready for work; getting in to work; staying in work; and finally, getting on in work. I am looking forward to hearing the detail and the outcomes and making sure that we act on them through the Congress and beyond.

Your experiences, your expertise, and your ideas are probably the most important asset that we have when it comes to improving the lives and experiences of disabled people. The work you do in highlighting key issues, mobilising public opinion, putting pressure on government and, crucially, helping us identify the solutions, will help us address these challenges, build on the progress we have made and ultimately make Scotland a better country, not just for people with disabilities but for everybody who lives here.

I want to end by thanking you on behalf of the government, but beyond that by thanking you on behalf of all the people of our country. By working together, we have been able to achieve a lot, but we can achieve so much more. One of the reasons I wanted to be here today was to give you my personal commitment on behalf of the government that we will continue to work in close partnership with you.

Such partnerships do not mean we always agree on everything. There will always be areas where you disagree with government policy or want us to go further and faster. That is the nature of democracy but, by working together, we have proven that we can make a difference. My personal commitment to you is that we will continue to listen, act, and collectively do what we need to do to make Scotland the best possible place to be if you live with a disability.

28

A HUNDRED YEARS OF WOMEN'S SUFFRAGE

Given to the Scottish Parliament
Holyrood, Edinburgh, 6th February 2018

> Leading a Holyrood debate to mark this important anniversary,
> NS honoured the memory of the Suffragettes by acknowledging
> her personal debt to the movement. Not content to leave their
> memory as a footnote, or even a chapter, in history, she allied
> their cause with the Me Too and Time's Up movements and the
> practical actions she, as the first woman First Minister, and her
> government, had taken to advance the cause in modern times.

There is an old Scots proverb which was used on suffragist and
Suffragette banners. The first part of which later provided the title
for a history of our suffragist movement. It says simply 'A guid
cause makes a strong arm'. The guid cause we are honouring today
was given further strength by the commitment of tens of thousands of women, as well as many men, from across the country. By
1914, there were suffrage associations from Orkney and Shetland
to Kirkcudbright and North Berwick.

If you look for them you will see powerful symbols of the suffrage
campaign across Scotland. When I was a student at Glasgow
University, I walked on countless occasions past the Suffragette
Oak in Kelvingrove Park. The First Minister's residence at Bute
House overlooks Charlotte Square, which was the starting point
for the Scottish suffragists' march to London in 1912. Occasionally,
I find myself wishing I could spend a few moments with those

women to pay tribute to their courage and sacrifice, and to thank them for enabling a woman like me to occupy the office I do today.

Charlotte Square is also where Elsie Inglis, one of the greatest of Scottish suffragists, went to school. This morning, with the Suffragette flag flying outside, I chaired a meeting of our gender-balanced Scottish cabinet in Saint Andrew's House, which stands on the site of the old Calton Jail, where many Suffragettes were imprisoned in the years before World War One. That last poignant fact is a reminder that many who campaigned for the vote made sacrifices that are beyond our imagination.

Some, especially those who adopted militant tactics in response to government intransigence, were not only jailed, but also horribly mistreated and even force-fed. Many more devoted countless hours of their time to their cause, and all Suffragettes and suffragists risked public disapproval, or anger, or contempt.

We, in this generation, know that even today it is not always easy for women to speak up in public life; but whatever the challenges we face now, it must have been more difficult then. The Glasgow and West of Scotland Suffrage Association described what a woman often went through: 'She defies convention and throws aside that much-prized virtue: respectability. She gives up friendships that she values; often she renounces all her past life.'

When I stand here in this chamber as a female First Minister, to be followed by a female leader of the opposition, my overriding emotion is one of deep gratitude. All of us, but women especially, owe an immeasurable debt to the Suffragettes and the suffragists that we honour today. For that reason, this centenary is being marked, not only by this parliamentary debate, but also by events and commemorations across the country.

The Scottish Government confirmed yesterday that we will provide funding for local projects which will mark the anniversary. We will also support the Glasgow Women's Library, which is developing a programme of commemorative events. In addition, we are organising a cross-party event for young people here at the parliament and will fund projects to improve women's representation and participation in public life.

These final two strands to the programme are important. These commemorations should not simply be about marking our past; they should also look to our future. Women secured the parliamentary vote a century ago, and have had equal voting rights to men for ninety years, but the uncomfortable truth is that gender equality remains an unwon cause that it is the duty of our generation to win.

A century on, the gender pay gap still stands at 9% in the UK, and almost 7% in Scotland. Women are more than half the population, but only make up 27% of members on the boards of the UK's largest companies. We still need to address the gender stereotyping that means just 6% of our engineering modern apprentices are women, while only 4% of our childcare modern apprentices are men.

It is worth thinking deeply about all of this. A key reason for women getting the vote was the contribution they made to the war effort, from the munitions factories of Clydeside to the field hospitals of the Balkans. They irrefutably demonstrated that women's competence and capability was equal to men's, but a hundred years later that equal capability is still not reflected in equal pay or equal status. In addition, we have been reminded all too recently that sexual abuse, sexual harassment, and sexist behaviour are still widespread across our society.

Inequality persists when it comes to political representation. When this parliament was first elected in 1999, more women were chosen to represent Scottish constituencies than had been elected to Westminster in the previous eighty years, but the hard reality is that there has been little progress since. The proportion of women MSPs in the parliament was 37% in 1999, and now stands at just 35%. In my own party it is 43%, which represents progress since 2011 but, as with all parties, we need to do more.

There are areas where this parliament has genuine grounds for pride. Just last week, every member of this chamber supported the Domestic Abuse Bill, legislation which has been acclaimed as setting a new gold standard in protecting women from coercive and controlling behaviour. Last week we also approved legislation to ensure 50% female representation on public boards, ensuring that the public sector will lead by example on appointing women to leadership positions.

This parliamentary session will see a massive expansion of childcare, which will help parents, particularly mothers, to return to work and pursue careers, and much of Scotland's international development work in Africa and Pakistan prioritises the empowerment of women, but we still need to do more. We can and should draw strength from these significant recent accomplishments but, looking at some of the wider social developments of the last year, such as the public response to stories of harassment and unequal pay, and the development of the 'Me Too' and 'Time's Up' movements, I think there is a chance to achieve even more significant and rapid change.

Public scrutiny of discrimination has never been higher, and public tolerance of it never lower, which gives all of us not only an obligation, but also an opportunity to make greater progress towards true gender equality. It is an opportunity we must work on together and seize.

When I was elected as First Minister in 2014, I commented that my niece, who was then eight years old, was in the public gallery, and that my fervent hope was that, by the time she was a young woman, she would have no need to know about issues such as the gender pay gap, or underrepresentation, or other barriers, like high childcare costs, that make it hard for so many women to work and pursue careers. This parliament can play a vital role in consigning those issues to history. I want young people in the future to see them in the same way we see voting rights for women, as a cause that was argued for, and won, by earlier generations.

We are here to honour the perseverance, courage and

self-sacrifice of the suffragists and Suffragettes but, ultimately, the best way of doing that is not through parliamentary debates or commemorative events, important though they are. It is by renewing our resolve to use the powers we have, which in many ways we owe to the suffrage movement, to make the world a better place for the girls and young women who are growing up today.

If we can add our strength to that guid cause, we will pay a fitting tribute in this centenary year. It falls on our generation through deeds, not words, to complete the work that the suffrage movement started, to ensure that gender will no longer be a barrier to women achieving their dreams. That, in my view, is the truly appropriate way of for us to repay our enormous debt to the heroic movement that we celebrate and honour today.

29

ON CHILD POVERTY AND CHILDREN'S RIGHTS

Given to the Chinese People's Association for Friendship with Foreign Countries
Beijing, 10th April 2018

On a five-day visit to China to promote business and academic links, NS met with Vice Premier Hu Chunhua to discuss the long and developing relationship between the two countries, with special attention to human rights violations by China. The following day she made the first of two speeches of significance at an event hosted by UNICEF. Considering the subject of human rights, specifically children's rights, she presented a sensitive and constructive discussion of Scotland's responses to the challenge while praising many of her host's. A point of note though, is her insistence on children's participation in decision-making, which is likely to be more practical in a democracy with a tradition of open debate. All the essential elements of practical liberal politics are present in these two speeches.

I am delighted to speak once again at the Chinese People's Association for Friendship with Foreign Countries [CPAFFC], and grateful for everything this organisation does to strengthen the ties between our Scottish Affairs Office in Beijing and the Chinese Government's State Council: just one example of the good work you do to forge friendships with countries around the world.

I am also delighted that this event is being hosted by UNICEF, knowing how important its work is in China and appreciating the work of its Scotland office, whose programme for rights helps Scottish schoolchildren accept and appreciate difference and diversity. The Scottish Government and UNICEF are currently exploring some exciting ideas about working together even more closely.

I have been asked to speak specifically about children's rights and equality, both issues of deep interest to CPAFFC and UNICEF who, last year, jointly held a consultation on cognitive capital. This is the term given to the set of skills and abilities, including communication and creativity, that allow people, especially young people, to interact, contribute to the world, and enjoy happy and fulfilling lives. That right is one we owe to every child, everywhere in the world. The consultation highlighted the importance of supporting development early in childhood, which helps improve brain development, increases future life chances, and enhances children's rights.

The summary of that event makes an important point. It says that investing in children 'fulfils a moral imperative' and is 'one of the highest return investments a country can make'. These two ideas underpin much of what I will say this morning. For China, Scotland, and indeed all nations, promoting children's rights, and tackling child poverty, is both a moral obligation and an economic necessity.

This is a particularly appropriate year to examine the issue of children's rights. In December, we will mark the 70th anniversary of the United Nations Declaration of Human Rights. That declaration, as well as upholding the inherent dignity and equal rights of all individuals, recognised that children are entitled to special care and assistance. The Declaration was followed in 1959 by the Declaration of the Rights of Children, and in 1989 by the UN Convention on the Rights of the Child.

As well as being the 70th anniversary of the Declaration of Human Rights, 2018 is also, for Scotland, our Year of Young People, in which we seek to celebrate the contribution that young people make to our society. The Scottish Government is considering how best we can strengthen children's rights, and support efforts to give children the same levels of protection as adults when it comes to physical assault. We are also considering how the principles of the UN Convention can best be reflected in domestic laws and policies and are committed to a three-year programme to raise awareness, including amongst children and young people themselves.

In doing so we are aware that children are dependent on their families, carers, and wider society for their development. How people's rights are respected in that wider society also has a big impact. Children do not simply have a right to protection from harm, vital though that is. Countries which sign up to the UN Convention also promise to provide positive support; they pledge specifically to encourage 'the development of the child's personality, talents and mental and physical abilities to their fullest potential'. They have a duty to support and cherish every child.

In China, that imperative is reflected in your National Programme of Action for Children, which recognises the importance of young people's rights, health, and welfare, and has led to some significant achievements. Since 2011, China has built 60,000 nurseries or kindergartens. In fact, early education is being provided to ten million more children than was the case seven years ago.

President Xi has pledged to eliminate absolute poverty by 2020. Poverty reduction, and addressing regional imbalances, will make a big difference to children and families. At last year's 19th National Party Congress, he gave strong indications that children will be a priority for China after 2020. In his address to the Congress, President Xi said that 'A nation will only prosper when its young people thrive', recognising that if children do not have a fair chance to flourish, it does not only blight their individual life chances, although that in itself is good enough reason for action, they are also less likely to contribute their effort, talent and ideas to society. In other words, child poverty does not only impoverish children, it impoverishes us all.

That is one of the reasons why, as UNICEF and our hosts pointed out last year, support for young children will be vital for China in the years ahead. As your population ages, and as economic growth moves towards a knowledge-based economy, it will become important to ensure that everyone can fulfil their potential.

Scotland is starting from a different position, and dealing with a vastly smaller population, but we still recognise many of the issues you face. We also have an ageing population, although people living longer is welcome and positive, and we are also moving to a knowledge-based economy. Making the most of everyone's talents is an even greater imperative now than in the past, and our over-whelming moral obligation is to ensure that every child has a fair chance to flourish. Therefore, we are providing additional targeted support to those who need it.

It is important to measure child poverty. You cannot fix some-thing if you do not know and understand the scale of the problem. In Scotland, we are determined to ensure not only that we do so, but also to be accountable for the steps we take to address it. Around a quarter of our children grow up in poverty, a number that has increased in recent years as welfare cuts imposed by the UK Government have frozen, reduced, or withdrawn the support available to families with children. Estimates suggest that, if we do nothing, the problem will grow further. By 2030, more than a third of children in Scotland could be growing up in poverty.

The Scottish Government's view is simple. It is not acceptable, and we are not willing to sit back and allow it to happen. That is why, last year, the Scottish Parliament passed a new Child Poverty Act, which sets a number of targets, requiring us to take action so that, by 2030, the number of children growing up in relative poverty will not be one in three. It will be reduced to one in ten. It is important to say that one in ten is still too many, but it will be a significant reduction to the scale of the problem.

Just two weeks ago, the Scottish Government published our first delivery plan for tackling child poverty, based on advice from our independent Poverty and Inequality Commission. The delivery plan sets out more than fifty wide-ranging actions we will take over the next four years to help children and families. From financial support for costs such as food, heating, and school uniforms, to helping parents improve their employment and career prospects so they can earn more to support their families.

My Scottish colleagues will be keen to share our fifty actions during the round table discussion later, but those new actions go alongside other work. There is evidence that children who have suffered a number of adverse childhood experiences, as they are sometimes called, physical abuse or the divorce of their parents, or poverty, are more likely to do badly at school, or struggle to find employment. We are making it a priority to provide better help and support for them and do so much earlier in their lives.

We are also reviewing our care system. The government owes a duty to children who, for whatever reason, cannot be looked after by their parents. In fact, this is one of the most important responsibilities a government can have. Those children need the best possible support and, perhaps most fundamentally, need to know they are cared for and loved. During the course of the review, we are making sure that we hear from the young people themselves, and I have promised to meet personally with as many as possible who have experienced the care system.

This is one of the ways we will ensure that children have a say in decisions that affect them, and the importance of children having a voice runs through all our work. Six weeks ago, the Scottish Cabinet held a joint meeting with members of Scotland's youth parliament and members of Scotland's children's parliament. We know that children cannot simply be passive recipients of rights. They need and deserve a voice and a role in the decisions which affect them, and which will affect them throughout their lives.

In all our work to improve support for children, Scotland (and again, this is an issue which is relevant in China) is striking a balance between targeted support and high-quality universal provision. The improvements we are making to universal services must benefit all children, but particularly children from deprived or disadvantaged backgrounds.

During this morning's discussion you will hear about our efforts to double the amount of free childcare available to all three and four year olds, and also about our major drive to raise attainment in schools, and close the gap between schools in the most affluent and the most deprived communities. Let me share with you another example of universal provision, of which I am very proud.

Since last August, parents of all new babies in Scotland have received what we call a 'baby box'. The baby box arrives two weeks before your child is born and it includes a range of essential items that every parent needs, such as clothes, thermometers, a range of basic items that all parents need and find useful but which, in some cases, they might not be able to buy.

The boxes encourage early contact between families and healthcare workers, but also have a symbolic value. Because baby boxes are provided to all babies, regardless of their background, they send out the important message that we value each child equally and will do everything we can to support and encourage their potential.

It is another way in which we are striving to live up to the spirit, as well as the letter, of the Convention on the Rights of the Child. We recognise the inherent truth set out seventy years ago in the first article of the Universal Declaration of Human Rights: 'All human beings are born free and equal in dignity and rights.'

The baby box is not a unique Scottish idea, we borrowed it from Finland, and that is an example of something which I think is important. In everything we do we are determined to share our experience, but we are also determined to learn from other countries across the world.

China and Scotland will inevitably sometimes have different perspectives and different starting points, but we have a strong friendship and partnership, as I have seen throughout my visit. We also share common interests and common challenges, such as how we implement and live up to the United Nations' Sustainable Development Goals. We both recognise that nothing is more fundamental to future success than the support and care we provide for our young people.

We know that by tackling poverty and promoting equality; by supporting education and childcare; and by recognising and strengthening children's rights; we can meet our moral obligations while laying the foundations for future prosperity and wellbeing.

30

THE IMPORTANCE OF INTERNATIONAL COLLABORATION

Given at an event organised by The Economist
Shanghai, 11th April 2018

After travelling around 900 miles between cities, NS gave a
second speech that was notable for its dovetailing with the first.
Having spoken in Beijing of child poverty and children's rights,
she now addressed the practical matters of business development
and partnership, eventually circling back on equality. The impli-
cation that economic advances should, would, and indeed must
accompany advances in human rights was obvious. Not only for
moral reasons but also because, as she asserted, it is less wasteful
and more energising.

It is a huge pleasure to be here in Shanghai, undoubtedly one of
the great global cities, and one which has strong historic ties to
Scotland. A Shanghai Scottish Society was established here in
1866, which we can confidently say was before the time of anybody
in this room today. The year before that, Thomas Sutherland, from
Aberdeen, established the first Shanghai branch of the Hong Kong
and Shanghai Bank.

Fittingly, a Scottish financial presence continues to this day.
In fact, Aberdeen Standard Investments is setting up a base
here, which demonstrates something that has been clear to me
throughout this visit. The links between Scotland and China, of

trade and commerce, education and culture, family and friendship, are probably stronger now than ever.

Since I arrived in Beijing on Sunday, I have met representatives of more than twenty Chinese businesses covering sectors such as textiles, technology, renewable energy, and food and drink, and seen significant new agreements signed between Chinese and Scottish universities. Just after this event, I am to meet Vice Mayor Weng, when we will announce that the Shanghai Festival's production of the 'Rite of Spring' will be part of the programme for next year's Edinburgh International Festival. On my first day I met twenty young Scottish students who are staying in China on scholarships, and who have been overwhelmed by the warmth of the welcome they have received. Those interactions between our young people augur well for the future friendship and relationship between our two countries.

My personal impression, that the friendship between our nations is flourishing, is borne out by the economic statistics. On average, Scotland's exports to China have grown by more than a third in each of the last four years and, in the last year alone, increased by 40%. That is higher growth than with any of our other trading partners. Inward investment to Scotland from China has also increased. More than 9,000 people from China now study in Scotland's universities and, as a result, communities across Scotland mark the Chinese New Year, just as Burns Night is celebrated regularly in Shanghai and Beijing.

Much of this upsurge in trade, investment and study is due to China's extraordinary economic growth in recent years, but it is also a testament to Scotland's own economic strengths. When Premier Li, at that time still Vice Premier Li, came to Scotland in 2011, he spoke at a welcoming reception at Edinburgh Castle. Almost the first thing he said was, 'It's great to be in Scotland. The land of invention.' The compliment was all the greater because of China's own history of invention and innovation. This is the country which gave the world the compass, paper and printing, and countless more inventions.

Premier Li was referring to the fact that people from Scotland have developed an astonishing proportion of the technologies that shaped the modern world. James Watt's steam engine, the television, the telephone, and beta blockers, are all examples. Our history of invention is a long and a proud one, but Premier Li was not simply talking about our past. He was also looking at the present and future. Scotland has more top-class universities per head than any other country in the world with one exception. Not China, but Luxembourg… but we have Luxembourg in our sights, and hope to pass them in the future!

Partly because of that influence, we are one of the world leaders in some of the key technologies of the future. Scotland is a major centre for offshore wind research, and home to the world's first floating wind farm. We also pioneer in wave and tidal power, with significant strengths in related areas such as battery storage and smart grids, which will be of increasing importance as the world moves to a low-carbon future.

In life sciences, we also see significant success, due to the quality of our internationally recognised research, and tomorrow I will attend an event where five Scottish universities will sign life sciences collaboration agreements with partners in China. We also have one of the largest clusters of data analytics researchers in Europe, and are seeing exciting developments in areas such as fintech, digital health and precision medicine. That is just one reason why Edinburgh was recently named the best city in Europe in which to start a technology company. Later today I will meet C-Trip, a Shanghai company which last year purchased Skyscanner, one of Scotland's most successful tech companies.

There is often remarkable innovation in sectors which are commonly seen as traditional, such as our textiles firms, which continue to make tartan cashmere for luxury brands, popular across the world… not least here in China. They also design materials which are used in artificial heart valves. Even our traditional companies in traditional sectors are innovating and growing into new areas, which helps explain why Scotland outperforms every other part of the UK, with the exception of London, for attracting inward investment. In research and development projects, we outperform even London.

To any in the audience considering investment, my message is that Scotland is open for business.

Alongside our reputation for innovation, we have what is, by some measures, the most highly qualified workforce in Europe working beside a strong and supportive public sector. Many of you will be familiar with my colleagues in Scottish Development International, who are always looking at how we can support companies with growth ambitions. We offer a fantastic quality of life, and the weather is not as bad as reported! Yes, it was snowing last week, but it was snowing in Beijing too!

Scotland is an ideal country in which to live, work, study or invest because, as you will have gathered, we have a strong and successful economy and real ambitions to grow it further. We also face challenges, but we are not unique in that, and one of our big challenges is the UK's decision to leave the European Union, which we did not vote for in the EU referendum, but which will affect us greatly. Not least in its impact on our economy.

Other challenges confront almost all countries across the developed and developing world: moving quickly to a low-carbon economy, adapting to an ageing population (a good thing but one that presents challenges for us all), ensuring secure, fulfilling employment in an age of increasing automation. In recent years, our economic growth has been lower than we would have liked. Partly, but not entirely, due to a slowdown in our oil and gas sector, which we will be focused on in the years ahead. Our productivity in the past decade has largely caught up with the rest of the UK but remains behind some of our European competitors. In the long term, that will impact living standards.

Many of those economic challenges are inextricably linked to social challenges. Although inequality in Scotland is lower than it is across the UK, it is still higher than anyone should be comfortable with. At an event in Beijing on child poverty[40], one of the points I made was that almost a quarter of children in Scotland grow up in poverty. That is unacceptable and is why we have launched a major new initiative to tackle child poverty.

The point I want to repeat is that poverty and inequality, as well as being morally unacceptable, are also economically damaging. The OECD estimated that between 1990 and 2010, rising income inequality in the UK reduced our economic output per head by nine percentage points, approximately £1,600 for everyone in the country. Low incomes reduce aggregate demand and restrict tax revenues needed for investment. Unequal economies are less resilient and more likely to depend on borrowing and credit, which means that growth is less likely to be sustainable. It stands to reason that we will do better as a society, if we can benefit from the skill, talent, and innovation of all our people.

I talked earlier about Scotland's history of invention. The reason many of the inventions that shaped the modern world came from Scotland was that we were one of the first societies, if not the first, to introduce universal free school education. By educating more people than other nations, we nurtured more individuals with the skill and talent to invent. At that time, it was almost exclusively men who could make full use of their talents, but the key point is that we gained a competitive advantage.

To make the most of our potential in the 21st century we will have to maximise opportunities for all, regardless of gender or background. Promoting equality does not detract from our focus on innovation. It is an essential part of that focus.

In looking at economic development and inequality, China starts from a different position and will often have a different perspective. China's population is also, of course, vastly larger. Shanghai on its own has almost five times that of Scotland, but some of the questions we grapple with have resonances here.

40.   See Speech 29, On Child Poverty and Children's Rights.

When President Xi addressed the 19th National Party Congress last autumn, he pledged to address 'development's imbalances and inadequacies, and push hard to improve the quality and effect of development'. As part of that, he has pledged to eliminate absolute poverty by 2020. I know that China is also looking at regional inequalities. When Christine Lagarde[41] spoke in Beijing last year about the 'Belt and Road' initiative, she praised the fact that it would contribute to more balanced economic growth.

China also has a deep interest in how the international economy works. President Xi last autumn stressed the need to make globalisation 'more open, inclusive and balanced'. There is an important point here. Policies such as free trade and immigration will often bring benefits to the economy, but they also have the potential to disadvantage, or seem to disadvantage, particular areas and groups. We have seen some of the consequences in Europe and the USA in recent years, and the UK's vote to leave the European Union is a case in point.

The benefits of globalisation, properly managed, should outweigh the costs. We can only sustain support for a dynamic and open economy if we do more to build a fair and inclusive society. For all of these moral, economic, and political reasons there is growing interest around the world in promoting growth that is inclusive. Growth, which everyone has a fair chance to contribute to, and from which everyone can benefit.

The Scottish Government has been trying to take a lead. In 2015, when we revised our Economic Strategy, we ensured that it focused on increasing competitiveness and tackling inequality as twin aims. What that means in practice is that the Scottish Government recognises there is an economic case for many of our key social interventions, such as tackling poverty, increasing attainment in schools, and increasing childcare provision.

We encourage progressive employment practices by attaching

41. Then Managing Director of the International Monetary Fund. Later President of the European Central Bank.

a high priority to fair work, and support the living wage. That is a level of pay, higher than the legal minimum wage, which has been calculated to ensure that people who work can afford the basic necessities of life. We also promote gender equality in politics, wider society, and the workplace. This is something I spoke about on my last visit to China, pointing out that, for virtually all nations, empowering women is probably the single and most straightforward way in which they can sustainably increase their economy's productive potential.

In Scotland we are encouraging more women to become entrepreneurs. It has been estimated that if as many women as men in Scotland started and ran their own businesses it would add almost £8 billion a year to our economy. That would represent an increase of 5% in our GDP. Our major expansion of childcare, often seen as a social intervention, is also a hard-edged economic intervention, helping women to get back in the workplace and pursue careers. A point we try to get across is that gender equality and fair work are not only good for employees, although that is important. They are also good for employers and business.

It helps the bottom line to ensure the talents of all are recognised. So, we are trying to work with business to create a partnership for productivity in which government is supportive, and government and business together support a fairer, stronger, more prosperous society. Of course, we know that it is easier to encourage that sense of partnership if government is doing everything it can to create an environment which promotes enterprise.

We invested in infrastructure, committing to every home and business in Scotland having access to superfast broadband by 2021. We also set out important measures to work with businesses to promote growth. In particular, we want to further enhance our capacity for innovation. We are significantly increasing government support for business research and development and establishing a national institute to build on our current strengths in advanced manufacturing.

We are now in the early stages of establishing a national state investment bank, which can provide mission-led, long-term capital for ambitious companies and important infrastructure projects in key sectors. That mission-led objective is important. The low-carbon economy is an obvious mission to look at, but there is also scope and need in other areas. How we adapt to an ageing society, investing in places. The objective of the new bank is to provide strategic investment, and support more and faster innovation.

All that should give a sense of the work we are doing in Scotland, and why it is relevant to the world in which we live. My final point though, which has been apparent throughout this speech, is that virtually all the issues I have raised are faced not only by Scotland or the UK, but also around the world. It makes sense for the Scottish Government to work with other countries through trade, joint investment, collaborative research, and the sharing of experiences and expertise. That is why it has been so gratifying, throughout my visit to China this week, to see the partnership between our governments, universities, businesses, and people, growing stronger and closer than ever.

31

CATHOLIC EDUCATION IN SCOTLAND

Given to the St Andrew's Foundation for Catholic Teacher Education
Glasgow University, 4th June 2018

Thomas Winning (1925–2001) was only the second Scottish cleric to attain the rank of Cardinal since the Reformation, following Gordon Gray (1910–1993). He was a socially conservative figure but capable of reaching across boundaries. In 1975, as Archbishop of Glasgow, he attended the General Assembly of the Church of Scotland, playing his part in the healing of a great divide. 'What do brothers say to each other after years and, in our case, centuries of silence?' he asked. 'Surely they ask for forgiveness.'[42] In this lecture given in his memory, NS focussed on Thomas Winning's commitment to Catholic education, appreciating its many successes and confirming the Scottish Government's practical support.

It was a privilege to join you for mass this morning in the wonderful Glasgow University chapel, and pay tribute to the life and the legacy of the late Cardinal Thomas Winning, a man who was loved and revered, and deeply respected across Scotland and the world, not only by those in the Catholic faith but also by people of all faiths and none. It is the utmost privilege to deliver this lecture today and I thank you for the opportunity.

---

42. Article in *The Herald* of 27th October 2017 by the Reverend Finlay Macdonald, Moderator of the Church of Scotland 2002–2003.

It is always wonderful to return to the University of Glasgow. I have exceptionally happy memories of my time as a law student here, and there is no doubt that this wonderful institution helped make me the person I am. One of my fondest memories is of graduating in this hall. Although I should maybe add that some of my less fond memories, are of sitting exams in this same hall!

This university is a highly appropriate setting for this morning's lecture, for both modern and historic reasons. It is the home of the St Andrew's Foundation for Catholic Teacher Education, which, in various guises over several decades, has helped to train thousands of teachers and, by doing so, has made an immense contribution not simply to Catholic education, but to the Scottish education system as a whole.

Looking back further, Glasgow University was, like St Andrews and Aberdeen universities, founded by a papal bull, which is a reminder of the contribution the faith has made to Scottish history and Scottish education more specifically. As Pope John Paul II said at Bellahouston Park in 1982, 'The names of Bishops Wardlaw, Turnbull and Elphinstone remain inseparably linked with the foundation of your universities, of which this nation has always been so justifiably proud.'

When Pope John Paul II spoke those words, he was addressing what is thought to be the largest crowd ever gathered on Scottish soil. His visit, and also of course Pope Benedict's in 2010, at which I was privileged to be present, emphasised and celebrated not simply the historic importance of the Catholic Church, but also the contribution the Catholic community makes to modern Scotland.

The 1982 visit was also one of the crowning achievements in the career of Thomas Winning, who at that time was Archbishop of Glasgow. There was a real possibility that, without his intervention, the visit would have been postponed because of the Falklands War.

In 1994 Archbishop Winning became only the second Scottish Cardinal since the reformation. His elevation was a fitting recognition of Scotland's importance to the Catholic Church, the church's importance to Scotland, and the stature and achievements of Cardinal Winning himself. Those achievements include his work to establish better relations with other faith groups. His 1975 address to the General Assembly was a landmark in the Catholic Church's relationship with the Church of Scotland.

He was also a tireless crusader for people who were poor, vulnerable, or marginalised in our society. One of his last campaigns, shortly before he died, was to argue for better treatment of asylum seekers, a cause whose urgency and importance are undiminished today.

Cardinal Winning did not agree with everything that I believe in, or that any politician believes in, but there is no doubt that, as someone who has lived in Glasgow for all her adult life, I always recognised, respected and appreciated the strength of his passion for social justice, and his advocacy of the Catholic faith. I am therefore honoured to give a lecture in his memory, on the eve of what would have been his 93rd birthday.

An important strand of his passion for social justice was his commitment to the principles of Catholic schooling. He was president of the Commission for Catholic Education from 1977 until his death in 2001, and that takes me to the main subject of this morning's remarks. The reason I have been asked to deliver this lecture, in this particular year, is that we are currently celebrating the centenary of the 1918 Education Act. 2018 is also Scotland's Year of Young People, and we are celebrating their talents and achievements in a programme that has to a large extent been designed by young people themselves. So, I hope that for young people in Catholic schools this will be a doubly special year.

The centenary of the 1918 Act is being marked throughout the year by a series of events including a national schools' mass in Falkirk Stadium later this month, a national parent gathering in August, and a major European conference in October. The Scottish Government and the Bishops' Conference will also co-host a reception at Edinburgh Castle towards the end of the year, close to the centenary of the bill gaining Royal Assent.

The range and scale of these celebrations is entirely fitting as the 1918 Act helped shape modern Scotland, and for the better. For the population generally, it raised the school leaving age. It also established education boards and tried to create better routes from elementary school to university. For the Catholic community, its consequences were even more important. Between 1872 and 1918, the Roman Catholic community maintained its own schools at a time when parents were also, as ratepayers, contributing to the running of other schools.

That meant that Roman Catholic schools, which educated one seventh of Scotland's schoolchildren, were significantly under-resourced and that, in turn, meant Catholic children were deprived of educational opportunities that other children could take for granted. That was not acceptable and changed with the Education Act.

As a modern politician there are two things that seem especially worth noting about the provisions for faith schools in the 1918 Act. The first is that they represent a very courageous and far-sighted compromise. The Catholic community entrusted the state with running Catholic schools and the state, in turn, promised that religious education and observance in Catholic schools would continue, and that the church would have a say in the selection of teachers.

This inevitably led to some arguments about whether the church was retaining too much or too little control over the schools. Robert Munro was the Secretary for Scotland at the time, and I was struck by something he said in a speech about the bill. He said that 'neither party considers that the arrangement goes so far as they would like. Might that not be the best tribute to its equity?' What is certainly true is that the result was a partnership between church and state with few parallels elsewhere, and that might explain why it has lasted so well.

The second striking thing about the denominational provisions of the Education Act is that they were driven by a sense of national purpose. I mentioned earlier that Catholic schools covered one seventh of the population. It was widely recognised, to quote Robert Munro again, that it was 'not in the national interest that such a proportion of the population in Scotland should be left out... in their endeavour to raise the general level of education.' That lesson holds true to this day.

I have made closing the attainment gap, between children in affluent areas and children in poorer areas, the defining aim of my time in office. Not only because of the harm inequality causes to individuals, but also because inequality is bad for the country as a whole. All of us suffer when individuals, through no fault of their own, face barriers to fulfilling their potential. It means that they are less able to contribute their efforts, talents, and ideas to wider society.

Professor Sir Tom Devine[43] gave this lecture last year. He wrote in his history of modern Scotland about the social mobility that was made possible by better education for Catholics, arguing that the 1918 Act 'enabled the growth of a large Catholic professional class, fully integrated into the mainstream of Scottish society.' When you consider the immense contribution the Catholic community has made to Scotland in the last century, it seems unarguable that the settlement is one which brought benefits not just to the Catholic faith, but to all of us.

Many organisations have played a part in that success. I mentioned the St Andrew's Foundation earlier. It is also worth highlighting the role of the Bishops' Conference and, in recent years, the Scottish Catholic Education Service, which provides support to schools, parishes and dioceses. The contribution of local authorities is essential, and I want to put on record the Scottish Government's appreciation of all of them.

---

43. Historian recognised for his work on Scottish history since c.1600 and the global diaspora of the Scottish people. Author of The Scottish Nation (Penguin 1999), and many other titles.

However, the key reason for the success of Catholic schools is the expertise, passion, and commitment of teachers, headteachers and teaching assistants throughout the country. I am delighted that some of them are in the audience today and want to thank all of you for your efforts. It is because of you, your colleagues and predecessors, that this year's centenary commemorations are the celebration of a national success story. The partnership between church and state, which began in 1918, has not merely endured, it has prospered, and it has done so in a way which has benefited all our country.

It follows that my message in this morning's lecture is a simple one. The Scottish Government is an unequivocal supporter of Catholic schools. We value the contribution they make to modern Scotland and want it to continue in the years ahead. So, we will work with local authorities, the Catholic Church, and organisations such as the St Andrew's Foundation and the Scottish Catholic Education Service, to ensure that Catholic schools continue to flourish.

It is striking how closely the ethos of faith schools matches the key developments in Scottish society and education in recent years. One of the key principles behind Curriculum for Excellence is that it provides children and young people with a rounded education. We do not simply want young people to be successful learners, we want them to be confident individuals, responsible citizens, and effective contributors. We want them to make a positive contribution to their community and the wider world.

Catholic schools encourage that. They are not unique in promoting those values, all schools in Scotland play a full part, but they do have an important role to play that is especially significant given the social changes we have seen in recent decades. We have become a truly multicultural society, and the diversity of modern Scotland is now one of our great strengths. Catholic schools, because of the ethos they encourage, are an important and very welcome part of that diversity. I see that almost every day, and am proud to represent a constituency, Glasgow Southside, which includes many excellent Catholic schools, including a number of primaries and a secondary, Holyrood, which is one of the largest anywhere in Europe.

One of the many wonderful things about Glasgow Southside is that it is probably the most diverse parliamentary constituency anywhere in Scotland, and this is reflected in the intakes of the Catholic schools. Visit primaries such as Holy Cross or St Bride's and you will hear upwards of thirty different languages being spoken. In St Albert's in Pollokshields, one of the best schools I have had the privilege of visiting, the pupil population is predominantly Muslim, which exemplifies a wider point. Educating people in a way which is compatible with the Catholic faith and Catholic values does not isolate them. It goes hand in hand with encouraging and enabling them to contribute to their wider community.

I see that in other schools, too. When the Scottish Government expanded the First Minister's reading challenge into secondary schools last year, I visited St Andrew's and St Bride's school in East Kilbride. They contribute not only to their local community but also to the wider world. For example, they have a partnership with Damu Primary School in Malawi.

This sense of social purpose is showcased by the Caritas Awards, established by the Scottish Catholic Education Service following Pope Benedict's visit in 2010. The 2018 awards ceremony takes place next Thursday and will celebrate more than a thousand young people who, after reflecting on their faith, have engaged in activities (such as volunteering) which benefit wider society. They demonstrate an important truth. Catholic schools, like all good schools, do not just educate people to be good learners. They encourage them to be good citizens.

In doing that, Catholic schools, like all schools, adapt to the times, which includes ensuring that all children, regardless of gender, race, faith, disability, or sexual orientation, are brought up in a welcoming environment, without fear of discrimination or bullying.

The Scottish Catholic Education Service is a valued member of the Scottish Government's LGBTI Inclusive Education Working Group. This term, the Education Service, together with the Catholic Head Teachers' Associations for primary and secondary schools, has established a working group to develop learning and teaching resources focussed on prejudice-based bullying. One consequence is that the Service will, from the start of next term, offer resources focussed on LGBTI matters at every stage of a child's time in school.

In tackling prejudice-based bullying, the fundamental principles involved – equality, compassion, and respect – are recognised to be universal and enduring. All schools need to apply them to create a truly inclusive environment for all pupils. I warmly welcome the measures Catholic schools and the Catholic Education Service have adopted so far. They are necessary and positive steps towards ensuring a culture of respect and dignity for all students.

Having spoken briefly about Curriculum for Excellence, I also want to talk briefly about the importance of the education reforms we are planning and implementing at present. These changes, based as they are on the principles of excellence and equity, will be good for all schools in Scotland, and I believe will further improve our Catholic schools. For example, Catholic schools are among the beneficiaries of the funding we have allocated to closing the attainment gap.

I know that the Scottish Catholic Education Service has welcomed many of our reforms and proposals for our Education Bill. That Bill will give more power to headteachers, to ensure that they are free to meet the distinctive needs of their own school community. That applies to them as leaders of learning and teaching but also, in Catholic schools, as leaders in their faith community.

The Education Service has also welcomed the clear statement

in our consultation paper that parents are the main educators of their children.

The partnership between school and family that the Scottish Government is encouraging has been central to the ethos of Catholic schools for generations. Our reforms seek to strengthen that partnership and ensure that all parents may to contribute to the life and ethos of their children's school. That will be good for all schools in Scotland and means that the position of Catholic schools, which is already strong, is likely to strengthen in the years ahead.

For these reasons, I see the future for Catholic education in Scotland as a bright one. However, I am aware that the sector faces real challenges. Arguably, the most important relates to teacher recruitment. Teachers who want to work in Catholic schools should gain the Catholic Teaching Certificate. The course which leads to the certificate equips teachers for integrating professional, personal, and religious values.

In recent years, local authorities have had increasing difficulty recruiting teachers who have that certificate and estimate that, towards the beginning of the current school year, there were 150 teacher vacancies in Catholic primary and secondary schools. It is likely that the real number was even bigger. So, over the last two years we have worked with the university here in Glasgow to address this problem and, last year, a grant of £28,000 enabled Glasgow's Catholic Teacher Education course to be extended to students at Edinburgh and Strathclyde Universities.

Due to the success of that programme, I am delighted to confirm that next year we will increase our grant by a further £100,000. This will enable the course to be extended to Aberdeen and will further increase the number of teachers who undergo Catholic Teacher Education. Last year, the total was 276, 93 of whom were funded by the Scottish Government. This year it is 322, all of whom will be funded by the Scottish Government.

This is an area where relatively small sums can make a meaningful difference. By extending Catholic Teacher Training throughout the country, we will enable more student teachers in more locations to benefit from the excellent work which is led here at Glasgow. We can help Catholic schools across Scotland to continue to find the passionate and dedicated teachers they need.

It is one further way in which we can not only live up to the legacy of the 1918 Act but also ensure that a thriving Catholic schools sector brings benefits to the whole of Scotland. It is also, of course, a further way of recognising the legacy of Cardinal Winning. When he died in 2001, the Catholic Education Commission went so far as to say, 'No one in the history of Catholic education has made a greater contribution'. His lifelong passion for education was, of course, in keeping with his sense of the church's mission.

At the beginning of my remarks, I quoted from Pope John Paul II's address in Bellahouston Park in 1982. I want to end by quoting from the mass for young people that he held the day before at Murrayfield Stadium. He referred to Scotland's young people as 'the pride of your beloved country and the promise of its bright future'. This sentiment seems especially appropriate now, in Scotland's Year of Young People. As we celebrate their promise and potential, one of the things we should acknowledge and appreciate is the strength and vigour of the Catholic schools' sector. A hundred years after the Education Act, you are an important and valued part of Scottish life and it is right that we mark the centenary and celebrate the progress the Act enabled.

We should appreciate the contribution Catholic education makes to modern Scotland, and endeavour to work even harder to raise standards in Catholic schools and all schools. If we do that, we can ensure they continue to encourage good learners and good citizens, and we can ensure that 2018 is a truly special year for children and young people in the Catholic community, and for all of Scotland.

32

OUTWARD-LOOKING AND OPEN FOR BUSINESS

Given at a Burns Supper hosted by the Lord Mayor of London
Mansion House, London, 29th January 2019

The first ever Burns Supper to be hosted by the Lord Mayor of
the City of London was attended by more than two hundred
business leaders. It provided the perfect opportunity for NS
to promote Scotland as an ideal place for the financial services
industry to operate. In an entertaining speech she also took the
opportunity to celebrate the Scotland–London connection,
with their shared dependence on internationalism, which had
possibly found new impetus when both voted to remain within
the European Union.

It is an absolute pleasure to be here in these grand surroundings
with all of you this evening. I am grateful to you, Lord Mayor, for
hosting us, and I am grateful to all of you for attending. I do feel
as if we are partaking in something of an historic occasion this
evening: the first ever Burns supper in the Mansion House. I hope
it is not the last and think we should declare a tradition.

The Lord Mayor mentioned some of the many Scottish inventions, meaning both those that were invented by Scots, and those
that we claim were invented by Scots (I am not sure which list is the
longest): penicillin, the telephone, television, the pin number. We
also claim to have invented the Bank of England and the overdraft,
but nobody said all those inventions were good. Only recently I

discovered that Scots founded the state bank of India as well, so the list grows longer every day.

One of our greatest exports is Robert Burns, a wonderful poet whose words of wisdom on many different topics remain as relevant today as they were when he wrote them.

Along with many people from the Scottish and London business communities this evening, we are joined by diplomatic representatives from countries across Europe, from Mexico and New Zealand. That is fitting because Robert Burns was a proud and committed internationalist. In fact, and this is relevant to a point I will make later on, when the Scottish Parliament reconvened in 1999, one of the songs chosen for the opening ceremony was Robert Burns' 'A Man's a Man', which contains these words:

Then let us pray that come it may,
(As come it will for a' that,)
That Man to Man, the world o'er,
Shall brothers be for a' that.

Those words are perhaps more resonant today than when Robert Burns wrote them. So, to celebrate not just his legacy but his internationalism this evening, it is wonderful to be joined by people from across the globe.

Our other purpose is to celebrate and strengthen the ties between Scotland's financial services industry and the City of London. In a week like this it is impossible to completely avoid Brexit when reflecting on that. However, I am sure you do not want me to spend too much time on it this evening and, believe you me, I do not want to spend too much time on it either! Apart from anything else, the Scottish Government's view is well-known. We think leaving the EU will be damaging to the UK as a whole.

We would prefer to stay in the EU and, short of that, would prefer to stay in the Single Market and Customs Union. We hope that the prospect of no deal will soon be removed and, if necessary to avoid a Brexit cliff edge, we believe that Article 50 should be extended to allow parliament time to come up with a proper and managed way forward. However, and this is the message I want to emphasise this evening, regardless of what happens with Brexit, there is a bright future for financial services in Scotland.

I am sure this is the case in many parts of the UK, but certainly in Scotland we see a need to be more firm in our determination to look outwards, to build links and foster collaboration, and that is as true in financial services as it is in any other area. The sector in Scotland is flourishing, and the Scottish Government is working closely with business to help it flourish more in the years ahead.

We have seen good evidence of that in the last year. Many of you will be aware already of the decision by Barclays to invest in Glasgow. That hugely welcome investment could create up to 2,500 jobs. Perhaps more significantly, in what was a global field of options since the other centres are in New Jersey and India, it is a major vote of confidence in Scotland and our workforce.

In the last two years HSBC and Computershare have hired hundreds of additional staff in Scotland, and we will hear from George Quinn later about Zurich's major investment in Glasgow. What all these businesses, and many more besides, recognise is that Scotland is one of the best places in Europe to base financial services operations. That is why we are the UK's most important financial centre outside London, with strengths across a range of areas from asset management to insurance and banking.

First and foremost, that is because of our people. We have world-class universities and colleges. By some measures, Scotland has the most highly qualified workforce in Europe. More than 70,000 students are studying subjects relevant to financial services in Scotland's universities, but that skills base goes beyond financial services and is why businesses across a range of economic sectors, several of which are represented here this evening, choose Scotland for inward investment.

To take an example connected with finance, we are widely

acknowledged as a UK leader in data and informatics. We are also investing significantly in wider digital skills, which I know has been a major focus of your time in office, Lord Mayor. That skilled workforce is a major reason why Technation, last year, named Edinburgh as the best location in the UK for establishing a technology company and that, in turn, is why our fintech sector is gaining international recognition.

Having a devolved government allows us to respond rapidly to the needs of business and makes it easier for the public sector to provide co-ordinated support for inward investors. We offer a brilliant quality of life, with vibrant cities and beautiful landscapes, if not always fantastic weather. To build on these strengths, we work closely with businesses in Scotland. I co-chair our Financial Services Advisory Board with Scottish Financial Enterprise, and we have worked very closely together to produce the financial services prospectus that the Lord Mayor referred to. We also want to work with companies based in London, and with the City of London itself.

There is a point which I think is worth emphasising here. The City of London and Scotland can sometimes be rivals or competitors and undoubtedly, every now and again, that will be the case. Far more frequently, we will benefit from working together. As all of us know, London's scale is unique within the UK and indeed Europe, which gives you an important comparative advantage, but we also know that Scotland offers a fantastic range of expertise and facilities, and that office costs are significantly lower.

So, and many of you have direct experience of this, companies which already have big operations in London can benefit from offices in Scotland which complement their London bases. Working together is good for Scotland, but also brings benefits for London as well, which is why we established a new Scottish Government base in London in 2017. It demonstrates that, whatever the future holds, it will always be in our interests to encourage close ties with London.

It also symbolises something wider. In the last couple of years, the Scottish Government has established new bases in Dublin, Berlin, and Paris. Our enterprise agencies have doubled their representation across Europe and are strengthening their presence in other parts of the world. What that symbolises is a determination to be firmly outward-looking and firmly open for business.

I mentioned earlier how appropriate it is that there is an international dimension to this evening's event. That is because Scotland, like the City of London, benefits enormously from our connections with friends and partners the world o'er. We have world-class businesses which prosper by trading the world o'er and are determined to forge new partnerships and strengthen existing ones here on these islands, across Europe, and across the world.

That definitely applies to the partnership Scotland enjoys with the City of London. We believe it benefits the City, and benefits Scotland, and are determined to work with you, Lord Mayor, to strengthen that relationship further.

33

HONOURING THE EDINBURGH SEVEN

Given to the National Advisory Council on Women and Girls
Surgeons' Hall, Edinburgh, 30th January 2019

The manifesto of the National Advisory Council on Women and Girls reads: 'For generations, our history has been written by one gender. One perspective, one vision, one half of the population. Half of history is missing. For years, we have been striving for change. But now is the time to change for good. To design a future where gender inequality is a historical curiosity. With the voice of everyone we want to create a Scotland where we are all equal – with an equal future. Together, we are generation equal'. In welcoming the Council's first report, NS looked back in history for inspiration and example.

In many ways this venue, the Surgeons' Hall, is an appropriate place for us to gather and to talk about this report on gender equality. On your way in you might have seen a plaque on the outer wall, dedicated to the UK's first female undergraduate students. In 1869, 150 years ago, the 'Edinburgh Seven', as they became known, enrolled at the University of Edinburgh to study medicine.

Unsurprisingly, they were immediately subjected to a campaign of hostility and harassment from staff, students, and members of the public that culminated here in 1870. The seven women were to sit an exam in the main building but, when they arrived, were confronted by hundreds of male students who hurled abuse and threw rubbish. The women persisted and eventually managed to enter through the gates.

The Riot of Surgeons' Hall attracted huge publicity, galvanising support for the Edinburgh Seven, which won over many women and men to their cause. It stands as a landmark in Scotland's progress towards equal rights for women and gives an indication of how far we have come. Last year women accounted for 60% of entrants to undergraduate courses in Scotland. For medical degrees, the figure was slightly higher at 61%. We can take encouragement from the progress that has been made since then although, like so many other countries, Scotland has a long way to go before achieving true gender equality. Across our society, endemic and often systemic inequalities persist.

One of the things I pledged on becoming First Minister was to do everything possible to improve opportunities for women and girls, a commitment that is extremely close to my heart and that the government I lead has tried to do.

We have taken a range of measures to challenge gender stereotypes, help women's voices to be heard and tackle violence against women and girls. However, we need to do more to eradicate the persistent inequalities they still face in their lives. Inspired by the example of Barack Obama when he was in the White House, we decided to establish the Advisory Council on Women and Girls, and I am delighted to receive your first year report and recommendations.

I am so grateful to everyone who has contributed to this process: members of the Council, members of the Circle, and all those who participated digitally or through the Monthly Spotlight events. The result is a report of great insight and ambition, which I warmly welcome with its recommendations. The eleven recommendations are thought-provoking and challenging, exactly as I hoped.

At the first meeting of the Advisory Council we talked about the importance of not being content with tinkering around the edges but being bold and challenging and ready to push the envelope. In this report that is exactly what you have done.

I do not have time today to talk in detail about each of the recommendations. In any event, the Scottish Government will take the necessary time to consider them properly and carefully and will publish a full and considered response in due course. I do want to give you some of my immediate thoughts on the key recommendations.

Something I found encouraging is that some, not all, of the recommendations broadly align with work the Scottish Government is doing already and will help us advance and accelerate it. The report focuses, rightly, on the central importance of education. We are already taking significant action to ensure that our education system promotes gender equality and will look at how your recommendations can build on those efforts.

You have proposed improvements to the services we provide to victims of sexual violence. I agree absolutely that is hugely important. It also ties in with work that the Chief Medical Officer for Scotland, who is present and a member of the council, is currently taking forward.

Your proposal to incorporate the UN Convention on the Elimination of all forms of Discrimination Against Women into Scots Law is one that I welcome and is particularly timely. You will be aware that in December, the Advisory Council on Human Rights recommended that we embed human rights into a new statutory framework. I strongly support that overall vision and direction of travel and have already announced that we will establish a taskforce to take the work forward.

The report also recommends a further expansion of early years learning and childcare. Again, as you know, the Scottish Government is almost doubling the funded childcare entitlement to 1140 hours per year for all children. To put that into context, in 2007 the funded entitlement was just over 400 hours a year. A significant expansion is already underway with significant logistical and financial implications, on which I must be straight with you. Our immediate priority is that commitment but, looking forward to the next parliament, we will carefully consider future investments. Whether in after-school care, or a further expansion of childcare, and I confirm today that your recommendation will form a central part of that discussion.

Our policies on childcare are just some of the ways in which we try to support women in the workplace, an important issue the report addresses through your interesting proposal for a Gender Beacon Collaborative. The idea of creating such a network, to promote equality and share best practice across sectors, is one that I am enthusiastic about and that has real potential.

The Scottish Government wants to move as quickly as possible to implement the recommendation and will move quickly to explore with partners the best model for achieving it. The Council and the Circle will have a role to play advising and informing that work as we take it forward.

In a report of this ambition there are aspects to which we must give careful consideration if we are to do it justice. I am sympathetic to, and indeed hugely supportive of, your proposals around electoral candidate quotas and paternity benefits. The powers needed to deliver these proposals are not yet fully devolved to the Scottish Parliament, so we must carefully consider what we can do using existing powers. That must be the starting point, but, where necessary, we must also make the case for them to the UK Government. There is no doubt that the recommendations and analysis of this Advisory Council will add real weight to our efforts.

One of your other proposals is for the creation of a new body to review media output. My initial view is that this might not be an appropriate role for government to undertake, as it is vital that we protect the independence of the media and the freedom of the press. That said, the issue underlying the recommendation is an important one. The way in which the media portrays women, and on occasion men, is clearly a big factor in shaping harmful gender stereotypes.

There have been recent positive signs that the media is beginning to take this issue seriously. In December, the Advertising Standards Authority announced a ban on harmful gender stereotyping in advertising, which is a good example of the media using self-regulation to respond to public concern. It demonstrates why, as a society, we need to continue to draw attention to, and challenge, sexism, misogyny, and harmful gender stereotyping.

We will consider how we can advise in the spirit of this recommendation while respecting the independence of the media and the freedom of the press, and I think that illustrates a wider point.

The proposals in this report provide the government with substance to build on and accelerate the progress already made. That is exactly what I asked the advisory council to do and I am grateful that you have risen to the challenge so well, but I think we all agree that government action by itself cannot bring about the kind of change we need. Each of us, women and men, individually and collectively, have a responsibility to meet the challenge of tackling gender inequalities.

In setting me a challenge which I will undertake with enthusiasm, I think it is also important to set the same challenge to representatives from across our society: from business, education, the public and third sectors. I would encourage everybody here, and in our wider networks, to read the Council's recommendations and consider how you, within the spheres you operate, can help to achieve their underlying aims.

That could involve pushing and agitating for greater equality in the organisations you work, study, or volunteer in. It could mean looking for new ways to support other women through formal and informal networks, or it could mean seeking new opportunities to advocate not only here in Scotland but also internationally.

The events that took place in this Surgeons' Hall 150 years ago might seem today like a historical curiosity. The rights these seven pioneers fought for are the ones are largely taken for granted today, but those rights did not appear by accident. They required action. They required women and, crucially, men. I am a great believer that the resolving of gender inequalities cannot just be the responsibility of women; it is the responsibility of men as well as women.

Equality requires brave women and men to show leadership, to take a stand and persist, often against the odds. The example of the Edinburgh Seven is one we must follow if we are to make gender inequality a historical curiosity. The report you have produced will help us do that and I want to conclude by thanking you again for the work, the input, the imagination, and creativity behind this report and its recommendations. I want to thank you for your commitment to a cause that matters so much to us all and to the kind of society that we want to live in today and our daughters, granddaughters, and great-granddaughters to inherit.

34

THE MARINE ECOLOGY

Given to Scotland's International Marine Conference
University of Strathclyde, Glasgow, 20th February 2019

> The Scottish Government proclaims its vision of 'clean, healthy, safe, productive and diverse seas that are managed to meet the long-term needs of nature and people' in its consultation paper *Proposal to Designate a Deep Sea Marine Reserve* (2019). Understanding that any assessment of the world's affairs cannot ignore the sea, and that any sensible appraisal of the world's environmental crises, whether global warming, single use plastics, or the sixth extinction, must have the world's waters in a central position, NS addressed the International Marine Conference in Glasgow.

I want to thank Strathclyde University for hosting this event. Strathclyde is a leader in key aspects of marine research. The One Ocean Hub, which it leads, and which many Scottish universities are part of, includes more than sixty partners in Africa, the south Pacific, and the Caribbean, together with several UN bodies. We could not have a more appropriate venue for a conference which also is a significant landmark for the Scottish Government.

Scotland's economy, history, and identity have been shaped by our seas. We possess well over half of the UK's coastal waters. By some measurements, when you include our islands, inlets, and sea lochs, we have a longer coastline than India, and are home to globally important populations of sea birds, marine mammals, plants, lichens, and molluscs such as flame shells.

Our economy benefits from industries such as fishing, marine tourism, aquaculture, and energy, and offshore wind and tidal power help to lay the foundations of the carbon-neutral future we want to achieve. The management of our seas is fundamental to the health, wellbeing, and prosperity of everyone across our country and an event like this, where we can share expertise, information, and ideas about the marine environment, is hugely important to communities across our country and other countries around the world.

In addition to delegates from Scotland and the rest of the UK, there are representatives here from more than ten other nations, and I want to offer you the warmest of welcomes. I will not go into detail about all the conference themes in my remarks but do want to highlight three specific issues: marine protected areas, blue carbon, and marine litter. All are of relevance to this event, and all are areas where Scotland is trying to show international leadership.

Marine Protected Areas (MPAs), for example, are widely and rightly recognised as a success story. In the last seven years our network has doubled in size, providing better protection for birds such as the black guillemot and fish such as the common skate. The Scottish Government is consulting on creating several new areas to protect species such as basking sharks, Risso's dolphins and minke whales; and to preserve the flame shell and red lichen beds in Loch Carron.

I can also confirm that the Scottish Government will consult on creating two new historic MPAs at Lerwick and Scapa Flow[44]. The Scapa Flow site, where the German High Seas fleet was scuttled after World War I, will attract international interest and shows how MPAs can help protect our historic environment, together with our natural heritage.

In addition, we are looking to create a new marine reserve in the north-east Atlantic, where the waters are more than 800 metres deep. The proposed reserve is almost 150,000 square

44. Locations in Orkney.

kilometres in area, almost twice that of Scotland's landmass, and will almost double the overall size of our marine protected areas. Instead of covering 22% of our territorial waters, they will cover 42%.

That expansion illustrates a broader point. There is an international commitment under the Convention on Biological Diversity for marine protected areas to account for 10% of the world's seas. Scotland already comfortably exceeds that target, and our intention to go further exemplifies our desire not simply to meet, but to go beyond our international obligations. We are trying to demonstrate global leadership in our stewardship of the seas.

That is true also in the second area I want to highlight, blue carbon. We recognise climate change as the most important issue facing our planet and have almost halved our carbon emissions since 1990. With some of the toughest statutory climate change targets in the world we are in process of legislating to make those targets even tougher. It is hugely important to know more about the role of our oceans in storing carbon. Rising temperatures have a negative effect on ecosystems around the world, and it is known that climate change affects our oceans. However, our oceans also affect climate change. They absorb around a quarter our carbon dioxide emissions and produce more than half our oxygen.

Scottish Natural Heritage[45] estimates that the seas around Scotland store more than 2,000 million tonnes of carbon, the equivalent of around 200 years of our current carbon emissions. Research by St Andrews University backs that up, suggesting that more carbon is captured and stored in our sea lochs than in all our peatlands and forests. One sea loch on the Ardnamurchan peninsula stores almost 27 million tonnes of carbon.

Blue carbon, as the carbon stored in the sea is called, is still a relatively new area for detailed investigation and we need to know more about it. We need to understand how human activity affects

45.   Public body responsible for Scotland's natural heritage.

the ability of the oceans to store carbon. As part of that, we need to understand whether we can do anything to enable our oceans to store more.

That is why Marine Scotland has developed a new research programme for blue carbon, and why, last year, the Scottish Blue Carbon Forum was established. It coordinates research on the role of our oceans in sequestering carbon and will help us play a leading role in one of the most important, but least understood, elements of the carbon cycle.

The third issue I want to touch upon today is, again, a hugely important one.

Some of the scenes in 'Blue Planet 2', of the horrific impact marine litter can have on wildlife, caused worldwide uproar. Heart-rending in themselves, they also spoke to many people's own sense, from walking their local stretches of coast, of the plastics and waste we produce on land causing lasting damage at sea. It is entirely appropriate that marine litter is the theme for Day Two of this conference.

The Scottish Government is already taking a lead. We published a strategy for reducing marine litter in 2014 that includes more than forty actions to reduce the amount of waste entering our seas, and to change public and business attitudes to ensure further reductions in the future. We have taken further action since then. Our ban on micro-plastics in personal care products came into force last June, and we were the first government in the UK to commit to banning plastic-stemmed cotton buds. Tomorrow we will publish a detailed analysis of the consultation responses we received on introducing a deposit return scheme for bottles and other containers.

We are doing a lot and want to continue to move forward and make progress. I can confirm two further steps today.

Every day, across the UK, more than four million sanitary products are flushed down the toilet, making a major contribution to our plastic litter problem. The Scottish Government will work with Zero Waste Scotland[46] on a promotional campaign for reusable sanitary products and, in the last year, has become the first government in the world to provide free access to sanitary products for everyone in education. A growing proportion of those free products are reusable.

This new campaign marks a further step in our efforts to encourage people to move away from disposable options, and further reduce the volume of single use plastics. It is a relatively small measure, which could have an important impact.

In addition to marine litter, which has its origins on land, we also need to tackle the smaller, but still significant, proportion which comes from our marine industries. As many of you will know, the Scottish Government will soon publish a discussion paper on the future of fisheries management in Scotland. I can confirm today that one of the questions it will ask is how we can establish as an offence, fishing vessels of all sizes throwing litter overboard at sea. This is a measure which can help ensure that the fishing sector plays a full part in protecting the marine environment it relies on.

The most important way to address marine litter is to address the problem at source. To reduce, reuse and recycle as much plastic waste as possible. However, we must be able to clean our seas after they have been affected by plastic use and that is why we have worked with Zero Waste Scotland to encourage new approaches to collecting and recovering plastic materials.

We hope the fund that we have established, which is worth up to £1 million, can benefit sites which are being affected by litter sinks, such as Loch Long on the Firth of Clyde. We also hope that the plastics which are found will then be reused.

Scotland is committed to the development of a more circular economy, in which materials are kept in use for as long as possible. We think that it can create economic opportunities, as well as

---

46. Non-profit organisation to lead Scotland into using products and resources responsibly, focusing on the greatest impact on climate change.

helping us meet environmental obligations, and our work with Zero Waste Scotland is one of the ways in which we are trying to grasp those opportunities.

In all of this, Scotland, by taking strong and determined action at home, will demonstrate international leadership which, in turn, emphasises another key point. All these issues, protecting marine habitats, blue carbon, and marine litter, have strong international dimensions, and we have been clear that, regardless of Brexit, we will continue to maintain EU environmental standards. We will also comply with international agreements such as the OSPAR Convention, which protects the environment of the north-east Atlantic.

Of course, we will continue to work with, and learn from, partners across the globe and that is why, as I mentioned at the start, I am delighted to see so many international delegates here today. This event will influence policy making in Scotland, and I hope it can play some part in informing environmental policies around the world.

35

A CALL TO SERVICE

Given to the General Assembly of the Church of Scotland
Assembly Hall on the Mound, Edinburgh, 22nd May 2019

> The General Assembly is the supreme court and governing body
> of Scotland's national church. It meets annually to hear reports
> from councils and committees, make laws and set its agenda for
> the coming year. In its recent history it has listened to many fine
> orations, including from the great pacifist and founder of the
> Iona Community, George MacLeod, speaking against nuclear
> weapons. It has observed the entry of female clerics from 1969
> when the Rev. Catherine McConachie was ordained, and has
> deliberated, sometimes painfully, on such matters as gay clergy
> within its ranks. In 2018 it voted by an overwhelming majority
> to conduct equal, or same-sex, marriages. In the early years of the
> recalled Scottish Parliament (1999–2005), the parliamentarians
> sat in the Assembly Hall while the new building at Holyrood
> was under construction. This warm-hearted address by NS was
> positioned at the centre of its 2019 programme.

Let me begin by paying tribute to the Very Reverend Susan Brown,
former Moderator, who fulfilled her duties with style, humour,
humility, compassion, and distinction. I also, of course, want to
congratulate you, Moderator, on your very well-deserved appoint-
ment and wish you well in the year ahead. Lastly, my warm thanks
go to all of you for the deep honour of this invitation to address the
General Assembly this morning.

It is always a pleasure to return to this magnificent chamber, of which I have many happy memories, as well as some stressful ones, of the five years when the Scottish Parliament sat here. By a poignant coincidence it is exactly twenty years ago that, in this chamber, I made my first speech as an MSP, on the importance of free access to university education, an issue that remains close to my heart. So, to be speaking here today is special indeed.

More importantly, whenever I attend the opening of the General Assembly, as I was privileged to do again on Saturday, I am struck by the extent to which the Church is at the centre, not only of people's spiritual lives, but also of Scottish public life, as it has been for generations. For a long time after the Act of Union, the General Assembly was the most prominent forum in Scotland for bringing people together to discuss the important issues of the day. It served, in the words of Professor Tom Devine, as 'a kind of surrogate parliament'.

The Church of Scotland also helped to re-establish the modern Scottish Parliament when the 1989 Assembly endorsed the Claim of Right for Scotland. It was one of the first major civic institutions to do so, and passed a resolution calling for the creation of a democratically elected assembly. The Church of Scotland went on to play an important and active part in the Scottish Constitutional Convention in the years following.

The Scottish Parliament undeniably owes a major debt to the Church of Scotland, and to previous general assemblies. That said, the General Assembly in one respect at least owes an important debt to the Scottish Parliament. It is only because of us that the wooden benches were replaced by padded seats, and I suspect that some of you are grateful for that by this point in the week.

While our new parliament was finding its feet here in 1999, the General Assembly of that year, for the first time I think since the 1920s, was taking place elsewhere, at the Edinburgh International Conference Centre. The moderator that year was the Right Reverend John Cairns who said that, despite devolution, the Church 'should not think… that we in the Kirk are demobilised from playing an active part in addressing the great national issues of the day.'

A look at today's Church and Society report would have reassured him as it shows a Kirk which is passionately engaged in the great national and international issues of the day, such as investment in young people, social security, and gender justice. In recent years it has been deeply concerned with tackling climate change. Through its World Mission it builds connections with communities in countries across the world. It is, for example, a key member of the Scotland Malawi Partnership.

I also want to take this opportunity to applaud your invaluable support for, and encouragement of, interfaith co-operation. The Muslim community in Scotland greatly appreciated the expression of solidarity that the Church issued, together with other Christian churches, in the aftermath of the Christchurch shootings[47]. At a time when intolerance and bigotry appear to be on the rise in some parts of the world, it is vitally important, and hugely appreciated, that the major faiths in Scotland stand together in solidarity.

It is because of all of this that my main message this morning is a simple, but very heartfelt one. Thank you.

Thank you for the enormous and highly valued contribution that the Church of Scotland makes to communities across our country and around the world. Everyone Christian in Scotland, and those of other faiths and none, benefit from the work you do. It follows that the Scottish Government welcomes and indeed cherishes the role of the Church of Scotland in our national life, and it is important to emphasise that we appreciate your role even when, or perhaps particularly when, you say things that are uncomfortable for governments to hear. Indeed, that is often when your voice is most valuable and most important.

Today, I want to add the Scottish Government's perspective to

---

47. Two consecutive mass shootings at mosques in Christchurch, New Zealand, by a white supremacist, ended the lives of 51 people and injured forty others.

your ongoing debates and deliberations. You will be relieved to hear, I am sure, that I do not intend to go into the detail of the specific policies of the Scottish Government... unless you really, really want me to! Rather than talk about what we are doing, I want to say something instead about why and how we do what we do, and will touch on two trends or themes that I think will be of increasing importance in the years ahead, and which are directly relevant to this assembly.

The first is the increasing importance of all governments promoting a sense of wellbeing in our societies. When the government I lead first took office in 2007, we created, for the first time, a national performance framework. As part of that, we set out a clear purpose for the country.

We said that our national objective was to create opportunities for all of Scotland to flourish, by increasing the rate of sustainable economic growth. Last year we revised that framework and, in doing so, changed our purpose. We broadened our approach to focus on wellbeing alongside economic growth, reflecting the fact that economic growth, even when it is sustainable and inclusive, is not in itself an end. It is a means to an end by which we help people live happy, healthy, and fulfilling lives.

We made one other change to the framework which is worth highlighting, a new statement of values setting out our expectation that what we do will be defined by the values of kindness, dignity and compassion. Values it can sometimes be easy to lose sight of in the day-to-day whirl of government. To be frank, I am not sure they will be the first words you think of, if you were to catch any of First Minister's Questions later this afternoon, but these values should define the role of government ministers as surely as they define the role of parish ministers.

One example of how we are seeking to put these values into practice is the establishment of our new Social Security Agency for Scotland. The Church and Society Council discusses that in today's report.

Setting up a new agency, especially one which will deliver vital payments to millions of people, is a complex task requiring a major focus on IT capabilities, finance, logistics and many other things. However, we have tried to ensure that all this work is underpinned by a statement of values, by a deep respect for human rights and human dignity. Again, we seek to ensure we do not lose sight of what really matters. What we are finding, although I do not want to seem complacent, is that those values do not hinder project delivery. They help by providing a sense of common purpose that can inspire and unite a large team as they build something new and focus on improving the lives of the people they serve.

I also think, and this is the second area I want to touch on, that we would do well to think more about the values of kindness and compassion as we conduct our politics, how we discuss and debate the great issues of the day.

I mentioned earlier the General Assembly's role in helping to bring about the Scottish Parliament. During that process, the Church facilitated and encouraged dialogue on potentially difficult and divisive issues. Indeed, it played a valuable role in the run up to the independence referendum in 2014, providing a space where people could debate and discuss the issues of Scotland's future in a respectful and constructive way. Of course, the manner this assembly conducts itself in is a model of how big issues can be debated in a way that builds consensus rather than deepening division.

The issues that we confront at present, including how the UK responds to Brexit, how we can influence that, and what our constitutional future should look like, arouse strong passions. Rightly so, but I am also aware that the current political climate, exacerbated by some forms of social media, can be polarising and divisive. Convictions and firmly held beliefs should not be derided, but these days we can be too quick to retreat into political tribes, focussing on areas of conflict rather than agreement.

All of us, and political leaders especially, have a responsibility to resist the momentum for division and polarisation. That does not mean avoiding robust debate, this is Scotland after all, but it does mean we should work harder to air honest differences in a civil and respectful way, while seeking common ground and consensus. When politicians forget or fall short, as all of us sometimes do, the Church is well placed to remind us.

With an eye to that responsibility I recently announced the establishment of a Citizens' Assembly on Scotland's future, which will bring together a representative cross-section with an independent chair, to consider what sort of country we are seeking to build, how to best equip the Scottish Parliament for the future, and how we enable people to make informed choices.

The Citizens' Assembly will be different to the constitutional convention of the late 80s and early 90s. It will be made up of individuals, of many faiths and none, rather than representatives of institutions. However, the spirit in which the Citizens' Assembly is being convened, as part of a genuine attempt to find as much common ground as we can, is one I hope will strike a chord here.

Moderator, I began by quoting the remarks that one of your predecessors, John Cairns, made in the early days of devolution, and want to end by quoting something your most recent predecessor said at around the same time.

The Scottish Parliament, as you know, has a regular 'Time for Reflection' slot and Susan Brown delivered one of the very first of these, in this chamber. She reflected on the fact that MSPs, by being involved in a new parliament, were making a leap into the unknown. With her characteristic straight talking, she compared MSPs to her dog, which had leapt over a harbour wall and into the sea the week before! I will let you judge the accuracy of that comparison.

Susan closed with a message, a call to service if you will, which I think is common to this assembly and the parliament down the road. She said: 'Above all, remember the people whom you serve – their needs, their skills, their shared responsibility for this land.

It was in their name that you leapt and it is for their sake that you now swim.'

After twenty years of devolution, the Scottish Parliament continues to make new leaps and face new challenges. In adapting to those, we will inevitably make mistakes. All parliaments do... all people do... but, by remembering the people we serve, by remaining true to the values of kindness, dignity and compassion, we can ensure that we do not simply keep afloat. That we make progress on behalf of those whom we serve.

We can make progress towards a fairer and a more prosperous Scotland, and we can, I believe, improve not just the wealth, but the wellbeing of people and communities across the country. Striving to do that I, and indeed MSPs from all parties, draw strength from the support, and the challenge, offered by the General Assembly. Just as we take inspiration from the example of service shown by so many in the Church of Scotland, and from across Scotland's faith communities.

36

TWENTY YEARS OF DEVOLUTION

Given to Reform Scotland
Edinburgh, 18th June 2019

> Ever aware of historical context, NS reminisced on the recalled
> Scottish Parliament to the independent think tank, Reform
> Scotland, while laying down a likely agenda for its immediate
> future. Recalling such heroic figures as Donald Dewar and
> Winnie Ewing, and reframing a question famously posed by
> author and public intellectual Neal Ascherson, she anticipated
> the 'next phase of our national journey...whatever our views'.

Taking my place in the new institution [the Scottish Parliament],
as a new MSP alongside 128 others, is one of the highlights of my
life. I remember the mood of optimism within the parliament, that
prevailed in the country, and that was captured on the first day the
parliament sat, very well in my view, by Winnie Ewing. She was the
oldest elected member and, as such, convened proceedings, giving a
speech which ended with these words: 'It was said that 1707 was the
end of an auld sang. All of us here can begin to write together a new
Scottish song, and I urge all of you to sing it in harmony. Fortissimo!'

For all the inevitable ups and downs, the note of optimism
Winnie Ewing struck has largely been vindicated.

It was not universally predicted at the time. Before the 1997
referendum, William Hague[48] (former Conservative prime

---

48. Conservative member for Richmond 1999–2015. Leader of the Opposition
     in Westminster 1997–2001.

minister) argued that 'the tartan tax would lead to foreign investors saying no to Scotland', and a young, little-known journalist called Michael Gove said that devolution would lead to 'a brain drain, a flight of finance as well as skilled labour', and 'add to the burden of business taxation'.

Those warnings were comprehensively wrong. Devolution did not deter foreign investors, and Scotland, for the last few years, has been the top location in the UK for attracting inward investment outside of London. Devolution did not create a brain drain. We have benefited hugely from being able to attract workers and students from across the UK and overseas. Nor did it add to the burden of business taxation. It enabled this Scottish Government to create a small business bonus, which the UK Government later emulated.

Throughout the last twenty years, and this is to the credit of all the parties in the parliament, the institution has worked to make a difference to the lives of people across Scotland. In doing so, yes, it has made mistakes. All parliaments do. In some areas, some people will think it has not made as much progress as they would have wanted. Certainly not in the rocky, early years before the parliament building was completed, but overall, in the round, I strongly believe the record of achievement is a significant one.

The parliament might not always have sung in harmony, as Winnie Ewing hoped (although perhaps in a democracy we should never want complete harmony), but in our debating we have sought and often managed to reach consensus. We have shown that a proportionally elected chamber can do things differently from Westminster ... and do them well.

Land reform; the ban on smoking in public places; proportional representation in council elections; the most ambitious climate change legislation anywhere in the world; equal marriage; minimum unit pricing for alcohol: all of these and many more initiatives have helped, and are helping, to make this country better and fairer. Along the way we have gained new powers and built, or are building, new institutions. For example, a new tax agency and a social security agency that were not envisaged by all of us in 1999. That process is continuing and, two weeks ago, the parliament voted unanimously to create an enterprise agency to help with economic growth in the South of Scotland.

Work to establish the new Scottish National Investment Bank proceeds and has the potential to be one of the most transformative steps the parliament has taken.

Although this sometimes, and legitimately, provokes different views, the Scottish Parliament has, where appropriate, maintained, enhanced, or created universal services. Tuition fees and personal care for older people are examples. The baby box is more recent, and we have a substantial expansion of childcare underway right now. By doing all that, we have supported the idea of a social contract at a time when it has been threatened elsewhere.

We recognise that everyone contributes to our society, at different times and in different ways, so everyone should receive a level of support in return. These universal services not only make people's lives better, they also help to build the solidarity and cohesion essential to a good society.

I think the parliament can be genuinely proud of these achievements, and many more besides. It is perhaps telling that the most recent Scottish Social Attitudes Survey found that more than 60% of people trust the Scottish Parliament to act in the country's best interests. For the UK, the corresponding score is 21%.

Let me say this clearly, that contrast with the UK Parliament cannot and should not be a source of complacency. Not least because doing better than Westminster is not a particularly high bar to get over these days, but it is also the case that attitudes can and do change. To retain and grow trust, Holyrood must continue to make a tangibly positive difference to people's lives.

We must continue to improve our schools, a key focus of my government. We have a big job to do to ensure our health service can adapt to an ageing population. We must focus on our productivity as a country and do so in a way that is sustainable. We need also to live up to the focus on wellbeing, which we set out explicitly in the latest iteration of the National Performance Framework. Growth cannot be an end in itself; it must be the means by which we enable people to live happy, healthy, and fulfilling lives.

We need to do all of this while we adapt to the profound challenges that we, in common with other countries, face in the years ahead. I cannot go into all of those today. A speech of this nature is never going to do justice to issues like artificial intelligence, the impact of automation, and adapting to an ageing population, but they will require detailed and focused attention by the parliament in the years ahead. I do though, want to touch briefly on a couple of interlinked issues.

The first and most important is the climate crisis, which will be the defining challenge of the next twenty years, not simply for Scotland, but for the world. As a country we have made significant progress over the past two decades. We are, and are seen to be, a world leader in cutting emissions, but we need to do more. By the time our parliament marks its 40th anniversary, we must be on the verge of being a carbon-neutral economy. Only a few years after that, we must be a net-zero emitter of all greenhouse gases to live up to our international obligations.

The change required to achieve all that will be profound. It will affect the design of our cities, the way we travel, and the heating of our homes. It will require an end to throwaway culture, and a more circular economy. It will involve tree planting and peat restoration, alongside the development of new technologies. Our challenge is not just to do all that, but to lead the world as we do it.

There is a moral imperative since Scotland led the world into the carbon age, but there is also opportunity if we get it right. Many of the changes we need will not only help our environment but also create jobs and grow our economy. However, we have seen in previous economic transformations that it is too easy for people and communities to be left behind.

I grew up in Ayrshire in the 1970s and 1980s and remember vividly the impact of deindustrialization. The fear of unemployment was pervasive. Lasting scars were left on many communities, and elements of that legacy remain with us today. We cannot let that happen again. Instead, we must position ourselves to maximise the domestic economic potential of the renewables and low-carbon revolution, which is why we appointed a Just Transition Commission last year, to help ensure that the economic and technological change that lies ahead will create a fairer and happier society as well as a wealthier one.

Promoting equality and tackling poverty is linked to what I have been talking about and has been a consistent priority for the Scottish Parliament. We are the only part of the UK to have statutory targets for reducing and ultimately eradicating child poverty. That said, setting targets, in itself, does not deliver change, and while poverty and child poverty rates in Scotland are lower than in other parts of the UK, they are still too high.

We must recognise, perhaps more than we have done previously, that poverty and inequality damage all of us. We all lose when economic disadvantage stops people from contributing fully to society. That is why we are continuing to promote policies like the living wage. It is why we will shortly set out plans for a targeted income supplement to help deliver those targets on child poverty, and it is why we put so much focus on closing the education attainment gap and ensuring equal access to higher and further education.

It is a fact, of course, that we tackle poverty with one hand tied behind our back. UK measures like the bedroom tax and the benefits freeze run counter to what we seek to achieve and every penny we spend trying to mitigate these policies is money we are not able to invest more strategically and proactively. The UN Special Rapporteur on poverty recently described this as outrageous and unsustainable, and it begs this question. Why should we spend hundreds of millions of pounds mitigating the impact of

UK Government decisions, rather than taking the powers we need to make different decisions in the first place?

There are echoes here from the years before devolution, when social justice was so central to the campaigns of the 1980s and 1990s which helped create the Scottish Parliament. It was also linked to concern about a democratic deficit. People disliked policies being imposed on Scotland against the will of the majority and the poll tax became the totemic example of that.

By the end of October we could be heading not only for a damaging Brexit we did not vote for, but also a catastrophic No Deal Brexit. The votes of people in Scotland have been ignored. The Scottish Government's attempts at compromise were rejected. Votes in the Scottish Parliament, opposing Brexit and a subsequent power grab, were disregarded.

In 2014, the writer Neal Ascherson said he preferred not to ask people, 'Should Scotland be an independent country' but asked instead, 'Scotland, yes ... but what sort of Scotland?'

That is a question we must ask ourselves again because, instead of chaos, dysfunction, and the current political direction of Westminster, I strongly believe most people want a Scotland that is welcoming, tolerant, internationalist, and European, with a strong sense of social justice and responsibility.

My view is that we can better achieve that if our future is truly in our hands. If we can chart our own course at home, but, crucially, work constructively with other countries in the EU and across the globe. The crucial point is that, at this pivotal moment for the UK, it must be for the people of Scotland to decide. That is why we are laying the groundwork for another choice on independence, through the Referendum Bill introduced to parliament two weeks ago.

In doing that, whatever our views, as we look ahead to the next stage of our national journey we must be determined to learn and apply the lessons of Brexit. The current political climate, exacerbated by social media, can be polarising and divisive. I feel that as a participant and know it is how many citizens of our country feel. Those of us who care about the values of our democracy, informed decision-making and the quality of public discourse, cannot and must not give in to that momentum for division and polarisation.

The current situation requires us to discuss and decide Scotland's future, but we should strive to air honest and strongly held differences respectfully, while seeking as much common ground and consensus as we can. That is why I have offered talks to the parties who oppose independence, to discuss what powers they think Scotland needs to face the challenges of the future. If substantial proposals arise my hope is that the parliament can present them in a unified way.

It is also why my government announced the establishment of a citizens' assembly on Scotland's future. To bring people together to seek, not the divisions, but the areas for agreement. If this initiative is successful, I suspect we may see that model becoming a more regular feature of our decision-making in years to come.

I mentioned earlier that the parliament has often, not always successfully, worked to build consensus and seek common ground. That is the spirit in which we make these moves. The fact that we do not all agree within this room, or within the wider country, on Scotland's constitutional destination, should not prevent us from travelling as far as we can together.

I began my remarks by quoting Winnie Ewing during the first day of the Scottish Parliament and want to end by quoting Donald Dewar's at the official state opening, which took place a few weeks later. In my view, he gave one of the finest speeches of modern Scottish times, his finest in a very distinguished career. In it he said, 'This is about more than our politics and our laws. This is about who we are, how we carry ourselves'.

These are words we would all do very well to remember. The Scottish Parliament, by and large, has carried itself well over the last twenty years. In its procedures, its openness, its willingness to seek consensus, it has offered at times a contrast to Westminster. It has earned public trust and confidence and delivered substantive measures which have improved people's lives. The next six months could offer challenges greater than anything seen in those twenty years, which, in my view, will require greater powers for Scotland. Indeed, the full powers that come with independence.

As we discuss the shape of that and how we gain the powers we need, we must ensure that our debates are thorough, thoughtful, and constructive, and that we carry as many people with us as possible. If we can achieve that, to end on a note of optimism, I think we can surpass, rather than merely fulfil, the hopes of twenty years ago. We can ensure that Scotland's new song is of a greener, fairer, and more prosperous country.

37

THE COUNTRIES MOST AFFECTED

Given to the World Forum on Climate Justice
Glasgow Caledonian University, 28th June 2019

> With climate justice now at the forefront of many far-seeing
> minds, NS gave this deeply felt speech to an international
> audience in the city of Glasgow. The inaugural World Forum
> on Climate Justice was a conference of civic groups, academics,
> business representatives, members of the public, and policy-
> makers. Fellow speakers were Mary Robinson, former president
> of Ireland, and Patrick Bond, professor of political economy at
> the University of Witwatersrand, South Africa.

It is an honour to welcome delegates from thirty-five countries
around the world to such an important event. I am struck by the
impressive range of topics you will be discussing, from the role of
trade unions to the redefinition of Gross Domestic Product, from
gender justice in the Philippines to the redevelopment of New
York City's waterfront. The global climate crisis and climate emergency touches every aspect of our lives, and is the most important
and pressing environmental, economic, and moral issue facing the
world today.

Climate justice must be at the heart of our response. We must
recognise the imbalance between those who are most responsible
for climate change, and those who are most affected. When Mary
Robinson spoke this morning, I found it interesting that her
Foundation has concluded that climate justice, having been almost

an almost taboo subject in 2010, is now widely accepted. That is hugely important and hugely encouraging, and I like to think that we in Scotland have played our part in its acceptance as an important issue. In that year we became the first government anywhere in the world to establish a fund for climate justice, and in 2017 this university was first to establish a centre for climate justice. It seems fitting that Scotland is hosting the first ever global forum for climate justice.

I will talk about climate justice specifically in a moment, but I want to begin by stressing a point that I hope everyone is aware of, that is important to stress unequivocally. Scotland is determined to play a full part in the battle against climate change and we intend to win.

We have already reduced our greenhouse gas emissions by 40% since 1990 but have now determined to achieve net-zero emissions by 2045 having become carbon neutral by 2040. If this new target is approved by parliament, as I expect it will, we will have the most stringent and ambitious statutory targets in the world. Becoming a net-zero nation, as we intend, will require changes to virtually every aspect of everyday life. Decarbonisation will change how we travel, keep our homes and workplaces warm, and design our towns and cities in the future. We must move rapidly from a throwaway culture to a genuinely circular economy. To develop and apply new technologies, while also planting millions of trees and restoring peatlands.

This must be a truly national endeavour, and the Scottish Government over the summer will launch a Big Climate Conversation. We intend to arrange consultation events around the country; help communities to stage their own events; and reach as many people as we can through digital communications. We hope to reach thousands of people and organisations to hear about their concerns, priorities, and ambitions, in order to understand how they are already changing their behaviour and what further changes they are willing to make. Indeed, what further changes we all need to be persuaded to make and what action we can take as a country, to tackle the global climate emergency.

In doing this, we want to be clear about the scale of the necessary changes and the scale of the challenges. We want to set out the fact that the transition to decarbonisation can also bring opportunities and rewards. We can make our lifestyles healthier, our air cleaner, and our landscapes even more beautiful. We can develop new technologies and techniques which in turn, if we get it right, create new jobs and, if we ensure that the transition to a net-zero economy is just, making sure as far as possible that people are not left behind, we can ensure that Scotland is a fairer country as well as greener and environmentally friendly.

Last year, we appointed a Just Transition Commission, becoming one of the first countries to focus on the concept of just transition. It will consider the whole of our economy, and indeed the whole of our society, and make recommendations on ensuring that the benefits and costs of decarbonisation are distributed fairly. It is an important way of ensuring that a net-zero economy can bring benefits for everyone.

I have emphasised our domestic actions because doing the right thing in Scotland is, in many ways, the most important contribution we can make. These domestic policies lend weight to our support for global action and mean we are leading not only with our rhetoric, but also with the strength of our example. We cannot expect others to reduce emissions unless we are serious about doing so ourselves.

In addition to action here in Scotland, we will directly help other countries where possible. The climate crisis is becoming increasingly evident in developed countries, who are seeing more extreme weather events such as severe storms and droughts. However, the consequences are more serious in many developing nations. For island and low-lying nations, it poses a genuinely existential threat with others facing humanitarian emergencies from drought or flooding which, of course, can lead to mass displacements of population.

The countries most affected by climate change are usually those who have done least to cause it. The individuals most affected are often the most vulnerable, the old and the young with women, too, disproportionately affected. Climate change can cause poverty, and resource scarcity increases the burdens that women face in supporting their families. Walking further to get water they are at greater risk of gender-based violence.

It is impossible to properly tackle the climate crisis without putting climate justice at the heart of everything we do. Countries, like ours, which have become prosperous partly because of greenhouse gas usage, must help those being impoverished as a result.

In Scotland we are determined to do our bit, to play our part, to live up to our moral responsibility, and in 2012 created the world's first ever climate justice fund. It supports projects in Malawi, Rwanda, and Zambia and, in recent years, has provided not only access to clean water for more than 70,000 people but also renewable energy for 80,000. We are working with village communities in south Malawi to restore water points, and to train people in the use of energy efficient stoves. We trained farmers to use methods which reduce their vulnerability to the fall armyworm, a moth larva which can destroy a range of different crops. We are helping build a network of Young Malawian Climate Leaders; we want young people, who will be most affected by the climate crisis, to have a stronger voice here at home and internationally.

As you probably know, our Climate Justice Fund is small when viewed in comparison to the overall scale of the problem, but it does bring significant benefits to tens of thousands of people who are directly affected by climate change. It helps to empower communities to adapt to the crisis and sends a signal to other countries around the world.

I mentioned earlier my hope that, by ensuring a just transition, the move to a net-zero economy could make Scotland a fairer country as well as a greener one. As the sustainable development goals acknowledge, that is an ambition we should share with the whole world. The world must become fairer, as well as more sustainable, and promoting climate justice can help us achieve that goal.

The final point I want to make is that the Climate Justice Fund is important, not only because of what Scotland is doing, but also because of how we are seeking to do it. It achieves a disproportionate impact because we work alongside others in partnership. In Malawi, for example, it is backed by a network of individuals, schools, universities, colleges, faith groups and non-governmental organisations.

In all the work we are doing to address climate change, setting and striving to meet strict targets; developing new technologies; supporting a just transition; promoting climate justice, we try to make working in partnership a key principle.

That, of course, includes partnership with governments and organisations in other countries. We believe we have a great deal to offer the world, but we also know that we have a huge amount to learn from countries all across the globe and it is heartening to see experts from so many different countries here. I hope that your discussions will prove stimulating and productive, and that you gain long term benefit from new contacts, from the information you are gathering and the experiences you share. Do that, and this conference will be a success not only in its own terms, but also in terms of the action it can spark for the future.

38

GROWTH IS NOT AN END IN ITSELF

Given at a TED Talk
Edinburgh, 29th July 2019

> In this TED Talk, NS discusses the essence of wellbeing
> thinking and finds historical connection with two famous books
> by Adam Smith. The Wellbeing Economy Governments partner-
> ship (WEGo), to which she refers, is a collaboration of national
> and regional governments promoting the sharing of expertise
> and transferrable policy practices. Comprising Scotland, New
> Zealand, Iceland, and Wales, (Finland would join in late 2020)
> it recognises that 21st-century development entails the delivery
> of human and ecological wellbeing. A month earlier she had
> opened a series of policy labs at Panmure House, welcoming not
> only representatives of Iceland and New Zealand but also the
> Organisation for Economic Co-operation and Development.

Just over a mile from here, in Edinburgh's Old Town, is Panmure
House, the home of the world-renowned Scottish economist Adam
Smith. In his important work *The Wealth of Nations*, Adam Smith
argued that the measurement of a country's wealth was not just its
gold and silver reserves. It was the totality of the country's production and commerce. I guess it was one of the earliest descriptions of
what we now know today as Gross Domestic Product.

In the years since, that measurement of production and
commerce, GDP, has become ever more important, to the point
that – and I do not believe this is what Adam Smith would have

intended – it is often seen as the most important measurement of a country's overall success. My argument today is that it is time for that to change.

You know, what we choose to measure as a country matters; it really matters because it drives political focus, it drives public activity and, against that context, I think the limitations of GDP as a measurement of a country's success are all too obvious. GDP measures the output of all our work, but it says nothing about the nature of that work, about whether that work is worthwhile or fulfilling. It puts a value, for example, on illegal drug consumption, but not on unpaid care, and values activity in the short term that boosts the economy, even if that activity is hugely damaging to the sustainability of our planet in the longer term.

When we reflect on the past decade of political and economic upheaval, of growing inequalities, and when we look ahead to the challenges of the climate emergency, increasing automation, an aging population, then I think the argument for a much broader definition of what it means to be successful as a country, as a society, is compelling, and increasingly so.

That is why Scotland in 2018 took the initiative in establishing a new network called the Wellbeing Economy Governments group, bringing together as founding members the countries of Scotland, Iceland, and New Zealand. We are sometimes called the SIN countries, although our focus is very much on the common good.

The purpose of this group is to challenge that focus on the narrow measurement of GDP. To say that, yes, economic growth matters, it is important, but it is not all that is important. Growth in GDP should not be pursued at any or all cost. In fact, the argument of the group is that the goal, the objective of economic policy, should be collective wellbeing: how happy and healthy a population is, not just how wealthy a population is. I will touch on the policy implications of that in a moment, but I think, particularly in the world we live in today, it has a deeper resonance.

When we focus on wellbeing, we start a conversation that

provokes profound and fundamental questions. What really matters to us in our lives? What do we value in the communities we live in? What kind of country, what kind of society, do we really want to be? And when we engage people in those questions, in finding the answers to those questions, then I believe that we have a much better chance of addressing the alienation and disaffection from politics that is so prevalent in so many countries across the developed world today.

In policy terms, this journey for Scotland started back in 2007, when we published what we call our National Performance Framework, looking at the range of indicators that we measure ourselves against. Those indicators are as varied as income inequality, the happiness of children, access to green spaces, access to housing. None of these are captured in GDP statistics, but they are all fundamental to a healthy and happy society, and that broader approach is at the heart of our economic strategy, where we give equal importance to tackling inequality as we do to economic competitiveness. It drives our commitment to fair work, making sure that work is fulfilling and well-paid, and is behind our decision to establish a Just Transition Commission to guide our path to a carbon zero economy. We know from economic transformations of the past that, if we are not careful, there are more losers than winners and, as we face the challenges of climate change and automation, we must not make those mistakes again.

The work we are doing here in Scotland is, I think, significant, but we have much to learn from other countries. I mentioned our partner nations in the Wellbeing network: Iceland and New Zealand. It is worth noting, and I will leave it to you to decide whether this is relevant or not, that all three of these countries are currently led by women.

They are doing great work: New Zealand, in 2019, publishing its first Wellbeing Budget, with mental health at its heart; Iceland leading the way on equal pay, childcare and paternity rights. These are not policies we immediately think of when we talk about creating a wealthy economy, but policies that are fundamental to a healthy economy and a happy society. I started with Adam Smith and *The Wealth of Nations*. In Adam Smith's earlier work, *The Theory of Moral Sentiments*, which I think is just as important, he made the observation that the value of any government is judged in proportion to the extent that it makes its people happy.

I think that is a good founding principle for any group of countries focused on promoting wellbeing. None of us has all of the answers, not even Scotland, his birthplace, but in the world we live in today, with growing divides and inequalities, with disaffection and alienation, it is more important than ever that we ask and find the answers to those questions and promote a vision of society that has wellbeing, not just wealth, at its very heart.

You are right now in the beautiful, sunny capital city of the country that led the world in the Enlightenment, the country that helped lead the world into the industrial age, the country that is now helping to lead the world into the low-carbon age. I want, and am determined, that Scotland will also be the country that helps change the focus of countries and governments across the world to put wellbeing at the heart of everything that we do.

I think we owe that to this generation, and certainly believe we owe it to the next and all that come after. If we do it, led here from the country of the Enlightenment, then I think we will create a better, healthier, fairer and happier society at home, and play our part in building a fairer, happier world as well.

39

THE IMPORTANCE OF LITERATURE

Given to Northern Lights Literature
Edinburgh International Conference Centre, 25th August 2019

> With a lifelong dedication to reading and literature, NS regularly tweets about books she has enjoyed or is currently reading. She has befriended many of the world's most famous authors and is a frequent interviewer at the Edinburgh International Book Festival (EIBF) where she has had public conversations with Chimamanda Ngozi Adichie, Arundhati Roy, and Ali Smith. In 2016 she founded the First Minister's Reading Challenge (for primary age children) with the Scottish Book Trust and in 2019 spoke at the Publishing Scotland Conference in Surgeons' Hall, Edinburgh. Later in the year she gave the following speech to Northern Lights, a collaborative project between the EIBF and Bradford Literature Festival designed to bring together publishers based in Scotland and the north of England. By this time, the word 'diversity' had joined 'wellbeing' in her essential lexicon.

Let me begin with a large and heartfelt thank you to the Edinburgh International Book Festival together with Bradford Literary Festival for organising this event. I am genuinely delighted to be here. Attending events like this, meeting and speaking with people whose work is so close to my heart, is one of the perks of my job as First Minister.

I have just chaired a roundtable of Scottish publishers, reflecting not only on the successes in the sector but also some of the challenges it faces, and considering collectively what we can do to ensure that, here, in the birthplace of the Enlightenment, books, literature and reading will remain an integral and vibrant, essential part of who we are as a country.

That really matters to me. Even a brief look at my Twitter feed will show that reading books and discovering new authors is hugely important to me, one of the great passions of my life. Reading books, particularly literature, is fundamental to my life and essential for my wellbeing, but it is also vital to the perspectives I bring to bear in my work as First Minister. Lives and experiences beyond direct knowledge, and the empathy that comes with them, are core to the work of any leader, especially any political leader.

Being here with you today, and with these distinguished panellists, is a huge honour. I am also delighted that we are discussing such an important topic, because this *is* an important topic. Important in its own right, but, given the fractious nature and increased polarisation of the world, how we have more voices heard, bringing together disparate and diverse perspectives, and deepening our mutual and collective understanding is, I think, more important than it has been in my lifetime.

Earlier this week, as part of the Edinburgh Book Festival, I was lucky enough to interview Arundhati Roy. For me, and for the assembled audience, it was an obviously fascinating experience to hear one of the world's great writers speak about her career, her writing, and the political situation in her home country of India. It was a typically wonderful evening at the Book Festival but, as I looked around at that audience, I was reminded again as I am so often, of the incredible power of literature.

Every person in that room was in the palm of Arundhati's hand. Everybody was touched by her work, by the themes of her writing. Her books have opened our minds to new ideas, new stories and new perspectives and, as a result, and certainly as a result of that event, all of us were a little more aware and had a little more understanding of different lives, different cultures and the world around us.

It is impossible to overstate the value of that, to all of us as individuals and to the wellbeing of our societies. It is why I believe that having a strong, diverse literary and publishing scene is essential for any country. It is also why I think the work that you do is so important. You play a central role in finding and providing a platform for new literary talent and, in doing so, bring joy and enlightenment to countless people and make our society more interesting, vibrant, and outward-looking. It is an extraordinary contribution to make, and one which I as First Minister want to do all I can to support.

We try to support publishing and writing through the Edinburgh International Book Festival, organisations like the Scottish Book Trust, and Publishing Scotland. I have established, through Scotland's schools, something called the First Minister's Reading Challenge[49]. All of that is intended to develop, maintain, sustain, and grow a strong reading culture across our society, and is why I so warmly welcome the Northern Lights initiative and the idea of greater collaboration between Scotland and the North of England. To provide in practical terms a counter to the gravitational pull to the south we have experienced for so long.

I particularly welcome your focus on greater diversity. For all its undoubted strengths, this is an area where we know publishing needs to do better. It is clear from a range of evidence that the industry is still not as diverse and inclusive as it should and could be. Research from the ROAR[50] project in 2017, for example, found that only around a third of the books published in Scotland were written by women.

We know that black and minority ethnic writers are significantly underrepresented. A couple of years ago it was reported that fewer than one hundred books by non-white British authors were published over the whole of 2016. There are also regional and

---

49. To help children and young people discover the power of reading.
50. Founded in 2016, ROAR stands for Represent, Object, Advocate, Rewrite.

geographic disparities. I do not need to tell any of you that the industry does remain very much geared towards London and the South East.

Socio-economic inequalities are also evident. Researchers from the Universities of Edinburgh and Sheffield estimate that just 12% of people involved in publishing, including writers and translators, are from working-class backgrounds. That touches on an important point. It is not just in the output of publishing, or the range of authors being published, that we see a lack of diversity. We also see it in the industry workforce and particularly in senior positions. Of course, publishing is not unique in that respect, and all of this is interlinked. If we have a narrower range of voices influencing decisions, then inevitably it will have an impact on the kinds of writers and books which are published.

These are issues which publishing needs to tackle. Doing so is a matter of basic fairness and equality, but the economic case is also important. In publishing, as in any other walk of life, equality is good for competitiveness, quality, and the profits that you will make. So, we should not see it in a warm, fuzzy sense, we should have a hard-headed focus as well.

We have seen some encouraging signs in recent years that the industry is ready to act. The launch of the Publishers Association's Inclusivity Plan a couple of years ago was a positive development. We have also seen firms taking steps to open the profession through things like paid internships and mentoring schemes, which was an issue that was raised at the roundtable earlier.

Here in Scotland, there are some recent examples of publishers embracing diverse voices and I think reaping the benefits of that. 404 Ink, who I know are here today, are a good example, BHP Comics in Glasgow is another, and Charco Press that is here today as well. All in terms of their output link to the diversity of voices in Scotland.

Alongside relatively new publishers, our more established publishers are taking this seriously. *Celestial Bodies*, written by

Jokha Alharthi[51] and published by Sandstone Press, is one of the year's great literary success stories. It is the first English translation of a novel by an Omani woman, and in May became the first book by an Arabic language writer to win the Man Booker International Prize.

These are examples of successes and progress that we should celebrate and should inspire us to do more. Firstly though, they are signs of a determination to tackle this issue. To go back to the point that Nick [Barley, director of the Edinburgh International Book Festival] made, and I refer to as well, part of what publishing needs to do is not simply be diverse for its own sake, but contribute to the economic sustainability and success of the sector.

I want to end where I started, by reflecting on my interview with Arundhati Roy last week. While preparing for that interview I was really struck by something she said in a Guardian interview, about the way in which she is sometimes described. She said this: 'When people say this business of "she's the voice of the voiceless", it makes me crazy. I say, "there's no voiceless, there's only the deliberately silenced … or the purposely unheard".'

One of the reasons I admire the work of publishing so much is that, often, you are the people who break that silence. By supporting new writers, you ensure that unheard voices are heard loudly around the world and I, along with millions of others, benefit hugely. The challenge now is to build on these strengths so that publishing better reflects the diversity of our society and the world we live in.

---

51. Translated by Marilyn Booth.

40

A CUP OF KINDNESS

Given to the European Policy Centre
Brussels, 10th February 2020.

> With the chiming in of the year 2020, Scotland was on the lip
> of removal from the European Union, and soon removed, not
> only against its democratic choice as expressed in successive
> referendums but also against the will of its elected parliament. It
> was a time for regret and reflection, as is apparent in this speech
> to the European Policy Centre just a few days later, but it was also
> time for a beacon of hope to be raised for the people of Scotland
> as well as colleagues, family, and friends across the continent.

It is always wonderful to be in Brussels, but today it is also quite
emotional. This is the first time I have been here, or indeed
anywhere outside Scotland, since the UK left the European Union
ten days ago.

Brexit was a sad matter for me, for many in Scotland and across
the UK, and some of the most affecting moments of the week
leading to Brexit occurred here in Brussels. I was especially struck
by footage from the Wednesday of the last session of the European
Parliament to be attended by MEPs from the UK.

The sincerity, grace, and goodwill from people such as Guy
Verhofstadt and Ursula von der Leyen was impressive but, for
many people, and perhaps particularly for many in Scotland, the
most moving moment was at the end, when MEPs from all parties
and all countries stood together to sing Auld Lang Syne. That scene

of solidarity and friendship encapsulated the values the Scottish Government and many people in Scotland most cherish about the European Union.

For me though, and I suspect many others in Scotland, hearing Robert Burns' words in that room at that time had another effect. It reinforced the sense that we have left a place where we belong. That we should still be participating in that chamber, rather than departing it.

At almost exactly the same time those scenes were taking place, the Scottish Parliament was voting to back a further referendum on Scottish independence. The connections between those two scenes form the basis of my remarks today.

I am going to set out, briefly, the ongoing regret the Scottish Government feels over Brexit and explain some of the ways in which we will respond. In doing that I will make clear our desire to return to the European Parliament as an independent nation, comfortable (as EU members have to be) with the idea that independence, in the modern world, involves recognising and embracing our interdependence.

As you know, 62% of voters in Scotland chose to stay in the EU in 2016. Subsequent opinion polls suggest that pro-EU sentiment has grown, and our desire to stay has been reaffirmed by three subsequent nationwide elections. In December, parties in favour of remaining in the EU, or holding a further referendum, gained almost three-quarters of the vote. Pro-European sentiment has very deep and strong roots in Scotland, and the basic principle of independent nations working together for a common good is one that appeals to many.

We also recognise the solidarity the EU offers to smaller member states. People in Scotland have seen, and will long remember, the support the EU has given to Ireland throughout the first stage of the Brexit process.

In addition, Scotland has day-to-day experience of the practical benefits of membership. EU regulations have made our rivers and coasts cleaner. Our universities collaborate with research partners across the continent. EU freedom of movement has given opportunities to people living in Scotland and encouraged new Scots to contribute to our economy and society. One of our priorities is to support those EU citizens to stay in Scotland.

Our businesses benefit from the single market. Figures last week demonstrated that over the last five years, Scotland's sales to the EU, which account for more than half our international exports, have grown by more than 4% a year. More than twice as fast as our exports to the rest of the world.

We are leaving the European Union, imperfect as it undoubtedly is, at a time when we have never benefited from it more, and leaving it, in my view, when we have never needed it more. In an age when intolerance and bigotry seem to be on the rise, the values of democracy, equality, solidarity, the rule of law, and respect for human rights are more important than ever.

The founding motivation of the EU, as a Peace Project, is too easily forgotten in the UK, but its importance has struck me regularly at memorial events for the two world wars. Most recently, just a matter of days ago, for the 75th anniversary of the liberation of Auschwitz.

At a time of climate crisis, co-operating with the EU improves our ability to tackle climate change at home and amplifies our voice in international negotiations. In an age of great trading blocks, the EU represents our best opportunity to benefit from free trade, without engaging in a race to the bottom. All of this is important, and helps explain why Scotland regrets Brexit, and why so many of us continue to feel European... but, of course, the real question, the one you will want me to focus on, is not what we have lost. It is what happens next. What practical steps can Scotland take to mitigate the effects of the UK Government's actions?

There are essentially two parts to the answer. Firstly, for as long as Scotland remains part of the United Kingdom, we will try to influence UK Government policy and, where possible, work constructively with the UK Government. That point extends beyond Brexit negotiations.

As many of you will know, the COP26[52] Climate Summit will take place in Glasgow in November and is due to be the most important climate summit since the Paris talks of 2015. Given the ever-increasing urgency of the climate crisis it may prove to be even more important.

There has been a lot of talk about the Glasgow summit recently, and about relations between the Scottish and UK Governments, so let me be clear about my approach. There is a strong argument that nothing happening anywhere in the world this year will be more important than making the Glasgow summit a success. The Scottish Government will do everything we can to make it so, and that includes working positively and constructively with the UK Government.

A similar principle applies to the UK's negotiations with the EU. We will do what we can to work as closely and as constructively as possible and, in doing so, will try to influence negotiations in a way which benefits Scotland, the UK and the EU. We will stress the value of having as close a trading relationship with the EU as possible.

The Prime Minister made a speech about this last week, insisting on the right to diverge from EU standards. In areas like social and environmental standards, on the other hand, the EU wants a guarantee that the UK will not regress: that the UK will not undercut the EU by adopting lower standards, an issue which matters hugely. As the EU continually makes clear, the more we diverge from its standards, the less access we will have to the single market. So, the right to diverge will come at a cost. In my view a cost that is too heavy.

In the areas where non-regression applies, the UK will always be able to opt for higher standards than those required by the EU.

52. The twenty-sixth United Nations Climate Change Conference was post-poned to November 2021 because of the COVID-19 pandemic.

Although the Prime Minister never explicitly said this, in fact he never gave a single concrete example of an area in which divergence could benefit the UK, the only possible reason for wanting the freedom to diverge is if you want to adopt lower standards. As things stand, there is a danger that the UK will significantly reduce our access to the single market, harming manufacturers and service industries across the country, because it wants the freedom to lower standards relating to health, safety, the environment, and workers' rights.

The Scottish Government will argue against that approach. We largely support the idea of a level playing field, removing the possibility of the UK adopting lower standards than the EU, protecting environmental standards and working conditions, and making it easier for Scottish businesses to export to the EU. We will continually make that case as negotiations proceed.

On past evidence, I am not overly optimistic about our chances of success, so we are looking to what we can do, using our devolved powers, to maintain the closest possible ties with the EU.

We intend to introduce legislation enabling Scotland to keep pace with EU regulatory standards where we have the power to do so. It is a way in which we can protect the health and wellbeing of people in Scotland, maintain the international reputation of businesses in Scotland, and make it easier, when the time comes, as I believe it will, for Scotland to return to the EU.

We will also, and this is the second part of our approach, work towards the most obvious and important step Scotland can take in response to Brexit. We will seek to become independent, and then seek to re-establish our EU membership. The case for us being able to seek independence is clear.

As most of you know, Scotland six years ago had a vote on whether to become an independent country. Opponents of independence repeatedly said that voting to remain in the United Kingdom was the only way for us to stay in the EU. That argument weighed heavily with many.

Since then, Scotland has been taken out of the EU against our will, and the UK Government dismissed the Scottish Government's compromise offer of keeping the whole of the UK inside the Single Market and Customs Union. Its approach to Brexit has consistently been contrary to Scotland's views, values, and interests.

Strong support for the EU is one of the main reasons that the party I lead did so well in the recent UK election, in which we won eighty per cent of the seats in Scotland, but we also put, front and centre, the right of the people to choose their own future. Between staying in the UK after Brexit or becoming an independent country. Since that election, opinion polls have shown majority support for independence, and there are large majorities for the principle that it should be for the Scottish Parliament, not the Westminster Government, to determine whether and when there should be a referendum.

I am a believer in democracy, in the rule of law, in the power of respectful persuasion and deliberation, and continue to believe that, as we press the case for Scotland's right to choose, we should agree a process between ourselves and the UK Government for a referendum, in line with the mandate given by the people of Scotland. None of this should be a matter for controversy with the UK Government. The UK is not a unitary state. It is a voluntary union of nations, and one of those nations, Scotland, has expressed majority support, time and time again, for remaining in the European Union.

It cannot be right that more than five million EU citizens should be removed from the European Union, after 47 years of membership, without the chance to have their say on the future of their country. That is why we are taking the steps required to ensure that an independence referendum can be held that is beyond legal challenge, so that the result is accepted and embraced both at home and internationally.

We are asking the Electoral Commission, the independent body that oversees elections in the UK, to test again the question used in 2014. The question that would be used in a referendum. We are inviting Scotland's elected representatives, MPs, MSPs, council leaders and recent MEPs, to establish a new Constitutional Convention, to broaden support for the principle of Scotland's right to choose. We will publish a series of papers, the 'New Scotland' papers, providing the information people need to make informed choices. Those papers will include our plans for membership of the EU.

We know, and some of the comments made by Donald Tusk last week confirmed this, that there is goodwill towards Scotland. We want to build on that goodwill and are keen to outline a clear route to re-accession, to show that that we understand what EU membership requires, and to demonstrate that we have much to offer.

Some of that should be relatively straightforward. Scotland already complies with the European Union's acquis[53]: its body of laws, obligations, and rights. As I have said, we are passing legislation to ensure that continues to be the case where practically possible. We welcome free movement because we know how much we benefit from it, and I hope that our overall approach as a constructive friend and partner is not in doubt.

Brexit has changed the context of the choice we intend to offer the people of Scotland, compared with the 2014 referendum. Fundamentally, do we believe it is better for our future, or not, to be part of the world's largest trading block and the shared values, and benefits of European Union membership?

Ultimately, when (and I believe it is a when) Scotland gains independence, I believe that the case for us joining the EU will be an overwhelming one.

That view is shared by many distinguished experts. In fact, Fabian [Zuleeg, European Policy Centre Chief Executive], you wrote a paper about Scotland and the EU last summer which put the basic issue well. You said that for Europe, 'rejecting a country

---

53. The body of common rights and obligations that are binding on all EU countries as Members.

that wants to be in the EU, accepts all conditions, is willing to go through the appropriate processes and follows European principles... should be inconceivable.'

We will rejoin not simply as a country with much to gain, but as one which has much to contribute.

That is made clear by the strategy document we published two weeks ago, giving Scotland's perspective on the key policy priorities for the EU as set out by Ursula von der Leyen, the new Commission President. Her support for an economy that works for everyone finds direct echoes in Scotland, a country which is increasingly focussing on wellbeing, alongside wealth, as a measurement of success.

Her emphasis on a Europe fit for the digital age is one we strongly support. Scotland is becoming one of the most important tech centres in Europe. Her desire for a Green New Deal is one we share. Scotland has some of the strongest statutory climate change targets in the world. We want to help lead the world into the net-zero carbon age and know our efforts are enhanced by membership of the EU.

The Commission's other priorities also speak of our shared values.

In all these issues, Scotland is a country which can and will make a difference. We will lead by example where we can, but we will also learn from the example of others and do so more effectively by working in partnership. I believe very strongly that our sovereignty will be amplified, not diminished, by membership of the EU.

I began by reflecting on the last appearance, for now, of Scottish MEPs in the European Parliament. When the old Scottish Parliament had its last sitting in 1707, proceedings were closed by the speaker, Lord Seafield, who said, 'There's the end of an auld sang'.

Those remarks found a curious echo in the scenes at the European Parliament two weeks ago. The singing of Auld Lang Syne marked the end of something which, although maybe not that old, has been precious to many people in Scotland... but our task now is to turn that end into a new beginning, to find our voice as an independent nation, and to take our place on the European and world stage.

When we do that we will speak up, together with our friends in Europe and around the world, for democracy, equality, and human rights. We will contribute to tackling challenges such as the climate crisis. We will work in partnership to enhance the wellbeing of people in Scotland, across Europe, and around the world.

For all those reasons, and many more, I look forward to the day when Scotland returns to where we belong. To EU membership with a place in the Council and the European Parliament. As an independent nation we will embrace international co-operation, and sing of solidarity and friendship not out of sorrow but with optimism and hope for the future.

A NOTE ON THE TRANSCRIPTIONS

The shift from one medium to another is always fraught with risk, and it is generally accepted that any translation from one language to another is necessarily a version. This might be of a novel or a poem, with poetry presenting special challenges. Music presents similar challenges to composers who extend their craft to adapt another's work for other instruments. Music is enriched by this practice but, to be frank, there is more to the process than arrangements. Some elements of interpretation are called for.

So it has been with these speeches and, as with the musical art, editorial integrity, to the originator, to the subject matter, to the reader, is essential. Meaning is sacrosanct. The point of this selection is to present the speeches as reading material, or essays, and allow a personality to appear that might be viewed as an unconscious self-portrait of their originator, in this case the fifth First Minister of Scotland, Nicola Sturgeon. Through them we can listen for her constant themes, played above the long ground note of independence for Scotland: gender equality, education, well-being, diversity, climate change and the oft-repeated point that social progress should come with economic advance. As argued in the introduction to this book, given the quasi-presidential nature of the post, we may be looking at the preoccupations of a nation with its eye to the future. Through its democratic processes it has chosen a leader, and this is where she chooses to lead. Again, a single election can change all that, as the lyrical symphony of Barack Obama's presidency was replaced by the unsettling dissonance of Donald Trump.

Only set piece speeches have been included, no press conferences or improvised discussions. A hundred and two received a first sweeping review and, of these, forty were chosen to represent a wide range of subjects given to an equally wide range of audiences from California to Beijing, and an economic range from the World Bank in New York to the Pierce Institute in Govan.

Any speech is likely to begin with a certain amount of throat clearing, and close with a friendly platitude. Therefore, many of these could be safely topped and tailed. Emphasis before an audience is often achieved by repetition or gesture, which are wasted on the reader. Frequently in the transcriptions the same effect has been sought through single sentence, possibly two sentence paragraphs, presenting important statements in a frame of white space. Similarly, the personal pronoun is used too frequently for the page, and the personal possessive. Short, punchy statements when re-paragraphed are seen to be developing thought. The word 'Scotland' seems to have been spoken at every opportunity, probably to press a basic premise home, where only once is sufficient for a reader rather than a listener.

How to refer to Nicola Sturgeon and her party had to be considered. Use of just the second name, Sturgeon, is the language of opposition when the politician is female. Too frequently it is not used respectfully. Not so with male politicians. The name Obama can be used without any such concern. Similarly, to simply use her first name would be too familiar, although Nicola is how she is best known in Scotland, a politician with a fond and trusting following. Too familiar also for an editor who has met her only twice (at the time of writing) and both times briefly. She has had no input into this selection. This book is unauthorised. In the end I settled for her initials, NS, which are unmistakeable and emotionally neutral.

Her party is the Scottish National Party, but in the preludes (to continue the musical theme) I have referred only to 'her party'. The reason for this is that I would wish this volume to be read as a discrete representation, a single expression that speaks of and for an individual who, in turn, speaks for a people for as long as she is in office. I would wish it to rise above the weekly knockabout of First Minister's Questions and the internal party divisions that any leader must deal with. I would wish it to speak to the future and let people there know what I wish our neighbours across the world to know now. This is what the people of Scotland cared about in the devolution era. This is what they aspired to be. This is what they did with the powers they had.

Robert Davidson
Highland Scotland
2020-2021

ACKNOWLEDGEMENTS

I wish to acknowledge my appreciation of the Sandstone Press core team who are a continual source of inspiration to me. Appreciation also of the wider team of editors, proof-readers, typographers, designers, salespeople, and distributors, without whom there would be no books. Special and unique thanks go to novelist, editor and publishing director, Moira Forsyth who read this text many times (as she reads all my work for publication), removed my usual tropes and 'frae mony a blunder freed me', along with daily gratitude for all the other good things she brings into my life.

Further thanks go to the many people of all parties and none, who dreamed that a Scottish Parliament was possible, who worked steadily towards it over a period of decades, and eventually willed it into existence. Special mention must be made of Donald Dewar in this respect, the most significant figure in its foundation, and Alex Salmond, for taking his party to a point where compromise and agreement were possible. There were many others.

These acknowledgements would be incomplete without a wholehearted appreciation of the team of original speechwriters[54] who have worked so hard, and in such detail, to meet the First Minister's requirements as she speaks for the nation. I salute my unknown colleagues.

Finally, I am grateful to Nicola Sturgeon for a government that probably comes as close to my own value system as any is likely to do, and for her vision of the future.

---

54. For an amusing account of life as a political speechwriter see *Thanks, Obama* by David Litt, published by Ecco Press, New York, 2017.

INDEX

NB: The suffix 'n' after a page number (e.g. '45n') indicates that the reference is to a footnote.

Aberdeen Standard Investments 217

Aberdeen University 226

Abusive Behaviour and Sexual Harm Bill (2015) 125

Access to Elected Office Fund 202

Adichi, Chimamanda Ngozi 4, 276

Advertising Standards Authority 244

Advisory Council on Human Rights 242-44

Air Discount Scheme 28

Alagiah, George 184

alcohol
  advertising of 76
  attitudes to 74, 78
  deaths related to 75, 76
  excessive consumption of 75, 78
  minimum pricing of 75, 76
  policy towards 74, 77

Alharthi, Jokha 280

Alliance Trust 39, 89

apprenticeships, rise in 23, 24, 37, 126, 127, 202, 207

Arctic Circle Assembly 142, 147, 148

Ascherson, Neal 259, 264

asylum seekers 59, 61, 121, 227

A9, dualling of 28, 85

'baby box' 143, 215, 261

Bahgat, Hossam 69

Ban ki-Moon 46, 129

Bannockburn, Battle of 158

Barbour, Mary 65, 73

Barclays Bank 227

Barley, Nick 280

BBC
  gender gap 183
  new BBC Scotland TV channel 186
  salaries of presenters 181-84

BBC Alba 184, 185

Bell, Torsten 114, 115

Benedict XVI, Pope 226, 231

Ben Lomond (California) 158

Berlin Wall, fall of 148

Beyond Borders 169, 172

BHP Comics 279

Biden, Joe 31n, 149

Big Climate Conversation 268

Bingham, Lord 67

Bishops' Conference 227, 229

Blair, Tony 31, 312

blue carbon 247-49, 251
Blue Gate Fields Junior School, Tower Hamlets 20
Blue Planet 2 TV series 249
Bond, Patrick 267
Book of Kells 150, 156
Bookbug reading project 53
Bord na Gaidhlig 81
Bradford Literature Festival 276
Brexit – *see also* referendum
  consequences of 138, 148, 154, 191, 236, 281
  dilemma for Scotland 176, 286, 287
  impact on climate change 168
  impact on free trade 154
  impact on higher education 161
  regret at decision 282, 283
British Council 44
British-Irish Council 140
broadband, provision of 27, 34, 85, 100, 192, 223
Brown, Gordon 2, 31
Brown, Jerry 167
Brown, Very Rev Susan 252, 257
Burns, Robert 236, 282
Burns Nights 218, 235
Bush, George W. 157

Cairns, Rt Rev John 253, 257
Calton Jail 296
Cameron, David 6, 61-64, 130, 132, 133, 199
Caritas Awards 231
carrier bag charge 89
Castlemilk Woodlands 100
Catholic Church

and education 228-32
place in Scotland's life 226, 227
relationship with Church of Scotland 227
Catholic Head Teachers' Association 232
Central Scotland Green Network 100
Centre on Constitutional Change 175
Chakrabarti, Baroness Shami 64
Challenge for Scotland's Biodiversity 98
Channel 4 TV 184-87
Charco Press 279
childcare
  expansion of 54, 192, 208, 222, 223, 242, 243, 261
  gender equality in 23, 111, 207
  free provision of 11, 18, 19, 126, 215
  investment in 34, 37, 44, 165, 216
child poverty, action against 211-14, 221, 263
Child Poverty Act (2017) 213
Children's University 59
China, business relationship with 218-20
Chinese New Year 218
Chinese People's Association for Friendship with Other Countries 41, 210
Christchurch shootings 254
Chu Guang 45
Church and Society Council 254, 255
Church of Scotland

General Assembly of 225, 227, 252, 253, 256
role in Scotland today 179, 253, 254, 257
Churchill, Winston 66
Citizens' Assembly on Scotland's Future 257, 265
civic nationalism 1
Claim of Right for Scotland 253
clearances 80
climate change
ambitious legislation on 90, 166, 248, 260, 288
defining challenge of 148, 166, 248, 266, 274
gender dimension of 46, 128, 146, 171, 270
loss of ecosystems 99, 167
Paris Agreement on 98, 143-46, 284
Climate Change Act (2009) 164
climate justice 16, 171, 267, 268-71
Climate Justice Fund 128, 143, 146, 155, 268-71
Clinton, Hillary 31, 36
Clovenstone Primary School 57
Cold War, end of 148
Commission for Catholic Education 227, 234
Commission on Developing Scotland's Young Workforce 23, 57
Commission on Widening Access 22, 111
Community Broadband Scotland 27, 85
community buyouts 29, 85, 86

Community Empowerment Act (2015) 29, 86
community empowerment, importance of 29, 228
Community Jobs Scotland 24
Computershare 237
Confederation of British Industry (CBI) 19
Connolly, Billy 52, 110
Constitution of Germany 130, 157, 165
constitutional change 132, 178, 256, 265
Convention of the Highlands and Islands (COHI) 26, 30
Convention on Biological Diversity 248
COP26 Climate Change Summit, Glasgow 284
Council of Economic Advisers 33, 135, 163
Creative Scotland 188
Cromarty Firth Bridge 26
Crown Estate 30, 86
Crown Office 125
C-Trip company 219
Curriculum for Excellence 17, 19-21, 49, 230, 232
Curtice, Professor John 176

Daesh (Islamic State) 121
Daily Mail 183
Daily Show, The (USA) 31
David Hume Institute 14, 16, 25
Davidson, Ruth 124n
decarbonisation 268
Delors, Jacques 115

Devine, Sir Tom 229, 253
Devolved Employment Services
    Advisory Group 202, 203
Dewar, Donald 2, 4, 10, 259, 265
Diamond project 184
Didcock, Carolyn 51
Directors Association 184
disabled people
  jobs for 72, 200-03
  valued in society 199
Doctor Who 187
domestic abuse 42, 124-26
  Domestic Abuse Bill (2018) 208
Dornoch Firth Bridge 26
Drumchapel Law Centre 3
Dublin University Philosophical
    Society 149
Dugdale, Kezia 124n

Early Years Collaborative 18, 21
early years learning 16, 18, 20, 22,
    34, 83, 165, 242
Edinburgh Castle 218, 228
Edinburgh International Book
    Festival 276-80
Edinburgh International Festival
    151, 218
Edinburgh International Television
    Festival 181
Edinburgh Old Town 272
'Edinburgh Seven' 240, 241, 245
Edinburgh University 160, 161, 233,
    240, 279
education
  aspirations for 25, 54-57
  Catholic 225-34
  free provision of 22, 221, 253

Gaelic medium 82-84
gender equality in 44, 45, 124, 128
  importance of 14, 16, 17, 24, 25,
    48, 49, 54, 216, 242, 253
  key to a better future 25, 54
  universal access to 16, 45n, 48, 49,
    67, 221
Education Act (1918) 227, 229, 234
Education Working Group 232
Egyptian Initiative for Personal
    Rights 69
Electoral Commission 286
Elphinstone, Bishop William 226
Empowering Scotland's Island
    Communities 29
empowerment
  of communities 27-29, 86, 112,
    202, 270
  of local authorities 27
  of women 43, 45, 46, 171, 208, 223
Equality Network 196
European Arrest Warrant 138
European Convention on Human
    Rights 64-72
European Customs Union 152
European Economic Community
    (EEC) 159, 221
European Free Trade Association
    (EFTA) 78
European Marine Energy Centre
    145
European Parliament 282, 288, 289
European Policy Centre 281
European Union
  and Scotland 152, 157, 281, 282, 286
  benefits of membership 115, 116,
    147, 159, 287

consequence of UK leaving 117,
134, 220, 222
EU nationals living in Scotland 117
immigration from 163, 164, 167
jobs for women 35, 37, 44
Scottish exports to 32, 283
Ewing, Winifred 1, 259, 260

Fair Start Scotland 203
Fair Work Convention 109
faith schools, importance of 228-30
fall armyworm 270
feminist writing 5
50:50 by 2020 campaign (for gender
balance) 36, 38, 39, 44, 89, 127
film and TV production in
Scotland, value of 187-89
Financial Services Advisory Board
Flanagan, Charlie 152
food banks 90, 91
Foods Commission 92
Forestry Commission 100
forests as carbon sinks 99, 248
Forsyth, Michael 2
free child care 11, 18, 19, 126, 215
free education 22, 221, 253
free movement of people 117, 118,
122, 126, 127, 147, 168, 203, 287
free school meals, introduction
of 20
free trade, benefits of 78, 122, 147,
153, 163, 164, 22, 2834
Fyfe, David Maxwell 66

Gaelic as part of our future 82
Gaelic College – *see* Sabhal Mor
Ostaig

Gaelic education 82-84
Gaelic language and culture,
support for 80-87
Gaelic Schools Capital Fund 82
Gate Interactive 39
Gender at Work Report (World
Bank) 34
gender- balanced boards 38, 39, 208
gender-balanced cabinet 3, 35, 38,
44, 124, 125, 169, 170, 206
Gender Beacon Collaborative 241
gender equality, progress towards
9, 34-37, 39, 41-43, 47, 157, 170,
208, 240-42
at Stanford University 164
good for employers 223
in China 42, 45
in Pakistan 128, 129
gender justice 267
gender pay gap 11, 37, 43, 126, 127,
170, 182, 183, 207, 208
gender segregation 23, 127
gender stereotyping 207, 241-44
General Assembly of the Church
of Scotland 225, 227, 252, 253,
256
General Election 2015 6, 31, 183
Glasgow and West of Scotland
Suffrage Association 206
Glasgow Central Mosque 94
Glasgow rent strikes 65
Glasgow School of Art 31
Glasgow University 16, 57, 103, 105,
160, 205, 225, 226
Glasgow Women's Library 206
Global Alcohol Policy Conference
74

Global Leaders' Meeting on
    Gender Equality and Women's
    Empowerment 45
Golden Gate Park, San Francisco
    158
Gorbachev, Mikhail 148
Gove, Michael 260
greenhouse gases 90, 96, 98,
    142-44, 146, 262, 268, 270
Grieve, Dominic 69
Grimsson, Ólafur Ragnar 143
Gross Domestic Product (GDP) 21,
    42, 136, 223, 272-74
Growing Up in Scotland Study 18
G20 Group 34, 44

Hague, William 259
Hall, Tony 183
happiness rating of countries 18, 274
Heggie, Stuart 51
Henry, Sir Lenny 183
Heriot-Watt University 160
Higgins, Michael 153, 155
Highlands & Islands Development
    Board 79, 84
Highlands & Islands Enterprise
    79, 84
Historical Sexual Offences (Pardons
    and Disregards) (Scotland) Bill
    (2017) 195
Hong Kong and Shanghai Bank
    (HSBC) 217, 237
Horsburgh, Florence 10
Hu Chunhua 210
human rights
    as a devolved issue 70
    as women's rights 42, 43

at heart of policymaking 172, 24,
    256
global application of 67, 69, 70, 72
National Action Plan for 71, 72
violation of 5, 210
Human Rights Act 64-72, 106
Human Rights Commission 71
Human Trafficking and
    Exploitation Bill (2015) 68
Hunter, James 79

Idlib, chemical attack on 166n
immigration
    benefits of 154, 164, 222
    campaigns against 134
    policy on 1, 161, 167, 168
    volume of 117
Inclusion Scotland 199, 202
income tax, role of 190-94
independence
    arguments against 114, 137, 265, 285
    arguments for 168, 179, 265, 285, 287
    debate on 1, 18, 138-1, 167, 176
    referendum 2014 2, 6, 14n, 28n,
        31, 72n, 162, 174, 256
    second referendum, calls for 116,
        162, 176-78, 264, 282, 286
Independent Living Fund 200
Inglis, Elsie 206
International Monetary Fund
    (IMF) 31, 38, 42, 222n
    International Union for the
        Conservation of Nature 97
    International Women's Day 123
    Invest in Young People Group 23
    Iona Community 252
Islamic State – *see* Daesh

Islands Area Ministerial Working
    Group 29

John Muir Way 199, 101
John Paul II, Pope 226, 234
Johnson, Boris 6
Jones, Carwyn 140
Juncker, Jean-Claude 120
Just Transition Commission 263,
    269, 274

Kakutani, Michiko 174
Kelvingrove Park, Glasgow 205
Kennedy, John Fitzgerald 4
Kenny, Enda 152
Kessock Bridge 26
Kilbeg development, Skye 80

Lagarde, Christine 33, 38, 42, 222
Land Reform Bill (2015) 29, 86
Lang, Ian 2
Lerwick Marine Protected Area
    (MPA) 247
Leyen, Ursula von der 281, 288
LGBTI community 195-98, 202, 232
Li Keqiang 218, 219
Liberty 64, 67, 68, 71, 107
Lincoln, Abraham: Gettysburg
    Address 103
Lisbon Treaty 62, 139
    Article 50 of 6, 139
Lloyd George, David 3
London Challenge (for schools) 20,
    21, 54

Make Young People Your Business
    campaign 24

Malawi, schools partnership with
    44, 146, 231, 254, 270, 271
Man Booker International Prize
    280
marine ecology 242, 246, 247
marine litter 248-51
Marine Protected Areas (MPAs)
    247, 248
Marriage and Civil Partnership
    (Scotland) Act (2014) 195
Mary Robinson Climate Justice
    Foundation 46
May, Theresa 6, 130, 136n, 183n,
    199
Mazucatto, Marianna 135
McConachie, Rev Catherine 252
McConnell, Jack 1, 2, 10, 123
Maclaren, John 158
MacLean, Sorley 86, 150
McLeish, Henry 2, 10
MacLeod, Lord George of Fiunary
    252
MacPherson, Mary 80, 86
Merkel, Angela 31, 59, 149
Meygen tidal array project 145
Mistura, Staffan de 171
Motherwell FC 142
Muir, John – see John Muir Way
Munro, Robert 228, 229
Murrell, Peter 4
Muslim community in Scotland
    231, 254

National Action Plan for Human
    Rights 71, 72
National Advisory Council on
    Women and Girls 240, 241

National Council for the Training of Journalists 184
National Film and Television School 188
National Health Service (NHS) 12, 120, 136, 191, 192
National Planning Framework 100
National Programme of Action for Children (China) 212
natural capital 97-102
Natural Capital Coalition 97
Natural Capital, Scottish Forum on 101
Neil, Alex 195
Neil, Andrew 182
Noble, Sir Iain 80
Northern Lights 276

Obama, Barack 6, 19, 133, 241, 291, 292
Ofcom 184, 186
Office of National Statistics 17, 32
One Ocean Hub 246
Organisation for Economic Co-Operation and Development (OECD) 15, 32-34, 77, 163, 221, 272
Orkney 27, 142, 145, 205
OSPAR Convention 251

Paris, terrorist attacks in 93-96
Paris Agreement on Climate Change 98, 143-46, 284
Paton, Sheila 51
Pelamis (film studio, Leith) 188
Pelosi, Nancy 147
people trafficking 60

Police Scotland 68, 69, 94, 196, 197
Poverty and Inequality Commission 214
Prospect North 143
Publishers Association 279
Publishing Scotland (formerly the Scottish Publishers Association) 276, 278
Pyramids (film studio, Bathgate) 188

Queensferry Crossing 14, 20
Quinn, George 237
Quorum Network Resources 39

Read Write Count campaign 56
Reading Challenge (First Minister's) 48, 231, 276, 278
Reagan, Ronald 148
Referendum on Devolution (1979) 2
Referendum on Devolution (1997) 2, 259
Referendum on EU membership (2016) 6, 114-16, 131, 132, 140, 149, 159, 163, 178
  lessons from 133-35
Referendum on Independence (2014) 2, 6, 18, 28, 112, 159, 177, 178
Referendum on Independence (second), calls for 116, 162, 175, 177, 282, 286
refugee crisis 59, 71, 72, 120, 121, 149, 150
  humanitarian response to 61, 167

Scottish welcome for refugees 95, 121, 171
Reform Scotland 259
Reid, Jimmy 3, 48, 52, 57, 102, 105, 106, 110-13
renewable energy
  economic benefit of 145, 166, 263
  potential for 85, 127, 144, 145, 270
  promotion of 155
rent strikes 65
Resolution Foundation 114, 118, 130
Rhine Capitalism 35, 108, 165
Rifkind, Malcolm 2
right to strike 106
ROAR project 278
Robeson, Paul 113
Robinson, Mary 41, 46, 79, 81, 151, 152, 155, 171, 267
Roosevelt, Eleanor 173
Rowling, J.K. 6
Roy, Arundhati 276
Royal Society of Edinburgh 14, 190
Rusbridger, Alan 174

Sabhal Mòr Ostaig 79, 80, 84-87, 151
St Andrew's Foundation for Catholic Teacher Education 225, 226, 229, 230
St Andrew's and St Bride's School, East Kilbride, partnership with Malawi 231
St Andrews University 160, 226, 248
St Colmcille (Columba) 149
St Jerome 156
Salmond, Alex

achieving majority government 2
and community buyouts 85
tribute from Nicola Sturgeon 10
voice of the nation 3, 4
same sex marriage 154, 195, 252, 253
Sandstone Press 280
Scapa Flow MPA 147
scholarship scheme 128
Scotland Act 2
Scotland, tax powers in 190
Scotland Week (USA) 257
Scottish Affairs Office, Beijing 41, 210
Scottish Ambulance Service 94
Scottish Attainment Challenge 21, 48, 54, 56
Scottish Blue Carbon Forum 249
Scottish Book Trust 276, 278
Scottish broadcasting 181, 185-87
Scottish Broadcasting Commission 185, 186
Scottish Business Pledge 109
Scottish Catholic Education Service 229-32
Scottish College for Educational Leadership 51, 52
Scottish Constitutional Convention 253, 287
Scottish Council of Jewish Communities 94
Scottish Council of Voluntary Organisations (SCVO) 24
Scottish Courts and Tribunal Service 125
Scottish exports to China, value of 210, 218-20
Scottish Financial Enterprise 238

Scottish Forum on Natural Capital
101
Scottish Government
  and climate change 166
  and human rights 167
  commitment to education 15
  economic policy 31, 42, 163, 221, 222
  limited taxation powers 190
  Programme for Government 27, 55
  Resilience Committee 94
  seeking to remain in EU 147, 156
  support for Gaelic 81
Scottish Green Party 123
Scottish Grocers Federation 88-92
Scottish Human Rights
  Commission 71
Scottish Land Fund 29, 86
Scottish National Investment Bank
  261
Scottish Natural Heritage 101, 248
Scottish National Party 2, 6
Scottish Parliament
  achievements of 261, 265
  and Church of Scotland 253, 256
  gender equality in 124, 125, 207
  opening of (1999) 10, 13, 236, 259
  rejecting Trade Union Bill 106-08
  seeking second independence
    referendum 177, 282, 286
Scottish Publishers Assiociation 279
  Scottish Social Attitudes Survey
    261
Scottish Survey of Literacy and
  Numeracy 52
Scottish Television 181
Scottish Trades Union Congress
  106

Scottish Wildlife Trust 97
Scottish Women's Convention 123,
  124
Seafield, Earl of 12, 288
sexual offences 125, 195, 196, 207,
  242
Shanghai Festival 218
Shanghai Scottish Society 217
Sheffield University 77
Shenu, Alan 59
Single European Act (1986) 115
Skyenet project 85
Skyscanner 219
Sleat Community Trust 85
Small Business Bonus scheme 89,
  191, 192, 260
Smith, Adam 101, 160, 190, 270, 275
Smith, Ali 4, 276
Smith, John 2
Smith, Sarah 182
Smith Commission 30, 72
smoking, banned in public places 3,
  155, 260
Snow, Jon 185
Social Security Agency for Scotland
  255
social security, provision of 72, 164,
  203, 254, 261
Standing Council of Experts 139
Stanford, Leland 158, 164
Stanford University (USA) 57, 160,
  163-66
Statoil (Norway) 145
Stewart, Jon 31
Stiglitz, Professor Joseph 33, 163
Strathclyde University 160, 174,
  176, 233, 246

STV2 television channel 185
suffrage movement 205-09
Suffragette Oak, Kelvingrove Park,
    Glasgow 205
sulphur dioxide emssions, reduction
    in, 119
Surgeons' Hall, riot of 240, 241, 244
sustainable growth, approach to
    26n, 29, 155, 193, 194, 285
Sutherland, Thomas 217
Swinney, John 4, 94
Syria
  civil war in 166, 167
  peace process 171, 172
  refugee crisis 59, 95, 121, 150
Syrian Vulnerable Persons
    Relocation Scheme 62
Syrian Women's Advisory Board
    172

Tahrir Square uprising (Egypt) 69
Tartan Day (USA) 157
Technation company 238
terrorist attacks 93-96, 254
Thatcher, Margaret 2, 3
Thomson, Roy 182
tourism, importance of 32, 85, 99,
    142, 247
Trade Union Bill, opposition to
    107-09
trade union law, devolution of 106,
    107
Transatlantic Trade and Investment
    Partnership 120
Treaty of Rome 158
Trinity College Dublin 149
Trump, Donald 157, 291

Turnbull, Bishop William 226
Tusk, Donald 287

United Nations Environment
    Programme 97
UN Capacity Building Initiative for
    Transparency 146
UN Committee on the Rights of
    Persons with Disabilities 200
UN Convention on Biological
    Diversity 248
UN Convention on Climate
    Change 143n
UN Convention on the Elimination
    of all forms of Discrimination
    against Women 242
UN Convention on the Rights of
    the Child 211, 212, 215
UN Declaration of Human Rights
    211, 215
UN Declaration of the Rights of
    Children 211
UN Mediation Support Unit 167
UN Millennium Goals 45n
UN Office of the Special Envoy for
    Syria 166, 171
UN Security Council resolution
    1325 166
UN Sustainable Development
    Goals 155, 166, 172, 216, 270
UNICEF 211
Upper Clyde Shipbuilders 103, 106

Verhofstadt, Guy 281
Virgin Money 39

Wallace, Jim 123

Wardlaw, Bishop Henry 226
Wark, Kirsty 182
Watt, James 219
wellbeing
  benefits of 14, 20, 47, 54, 56, 78,
    247
  of communities 87-89, 91, 100, 117,
    258, 275
Wellbeing Budget (New Zealand)
  274
Wellbeing Economy Governments
  Partnership 272, 273
Wester Hailes Education Centre
  51, 52
What Scotland Thinks website
  176n
wind power 145, 167, 219, 247
Winning, Cardinal Thomas 225-27,
  234
Winton, Sir Nicholas 61, 63
women, empowerment of 43, 45,
  46, 171, 208, 223
Women in Conflict programme
  166, 169
World Bank 29, 31, 33, 34, 38, 292

World Business Council for
  Sustainable Development 97
World Conference on Women 41,
  42
World Economic Forum 124, 170
World Forum on Climate Justice
  267
World Forum on Natural Capital
  97, 101
World Health Organisation
  (WHO) 74

Xi Jinping (President of China)
  212, 222

Yankovic, Alfred 'Weird Al' 149
Young Malawian Climate Leaders
  270
Young Scot programme 101
Younger, George 2
Yousafzai, Malala 41, 44

Zero Waste Scotland 249, 250
Zuleeg, Fabian 287
Zurich Insurance 237